HOLDING *pattern*

HOLDING *pattern*

how communication prevents intimacy in adults

Karen S. Falling Buzzard

Michigan State University Press
East Lansing

Michigan State University Press
East Lansing, Michigan 48823–5202

Printed and bound in the United States of America.

07 06 05 04 03 02 01 1 2 3 4 5 6 7 8 9 10

LIBRARY OF CONGRESS CATALOGING-IN-PUBLICATION DATA

Buzzard, Karen.
  Holding pattern : how communication prevents intimacy in adults / by
Karen S. Falling Buzzard.
    p. cm.
Includes bibliographical references and index.
  ISBN 0-87013-577-5 (pbk. : alk. paper)
  1. Interpersonal communication. 2. Interpersonal relations. I. Title.
HM1166 .B89 2001
  158.2—dc21
                                    2001000561

Cover design by Heather L. Truelove
Book design by Michael J. Brooks

Visit Michigan State University Press on the World Wide Web at:
www.msupress.msu.edu

Dedicated to my siblings Beverly, Clyde, Shirley, and Sharon—
Spring, Summer, Autumn, Winter

Contents

Acknowledgments

I am extremely grateful to those who agreed to be interviewed for the book. Without their contributions, this book would not have been possible. I also wish to sincerely thank Martha Bates at the MSU Press for her belief in the book. Finally, I wish to thank Patricia Illingsworth and Clyde E. Buzzard Jr. for their insights in reading the material and remarkable assistance in editing the project.

PART I
Intimacy and Adulthood

Introduction

The Lonely Heart in Middle Passage

The Life Cycle Revisited

While the older paradigm of the midlife "crisis" stills holds influence over much research, this paradigm assumes much that can no longer be taken for granted. It assumes that most have successfully navigated the perils of intimacy by midlife and are by this point settled in marriage, partnership, or some form of community. Many midlife myths of male or female menopause or crisis thus assume a background of marriage and family life that is no longer the only paradigm, nor even the most common one. According to the 1995 U.S. Census, one in four households was constituted by just one person, a dramatic change from fifty years ago, when only one in ten households consisted of a single person. Single-person households are expected to grow faster than all other kinds of households, an increase of 26 percent between 1995 and 2010, according to the U.S. Census as compared to an increase of 18 percent in overall household growth.[1] The midlife crisis paradigm also assumes that intimacy happens naturally and without struggle, similar to aging. This leaves those who are unmarried (whether divorced or never married) and those in marriages where intimacy is unsatisfying (perhaps this explains the 50 percent divorce rate in the United States) outside the model. For this reason we need to examine issues related specifically to nontraditional lifestyles that are now becoming more the norm.

What of those whose lives have not followed the traditional road map for life? In particular, what of those whose lives have veered from the beaten track and who find themselves on what may seem like the proverbial road less traveled? What of those who reach midlife transition and find themselves still single and somehow not forming the intimate relationships that they had innocently believed would "just happen?" These are the subjects of this book. So crucial is our need for intimacy to both our happiness and well being that for these people there is a sense of life having passed them by. Somehow their lives have fallen outside the dominant cultural script of marriage by twenty and

1

empty nests by forty. According to the 1997 U.S. Census only 35.7 percent of all families consisted of married couples with children under eighteen, the nuclear family. The last time the nuclear family constituted the majority of families was in 1967, with 50.1 percent![2]

It is with this in mind that I seek to examine those whose lives do not fit the conventional mold. Living outside expected conventions of a society and its social norms is difficult and not necessarily a happy choice—or even a choice at all—particularly if this was not part of the vision of how their lives would go.

My purpose is to offer a roadmap for intimacy by examining three communication and developmental passageways. A road map is always clearer if it is made concrete through illustrations. My road maps are accompanied by illustrated case studies of those who are struggling or have struggled to find psychological and communication markers, which function like geographical signposts, assuring us we are headed in the right direction in our journey toward intimacy.

A New Paradigm for Intimate Communication

What I offer here is a new paradigm for intimacy. This paradigm does not assume, as the older one does, that intimacy, adulthood, and marriage go hand in hand, but instead seeks to explain the many, no longer unique, who reach adulthood and are still alone—whether through never marrying or divorce. It is not an accident that the terms "old maid" and "bachelor" are no longer used to marginalize and stigmatize. Yet, the desire to share our lives with meaningful others remains an important part of a vital life and is one reinforced socially, emotionally, and physically.

As a scholar and teacher in the field of communication, I am aware of how deficiencies in communication skills sabotage the efforts of many who desire to attain intimate relationships. However, I feel a key dimension has been sorely missing in the research and training of communications skills, one critical to changing behavior. My paradigm seeks to provide a deeper understanding and a fuller insight into the individual passage to intimacy by examining problems in three critical communication processes—affectional, ethical, and authentic communication—as symptoms of more complex developmental passages. Together these communication and developmental passages serve as the foundation for intimacy.

Understanding problems in intimacy, the subject of this book, is timely. Many of the family and community structures that once nurtured intimacy and protected us from loneliness have been radically altered in the last half-century, making the achievement of intimacy a more personal accomplishment than it used to be. We are more transitory, both physically and emotionally, and we are impinged upon by a complex culture that, while providing more opportunities, provides less structure and security. Most seek a relationship, a community, a place where we belong, but it is more difficult to meet those needs when they are no longer supported by our established social structures.

Our Three Relational Needs

Psychologist W. C. Schultz identifies three basic interpersonal needs that we seek to meet in our relationships and that become the basis of relational communication. They are affection, control, and inclusion.[3] *Affection* is the degree of love needed. Each of us needs to love and to feel loved. *Control* is the need to affect and have power over those individuals and events that shape our lives. *Inclusion* is the degree of association needed, or how easily and how much we can let others know who we are. Each of these dimensions is a scale, along which an individual may be located, and each person may choose a different means of meeting these needs. We relate, or attempt to relate, to others in order to make sure these needs are met. If we succeed we feel psychologically comfortable. Understanding these needs and how we attempt to meet them is critical to understanding intimacy.

What Schultz has outlined are the basic communication yardsticks by which we can measure our capacity for intimacy: the affectional system, which shapes our capacity for affectionate communication; the control system, which shapes our capacity for ethical communication; and the inclusion system, which shapes our capacity for authentic communication. Each of these yardsticks involves learned sets of communication skills that have a developmental origin. Examining intimate communication only as a set of skills to be learned is like examining the branches of the tree rather than the roots. In order to develop an understanding of intimacy both our communications skills and our developmental models must be examined and understood. For example, it is not enough to point out that someone lacks swimming skills; we must also explore why that person fears the water.

Organization of the Book

Drawing on the work of W. C. Schultz, I illuminate in each of the three sections of the book a communication/developmental passageway that serves as a foundation for intimate communication: the three passageways are affectional, ethical, and authentic communication. In turn, each communication passageway is linked to underlying developmental processes critical for intimacy development.

Affectional communication I link to what researchers have called the stable base, or personal security, the process that gives us sufficient confidence to turn from our need to receive emotional nurturance and to give emotional nurturance to others. Our attachment styles are formed during the first critical years of life as we develop a template for future intimate relationships based on emotional interactions with our primary caregivers.

Ethical communication I link to our ability to take active control or responsibility for our circumstances and ourselves. This capacity is developed during our Oedipal phase, when we form a sense of self, take responsibility for this self, accept our sexuality, understand the world as complex rather than black and white, and develop coping strategies for dealing with new situations, where needs are disappointed, painful, or not satisfied.

Authentic communication, or our inclusion-exclusion system, I link to healthy identity or boundaries of the self. Boundaries determine the degree to which we are open or closed to influence by others or outside events and by our ability to receive appropriate feedback and make appropriate adaptations.

Through each of the three sections of this book I explore communications that are attempts to address these three needs, both healthy and neurotic. I explore these three needs in terms of their directionality—whether we are givers or receivers, whether we are active or passive in getting our needs met, and how open or closed we are to others. The task in meeting these needs is to find an optimal psychological balance or equilibrium. I explain communication directionality by examining the underlying developmental processes, both failures and successes, in their resolution. (See table 1.) My discussion of each critical passage to adult communication is accompanied by a case study that illustrates how the communication skills and developmental processes under study apply to successes and failures in intimate relationships in the lives of real people.

Those in anxious states assume too much (overactive) or too little (underactive) control or agency in assuring that these needs are met. They lack flexibility in direction and may choose behaviors that either exclude others or fail to protect the self. Schultz says, and many psychologists would agree, that an individual's expressed interpersonal behavior will reflect the behavioral experiences of his or her earliest interpersonal relations, usually with his or her parents.

The achievement of an optimum balance in intimate relationships requires negotiation. We want our affection for another to affect his or her behavior, yet we cannot expect the other to dedicate his or her entire life to satisfying our needs, nor can we afford to give all of our own time and energy to the process.

Table 1. Critical Passages to Intimacy.

Relational Need	Communication Markers: Directionality	Developmental Passages
Affection	Affectional Communication: From Narcissism (Self) to Other (Adult) Focusing	Attachment style
Control	Ethical Communication: Passive (Immature) to Active (Mature) Defenses	Oedipal resolution
Inclusion/ Exclusion	Authentic Communication: Too Closed or Too Open to Healthy Boundaries	Identity resolution

Since people differ in both their needs and capacities, a couple must, together, find a workable balance. The tricky part is that such negotiations occur mainly at a nonverbal level, by means of subtle clues given by gestures, tone of voice, and seemingly unrelated actions. Without verbal translation, our communication and motivation are rife for misunderstanding.

Adult Communication

Although communication patterns have roots in early periods of development, and some form of intimacy may be present in childhood, the intimacy of the child, because of its dependent state, is likely to be one-sided. In this book I focus on *adult communication,* by which I mean at communication that exhibit optimal mutuality, for the self and for others. Developmental processes that are adequate for the child may be inadequate for the adult, leading to distress in self and others. By focusing on how these adult processes develop, as well as how they become impaired, I attempt to restore to adulthood the possibility of changing earlier patterns.

I do not intend this to be a "self-help" book that offers "Ten Easy Steps." Yet, I do think that individuals may be able to critically examine their own behavior in terms of these dimensions in order to locate and understand problems in intimacy, perhaps with the help of a friend, counselor, or minister. Developmental processes are growth processes and therefore require time and effort. Change involves pain and discomfort, but the reward is great, even life-saving in some instances. It is unlikely that any human being truly does not want intimacy, though there are many who have adopted the defensive strategy of denying a need that they do not have the means to satisfy. When we are young we assume Mr. or Ms. Right will automatically come along someday, but if that has not happened and we are approaching middle age alone, an active and self-analytic approach to building intimate relationships is critical.

Methodology

My paradigm for intimate communication draws upon leading theorists in human development, psychology, philosophy, and communication. I am indebted to the work of Adler, Erikson, Freud, Horney, Klein, Bowlby, Winnicott, and Gilligan.[4] For their work on the ego processes involved in adult behavior, I am indebted to Robert Kegan and George Vaillant.[5]

For their work on aging, I owe my inspiration again to Erik Erikson, and to Thomas Cole.[6] For his work on boundaries, I owe credit to Ernest Hartmann.[7] This list would furthermore not be complete without mentioning Dan McAdams, to whom I owe my case study methodology.[8]

My approach stresses the complexity of the communication process for each individual. The capacity for adult communication emerges from the interaction of an internal organization with external social systems. Although the tapestry of each adulthood is woven with similar needles and threads, each has unique hues and designs.

Close examination of the language used in constructing our stories of the self is crucial to understanding how we make sense of our world. Each of us faces the task of bringing conceptual order to our own life narrative. Each assigns causes, creates stories, and breaks up the ongoing flow into punctuated sequences in order to give it meaning.[9] Understanding the manner through which people construct their existence is essential to understanding their level of development along each of the three dimensions of intimate communication I have outlined. Existentialists say we *are* our choices. Each story, and the shape given it, is a means of personal expression. Each life story expresses or communicates who the person understands him or herself to be. An examination of the implications of each life story unearths for each individual their assumptions about life, both acknowledged and unrealized.

Analyzing Our Life Stories

Following the work of Dan McAdams in *The Stories We Live By: Personal Myths and the Making of the Self*,[10] I conducted life-story interviews, choosing those stories whose personal myths best exemplified each of my three communication/developmental passageways. McAdams's theoretical constructs (italicized in the following) provide tools for analyzing communication processes and connecting them to developmental ones in each personal myth. A personal myth is a history of the self. It is an imaginative construction of the past in light of an envisioned future. While our selves are made within a social context, our identities include not only our sense of uniqueness and separateness but also our sense of connectedness. Identity is a search for unity and purpose. According to McAdams, we make sense of our lives by creating heroic narratives, starring ourselves. These stories embrace "the facts," but use them to construct larger themes of past, present, and future. They reveal the motives, values, and coping mechanisms that keep us going. McAdams says, "Making life into myth is what adulthood is all about."[11] I would add that adulthood is also about making myths into reality.

Peak and Nadir Experiences

I asked subjects to divide their lives into chapters. The method they used, whether chronological or thematic, provides clues to their inner lives. The narratives that the subjects provide identify high and low points. McAdams identifies what he calls peak and nadir experiences as crucial to understanding the self. *Peak experiences* are times of physical or mental strengthening, when we realize our own power and impact on others, while *nadir experiences* are low points, which have the potential to lead to redefinition.

Our Narrative Tone

Even infants unconsciously gather material for personal myths. Their relationships with their early caretakers determine their capacity for love and trust in later relationships. The infant experiences emotion and studies the reaction of the caregiver—a process known as mirroring. This affirms (or denies) the infant's sense of agency, power, and goodness, and basic attitudes of hope or despair may be formed before we have either the experience or language ability to help us evaluate reality.

The early influence of our caretakers determine what McAdams calls the *narrative tone of* our stories. Narrative tones range from hopeless pessimism to boundless optimism. As we shall see, secure attachment with a caregiver provides enduring faith in the goodness of the world and a sense of hope for the future. Such faith, or the lack of it, determines whether we see our wishes, hopes, and dreams as attainable. Insecure attachment creates a pessimistic belief that human beings do not get what they want, or that the world is capricious and unpredictable. Optimists are more likely than pessimists to take positive steps to confront challenges in life, and to develop more life-affirming strategies for coping. Narrative tone is the most pervasive feature of our personal myths in adulthood. The narrative tone is revealed through the content and manner in which each story is told.

Our Key Images: Theme, Plot, and Motivation

Before story plots are within our cognitive grasp, we make sense of the world through emotionally charged symbols. Throughout our earliest years we collect the central *images* that will animate our personal myths, images that are pre-verbal and prelogical. Family and culture provide the raw material, which become incorporated into our myth. Some images are modified or pass into oblivion, while others survive into adulthood and are incorporated into a continuing personal myth. As the child approaches school age he or she begins to develop the ability to think logically and to create stories with *themes* and *plots*. These themes and plots establish *motivational* patterns that determine how a person will perceive new experiences. A child who has developed a skeletal theme of disappointment and failure will tend to bring new events into that same theme—he or she will be predisposed toward a pessimistic story.

Following David Bakan, McAdams believes there are two fundamental motives: our need for love (communion) and our need for power (agency).[12] Communion is the individual's striving to lose his or her own individuality by merging with others, forming unions, and relating to others intimately. Agency is the striving to be separate from others, to become a powerful and autonomous force that masters and controls the environment and others—requiring a distant or objective attitude. Motives organize behavior and provide energy. They organize the personality as themes organize a story. Psychologist Carol Gilligan suggests that males frame ideas of human growth and development within the context of self-sufficiency and fulfillment (agency), while females concentrate on meaningful connections to others and commitment to the world (communion).[13] Since the goal in this book is to better understand the barriers to intimacy, the focus will be on our need for communion, but it will be impossible to exclude the need for agency because these two needs are inextricably connected.

Adolescence: Creating an Identity and Ontology of Self

According to McAdams, life becomes mythic during our teenage years. We become active mythmakers when we must confront the problem of *identity* head-on. Although one's sense of self is developed in early social interaction, identity is the attempt to make sense of it. Mythmaking begins when we realize we are no longer children. Using our newly acquired ability to reason, we attempt to make sense of who we are. From adolescence on, we face the central psychosocial task of forming and re-forming our identities. In adolescence we develop teleological and religious beliefs to give our identity an enduring and stable purpose or direction.

McAdams calls these beliefs about causation the *ideological settings* for our mythmaking. These ideological settings remain relatively intact for the rest of our lives, but may be changed by traumatic experiences.

Ideological settings, McAdams believes, are strategies we develop to explain how and why events transpire. Agnes Hankiss calls such strategies "ontologies of the self." She cites four dominant thematic possibilities: First, a good past gives birth to a good present, or what she calls the dynastic narrative. Dynastic narratives stress continuity between childhood and adulthood. A second theme she calls the antithetical narrative, where a bad past gives birth to a good present. Antithetical narratives include Cinderella stories, rags-to-riches motifs, and even the American Dream. Both the dynastic and the antithetical narratives are optimistic in seeing an ultimate "happy ending." A third narrative theme is the compensatory, where a good past gives birth to a bad present, and a fourth is the self-absolutory, where a bad past gives birth to a bad present.[14] Compensatory narratives stress the theme of peaking early, after which "it's all downhill from here." Self-absolutory narratives focus on severe disadvantages rarely transcended, on never having had a chance. Although both the compensatory and the self-absolutory narratives are pessimistic in essence, the self-absolving narrative is slightly upbeat, suggesting that "it could have been worse." As we shall see, the individuals whose stories we examine who are still single or feel unsatisfied in their relationships at midlife do not envision their pasts as happy ones. They see their lives either as antithetical or self-absolutory. Those who do manage to forge happy intimate relationships by midlife typically see their lives as antithetical—they have overcome a difficult past, often struggling through adolescence and adulthood to put together a sense of self that permits the intimacy they desire. Those who have yet to find the intimacy they desire more commonly see their narratives as self-absolutory, viewing their pasts as difficult and the present as a continuing struggle to find the emotional tools necessary to unlock the door to a different future.

Myths of older adolescents or young adults sometimes pass through a period of exploration and experimentation with life stories and roles, called *moratorium*. A moratorium is a period of hesitation during which a variety of identity possibilities are considered.[15] Ideally these explorations lead to choice and commitment, and those experiencing them emerge with a clear sense of personal identity, ready to work and make commitments in love and friendship.

Imagoes: How We See Our Self

Young adults create and define main characters that are personal and idealized concepts of self—what McAdams calls *Imagoes*. Imagoes are core personality traits and recurrent behaviors organized into such roles as caregiver, explorer, survivor, wanderer, warrior, sage, healer, or teacher. During the moratorium the hero tries on many such roles, and, ideally, selects the best fit.

Identity: Composing a Beginning, Middle, and End

All good stories require a satisfying ending, and as we reach midlife we have our first view of the end. We become aware that our personal story must end, but also that we might leave a legacy so that our story may in some sense go on. We must use this stage in our lives to refashion our myths so that something of personal importance may be passed on. The goal is to discover or compose a story for our life that integrates the past, present, and future into a unifying, and therefore continuing, narrative. This unification is called *identity*. A good story necessarily involves mistakes, failures, and contradictions (otherwise there is no excitement, no drama), but it also seeks reconciliation and harmony, a sense of completion. It seeks what McAdams calls generative integration, and what Aristotle called a beginning, middle, and an end. A good ending means having functioned in a productive and contributory way to the larger society, providing substance and direction for the next generation.

Unlike Erikson, and following McAdams, I understand intimacy development to be a lifelong concern. Like Erikson, however, I believe identity resolution is critical to intimacy. It is the formation and reformation of identity that becomes the central psychosocial task of our adult years. Fluctuations and changes occur as we pass through phases of exploration and commitment. During periods of exploration we may revise our self-definition in significant ways. Our task is regenerative, to create a self that remains purposeful, in order to give continued coherence and meaning to our lives.

Any study of adult development must assume that maturity and healthy development are shaped by cultural assumptions. In a Western culture, mature adults shoulder responsibility for their lives, assume productive roles in work and society, and make commitments in love and friendship. Adulthood, as we shall see from the case studies in the book, is a stage, not an age. It should also be noted that our models of marriage have shifted. The ideal relationship of the fifties was role-bound, and emphasized discreet and tactful communication. Today this model has shifted to a process-oriented one characterized by openness, expressiveness, and honesty in communication. Expressive communication has become the hallmark of modern relationships.

What Is a Communications Approach?

What is the value of approaching problems in intimacy from a communications perspective? No better answer has been provided than that of Watzlawick, Beavin, and Jackson in their classic work, *The Pragmatics of Human Communication.* "The pragmatics (or behavioral effects) of communication are not only words, their configurations, and meanings, which are the data of syntactics and semantics, but their nonverbal concomitants and body language as well." In other words, we must understand communication by examining both the verbal and nonverbal dimensions of behavior. In addition, I would add to these two dimensions the clues inherent in the *context* in which the communication occurs. "Thus from this perspective of pragmatics, all behavior, not only speech, is communication and all communication . . . affects behavior."[16] Thus, the terms *communication* and *behavior* may be virtually synonymous. As Watzlawick et al. put it, "You cannot not communicate."[17]

Communication investigators understand the value of this approach as observing the manifestations of *relationship* in its widest sense rather than the more individualistic view of man developed by psychology. Researchers in psychology have tended to oversimplify complex patterns of relations and interactions for convenience of research. As a result, qualities are studied in isolation rather than as an ongoing set of relations affected by the behavior of others. For communication researchers, all behavior occurs within a context or environment that is, practically speaking, a part of the communication. A statement made in the privacy of the bedroom has a quite different meaning from the same statement made in a public forum.

Human beings are not the only organisms to use non-verbal communication extensively. Nonverbal communication is inherited in part from our mammalian ancestors, but human experience adds a new dimension. In courtship, love, marriage, parent-child relationships, and work relationships nonverbal communication has greater significance than does verbal.[18] The importance of nonverbal communication to relational communication means human beings must constantly translate from one language to another in order to understand the full message. Although the focus in many studies of communication has been on verbal skills, a problem in human communication often is that our primitive nonverbal skills are insufficiently developed, both in sending and receiving nonverbal messages. Both our own nonverbal skills and our translations of others' skills may be deficient. Like an iceberg, intimate communication occurs mostly below the surface of verbal communication.

To the verbal and nonverbal dimensions of communication, Watzlawick et al. add a third—what they call paradoxical communication.[19] This is communication that crosses verbal and nonverbal contexts. The most common form of discourse, it includes complex structures such as humor and art. It involves toleration of paradox, ambiguity, and anomaly, which, as we shall see, are central to adult development in permitting us to use mature defenses and to tolerate life's shades of gray.

The Life-Span Approach

The life-span approach used here emphasizes the lifelong nature of human development and stresses that our understanding of human behaviors at any particular point is enhanced by taking into account an individual's past history and his or her future expectations. Since our concern is adult intimacy, the life-span approach is critical, for every adult has a long history of past behavior.

Let us turn, then, to some important questions. How are communication and intimacy related? What is my new paradigm for intimate communication? Why do I see intimacy as not just a communication process but a developmental passage? And finally, why is it still possible as adults to learn to be intimate?

1

Ur-moments in Communication: Developing an Adult Perspective

Communication difficulty is one of the most frequently cited reasons for the breakup of relationships. It almost always lies at the heart of problems in developing and sustaining relationships, friendships, even manager-employee relations. When we complain of problems in communication, we usually mean those skills that permit intimacy or connection with others, that lead to satisfying relationships in work and love.

This is not to say that communication and intimacy are synonymous. By intimate communication we obviously do not mean the casual communication that we use to order a meal or give directions, or even those public feelings that we may express in saying, "I'm not impressed by Senator Smith and don't plan to vote for him next term." Communication occurs for a variety of purposes, but we are concerned here with intimacy. By intimacy we mean communication leading to satisfying personal relationships exhibiting trust, commitment, and mutual comfort. For this special purpose I have previously defined the term *adult communication*. This may include sexual intimacy, but extends well beyond that to include emotional involvement of persons. In most instances intimacy is a two-person matter, but we will find that the issues generalize to include the entire web of close social relationships that we have with family, friends, lovers, and work relationships. In brief, the problems or skills that a person has in one area are likely to be seen in many other areas as well.

Learning the Language of Intimacy

Human relationships are the core of life, as essential as our biological needs for food or air. But we are born with only an innate capacity for meaningful relationships, not a fully formed capability to bring this capacity to fruition. Like all developmental processes, intimacy and the set of behaviors that make it possible must be acquired over time, just as we acquire language, physical skills, and factual knowledge. This means that some people, as a result of their unique experiences, acquire the ability for intimacy more easily or more quickly than others, and some, whose development was hindered or halted prematurely, have difficulty. There may be innate limits to our capacity for intimacy, just as we are born with greater or lesser abilities in other areas. However, it is reasonable to assume that all of us can achieve a satisfactory level of intimacy, just as we assume that all of us can learn to walk and talk.

That the skills required and the capacity for intimate communication have a developmental origin, in the same sense that language itself is acquired developmentally, is a unique idea for many. Just as there is a period in early childhood, roughly between the ages of one and five years, when children learn language almost automatically if they are exposed to accomplished speakers, so, as we shall see, there are three critical periods where we are emotionally wired for intimacy. As many of us know all too well, it is not impossible to learn a foreign language later in life, but we do not learn it automatically; only with conscious effort can such a skill be learned at a more advanced age. Although some people learn additional languages more easily than others do, none learn new languages with the same ease as the child. Similarly, the processes that enable us learn the skills of intimate communication occur with relative ease if we accomplish them at the right times in our lives. Many of us develop close relationships in our early twenties. This is traditionally the time we form lifelong friendships, fall in love, and, in some instances, marry. It is not impossible to learn intimacy at another age, but as with learning a foreign language, it is likely to require more conscious effort as the years go by.

Most psychologists and therapists agree that communication skills are central to adult relationships. Yet, these are not simply skills to be learned—they are also capacities that must be developed. Being able to communicate in adulthood requires a knowledge of how to connect with others at a fundamental and primitive level, but it also implies a tolerance for doing so. For many adults the problem may include both a lack of skill and a lack of capacity for risk taking. To become close to another is to bare oneself, which is far more difficult emotionally than physically. For this reason more scrutiny needs to be given to the developmental processes that underlie or create the capacity for adult communication, and that is what I propose to do here.

Our communication skills are markers of earlier developmental processes, processes whose resolution facilitates or inhibits intimacy. Intimacy, for this reason, must be understood not as a process which unfolds naturally and uniformly, like aging, but, as the case histories in this book demonstrate, as a capacity which results from having successfully traversed a set of developmental processes that enable the development of these communication skills. Erikson has written that our capacity for intimacy is first integrated in young adulthood. To achieve intimacy, this integration must include a shift in direction. (See table 1, p. 5) It is this shift in the directionality of our communication skills, in turn, which, in part, creates this capacity for intimacy. This shift involves learning to be givers as well as receivers (what I call affectional communication); learning to be active as well as passive (what I call ethical communication); and learning to be open enough to others to receive feedback and let others know who we are, but not so open that we lose our sense of self and not so closed we keep others away (what I call authentic communication). It is this shift that unconsciously signals to others our capacity for adult intimacy. Each set of skills develops in a social context, an ethical framework, and results from successful resolution of earlier conflicts requiring negotiation, compromise, and mutual understanding.

What Is Intimate Communication?

Intimate communication is a complex concept, and any consideration of it requires more than a brief definition, but Abraham Maslow's concept of hierarchy of needs provides a point of departure. Maslow says that when we have satisfied our sustenance needs, we turn our attention to higher social and spiritual needs, many of which can be achieved only through communication.[1] Erik Erikson similarly postulates that the central psychological task facing a person entering adulthood is to establish intimacy. Erikson defines intimacy as the capacity to commit oneself to concrete affiliations and partnerships and to develop the ethical strength to abide by such commitments even though they may call for significant sacrifice and compromise.[2] Without intimacy we experience only impersonal and superficial relationships and feel a deep sense of isolation. Intimacy enables us to conceptualize and articulate emotional experience in terms of other people.

Deficiencies in intimate communication can be traced to failures in development. Three critical developmental processes are necessary for intimate expression and serve as a yardstick of maturity. Though I do not pose an age/stage model, it is worthwhile to examine and pinpoint some reference points for adult growth that are necessary and predicable as the foundation of our individual capacity for intimacy and which form a rudimentary language of intimacy. I assume, following Erikson, that ego development continues throughout life, as opposed to Freud's emphasis on childhood as the template for the entire life span.[3] I also focus on the normal rather than the pathological. This is not to deny, or even to minimize, the fact that the foundation of our adult personalities is crystallized while we are young. Neither does this deny that basic personality tendencies continue for the rest our lives—saving some kind of intervention by self, by others, or by events. Yet, like Adler, I take the optimistic view that each personality can be shaped by the creative power to change (or, more accurately, to modify) determinants in the past.[4] We can never free ourselves entirely from our early life experiences, but we can build on strengths to limit the less desirable effects.

The Fundamentals of Adult Intimacy

Placing the development processes in a communication model, following Schultz, I identify three kinds of communication—affectional, ethical, and authentic—as significant in intimate situations. Our ability to engage in each of these kinds of communication is determined by our success in coping with childhood and adolescent psychological issues that are important and present in our nonverbal communication.

Affectional Communication: From Giving to Receiving

Affectional communication in my paradigm measures the ability to give and receive. The consolidation of our affectional self is developmentally linked to what British psychologist John Bowlby and others have called a secure base.[5] The pattern of attachment that a child develops with his or her caregiver determines both our quality and our capacity for affection. Those whose parents provide a secure base or stable bond are able to focus outward, or away from the self toward others. Unhealthy self-absorption, which Otto Kernberg and Heinz Kohut call narcissism, reflects a failure in this early caregiving, with a resultant lack of self-confidence.[6] Adult intimacy requires that one learn to nurture others as well as the self. If the caregiver is inattentive or inconsistent, the child becomes insecure and uncertain about other people and cautious about reaching outward for affection. Conversely, a stable childhood bond permits one to focus beyond the self.[7]

Ethical Communication: From Passive to Active

A second critical communication process, ethical communication, is the ability to take responsibility for our actions rather than remaining a passive victim of circumstance. This process rests upon success or failure in resolving Oedipal issues and establishing the capacity for sexual communication—which here has a much broader meaning than just the sexual act. If we are successful in dealing with Oedipal issues, we learn not to divide people or events into black or white, good or evil, but to tolerate ambiguity and imperfection in ourselves and in others. We are then able to control the fluctuation of our emotions as the superego (the conscience) is consolidated. This process is critical to the ability to handle conflict, an inherent part of all relationships, and even essential to the ability to become involved with others in the first place.

The integration of our conscience typically comes about during a developmental stage that Margaret Mahler calls rapprochement.[8] A satisfying rapprochement permits the child to explore, yet to regress and reunite with the primary caregiver if needed. If unsuccessful in this stage, a person may permanently split the world into good and bad objects. Mahler attributes this to a failure in separation or individuation. If we see ourselves as bad and others as good, we will have low self-esteem. If we see ourselves as good and others as bad, we will have difficulty with trust. If we flip back and forth between seeing a person as all good or all evil, we will be unable to find any stable basis for a relationship. Rapprochement leads to the development of object constancy, setting the stage for the Oedipal processes. Object constancy is the ability to hold antithetical beliefs about an object and thus to recognize shades of gray rather than only black and white. This permits a healthy sense of identification and ego strength, since it gives us a certain objectivity in evaluating our experience. The result is that we are able to handle conflict by selecting a mature defense rather than an immature one. Immature defenses isolate us and prevent satisfying relationships. Successful resolution permits a healthy process of differentiation from our families and better control over our emotions.

Defenses are the strategies a person employs to avoid being overwhelmed by sudden or unbearable stress. Harvard researcher George Valliant found that those who use mature defenses (suppression, sublimation, and humor) and what he calls the "kismet of finding supportive spouses" are more apt to be emotionally resilient and happier. They have better control of their impulses, are more likely to plan ahead, and tend to stress the positive aspects of an event or situation. They are less likely to respond to others with bitterness or prejudice, by blaming or projecting insecurities onto them, by denying reality, or by chronic complaining.[9] Those who use immature defenses, such as passive-aggressiveness, denial, displacement, and acting out, tend to have more problematic relationships. Unproductive patterns of conflict reflect a preoccupation with self and a disregard for others. The defenses we choose can be instrumental in our ability to get our lives on track by midlife. The Oedipal period also begins our acceptance of our maleness or femaleness, initiates our individuation from the family, and determines how confident or certain we feel about who we are, or what psychologists call our ego strength. It is our ego strength or sense of self that allows us to choose mature rather than immature defenses.

Successful intimate communication requires that we take responsibility for our life choices. Adler calls this dimension our activity versus passivity in resolving problems.[10] Karen Horney calls it hope versus dread.[11] When we are active, we use conscious reflection and deliberate action; when we are passive, we use the reverse—a lack of reflection and consequent inaction. The active person analyzes a situation, determines a best course of action, and takes responsibility for the result. The passive person prefers to think that he or she is a "victim of circumstances" and falls back upon unconscious coping mechanisms, such as rationalization and denial. Our coping mechanisms critically affect how we communicate, and especially how we deal with conflict. Healthy strategies require conscious effort and divert energy from primitive emotions to culturally acceptable ones. Passive defenses (e.g., constant complaining) remain unconscious and irritating to others and involve self-deception. The capacity for intimate relationships requires that we recognize and take responsibility for our choices.

Authentic Communication: From Unhealthy Extremes to Healthy Closeness and Distance

The third communication process, authentic communication, is the ability to permit others to know us through self-disclosure. In order for this to happen, we must develop and maintain healthy boundaries to regulate distance or closeness with others. This capacity is tied to our degree of identity resolution, a process that occurs throughout life but that can first be integrated during adolescence, when all critical components first become available. Psychoanalyst Ernest Hartmann makes distinctions between what he calls the thick-boundaried and the thin-boundaried. Hartman says that individuals with thick boundaries are armored and thick-skinned. They are rigid and difficult to get to know. Repetitious in their reactions, they fail to learn from experience and see the world as black or white. Characterized by repression and amnesia about childhood events, they have primitive defenses. They tend to awaken alert, with little dream recall. On the other hand, those with thin boundaries are fluid and permeable, tending to be vulnerable, open, and trusting. Because they have less repression, they dream more and remember more details about their dreams. They see the world as diffuse and fuzzy, attending to many things at once.[12]

Obviously, neither extreme is desirable; some healthy balance is required. Fixed ideas about who we are (thick boundaries) prevent us from getting what we want, but a lack of self-definition (thin boundaries) leaves us victim to passing whims and experiences. The healthy boundary allows us to see and be seen for who we are—to have no disparity between inner and outer self. A secure sense of identity and flexible boundaries allow us to both receive and send relational information, critical to intimacy.

Our stable base, Oedipal, and boundary issues are traversed nonverbally; therefore their successful resolution has an impact upon our ability to communicate nonverbally. Early failures in affectional, ethical, or authentic communication impede the development of intimate behavior by limiting our ability to feel or express caring toward others, by hindering the productive resolution of conflict, and by limiting our ability to give and receive feedback appropriately. Successfully navigating these three stages prepares the foundation for adult intimacy. Having had enough essential nourishment, we feel personally integrated, personally intact, and therefore free to focus on the world outside ourselves, moving from self to others. The integration of these three communication/developmental passageways determines our ability to be genuinely intimate and to find relationships that encourage intimate expression. Yet, since these processes occur nonverbally, for the most part, they have not been examined fully nor fruitfully to help untangle the communication issues that beset relationships.

Adulthood and Intimate Communication

Why do we consider intimacy an adult developmental task? The word *communicate* comes from the Latin *communicare,* "to make common." We share fellowship or communion when we see ourselves as part of a larger community. When we share, or find common ground with, another individual, we create intimacy. This is a single step, but a giant one, toward creating a community beyond the self. While the roots of our adult life grow from earlier life experiences, my thesis in this book is that communication skills crucial for intimacy may still be learned as adults. This challenges a popular belief about human development, namely, that our adult attachment styles are irrevocably determined by our early interactions with our primary caretakers. What happens to infants is important, but the notion that early interactions are frozen into the brain, unmalleable by later experience, is clearly refuted by the life experiences of the case studies offered in this book. The critical factor in human development is not security of attachment at age one but subsequent experiences. These include not only parental factors such as divorce, death, and accidents, but also other important relationships, such as those with siblings, friends, mentors, and supportive significant others.[13] Also critical is our ability to make the shift from immature and unconscious communication processes to conscious and mature ones. If we can uncover the roots of developmental processes that have shaped our capacity for intimacy, we have an opportunity to improve intimate communication. An understanding of the reasons behind a problem may or may not lead to immediate solutions, but it will allow critical insights that may permit behavior to become unstuck and move forward.

Like Erikson, I believe that adulthood is the crucial period in which intimacy occurs, and in which it is needed. The focus of emotional development in childhood and adolescence is on consolidating and integrating the self. In adulthood the focus shifts to connecting outside the self, in love, in work, and in community. Although the seeds are present in all of us, without appropriate nurturing and modeling in the family, intimacy cannot be brought to fruition in adulthood. Our deficiencies in intimacy are reflected both through our unresolved developmental issues and our faulty communication skills. Often, these skills and their underlying processes, not fully needed in childhood, lay dormant until adulthood, when we attempt to employ them to form intimate relationships. We must then reintegrate the missing pieces of our childhood by examining our strengths and our weaknesses in relationships.

Determining the causes of success and failure and what constitutes mature or adult communication is important not only to individuals who may be seeking better relationships, but also to society, since it is adult men and women who are responsible for the well-being of both the young and the old. Understanding intimate communication fully may in the long term help us to identify what processes are at work in cognition, language, regulation of emotion, belief systems, and attitude change. Uncovering the roots of problems in intimacy provides us with better gender and relational skills as we explore our own communication processes. Virginia Woolf, in her novel *To the Lighthouse*, said that one of the signs of passing youth is a sense of fellowship with other human beings. Learning to be intimate is sharing with a larger community beyond the self, a recognition of the basic fact that we are all more alike than different.[14]

To assist us in understanding issues and problems in adult communication, I turn next to a fuller development of each of the three critical communication/developmental passageways—affectional, ethical, and authentic communication—and a discussion of how each is manifest in the life of real individuals. My concern, of course, is not just with these individuals, but with the larger issues of human development and community. The question that I strive to answer in each case study is how the capacity for intimate communication is developed, and how problems in development lead to failures in community and communication problems in adulthood. I also examine how a complex pattern of relations and interactions may become mistakenly viewed as part of individual personality. Once we understand that these processes are not traits of personality but are part of an ongoing set of relationships (that is, they are social interactions and not personal traits), change becomes more possible, because social interactions can be examined and changed more easily than can personality.

Second Acts

F. Scott Fitzgerald said, "The problem with American lives is that they have no second act."[15] He meant that most people lose control of their story sometime between youth and old age. They begin with a first act of high expectations (virtually required in our culture) and they look forward to an old age of quiet contemplation and rewards. Yet somewhere in the middle passage they become frustrated, uncertain, and often isolated. This isolation is precisely the problem we attempt to deal with here. Our subjects are those in "middle passage," men and women who have survived childhood and adolescence, who have knowledge and abilities and achievements, but who now glimpse the end. Their problem is that they require other people, a "family" and "community" of some kind that offers appreciation and support. It requires their reaching out to significant others to form relationships in order to fulfill their lives.

Ur-moments, or How Does Change Occur?

Healthy modeling is fundamental for development. Children learn from parents, peers, and school, all provide less-than-ideal models. Not many of us have been fortunate enough to grow up in homes with ideal parents, and we imitate the unhealthy communication strategies that we saw as children as well as the healthy. Just as our early environment and relationships help to shape our communication strategies, so loving partners, supportive friendships, and nurturing therapists can provide environments conducive to new growth. Even with healthy modeling, we must make conscious choices that sometimes involve a struggle. I here call these choice-points Ur-moments, those moments when we realize that the communication strategies we use will fail to produce a desired outcome. We must actively decide whether to toss out those communication strategies that prevent us from getting what we want and learn new ones, or resign ourselves to repeating those tactics that have failed to meet our needs in the past. New strategies do not come easily, because older strategies exert a negative pull, as a well-worn rut holds a tire in its grip. Sometimes we must unlearn, often with difficulty, those strategies that hinder our continued development. If communication difficulties are rooted in traumatic events, growth may be difficult and distressing, especially at crisis points such as divorce, loss of employment, or the existential crunch of midlife. Ur-moments disrupt the equilibrium of identity, and change may require redefinition of the self.

In the Ur-moment, conflicting emotions must be balanced against each other. Intense emotions push and pull us between our best and worst impulses. Old patterns and behaviors may conflict with our presently desired outcomes. A child may manage conflict by crying or throwing a fit, but these tactics don't work for adults as a regular strategy. Freud portrayed the mind as a battleground of instinct, reason, and conscience, wrestling each other for control.[16] Such battles may cause great pain, but they also offer opportunity for growth and may create excitement about the future. So long as we are still fighting, we can at least know that we are alive, and we can remain hopeful even in the darkest hour.

Critical to the capacity for intimate communication is the ability to navigate and resolve intense and destabilizing crises. Mature resolution means choosing and operating from an active, outward, and appropriately open perspective. To be the best possible self is the fundamental goal. Carl Rogers observed that the good life is always a process, not a state of being—a direction, not a destination.[17] In these Ur-moments the individual is open to new insights and awareness but also vulnerable to fear, anxiety, immobilization, dependence, rage, and sorrow. If a crisis is resolved satisfactorily, positive new skills are integrated into our personality and become available in the next crisis. If the conflict is not resolved satisfactorily, the ego is damaged and we may revert to old strategies that have already failed. When we fail to rise to the challenge, we choose to stay the same, perpetuating the conditions of our impoverishment. It is, therefore, a necessary part of change that we take small steps that are likely to be successful rather than attempting global change that is unlikely to succeed. One of the advantages of having a guide—a therapist, minister, guru, or friend—is that such a person can help us choose intermediate strategies that provide gradual growth and steady success. The objective perspective of a guide helps us avoid unrealistic or too rapid change.

The value of the journey of life must be sought in the process of discovery, and discovery may come through various means. Here I integrate three separate approaches to meaning-making in our lives. The genetic approach reconstructs the way that emotional disturbances are rooted in early traumatic events, which exert a repressive pull on the present. The developmental approach makes us aware of process, of the fact that change continues at all stages of life. Communications theory calls our attention to present strategies, effective and ineffective, which we have learned from our past.

Some face their Ur-moments and are unwilling to take the steps necessary to create a new life. The crisis threatens a part of them that they are not willing to let go. Others remain unaware of their own complicity in not attaining the lives they seek and are aware only of a vague unhappiness or sense of loss. They provide a great deal of rationalization for their chosen lifestyle, but accept none of the responsibility for it. In a recent Oscar-nominated movie, Jerry McGuire (Tom Cruise) plays a cocky, successful, sports agent living a superficial fast-track life that lacks authenticity. He has a crisis of conscience that costs him his job. He makes a decision to live an authentic life and to develop relationships with depth, like the relationship he develops with his one professional client, a football player (Cuba Gooding Jr.), and his one devoted female employee (Renee Zellweger), who becomes his wife. It is a struggle to make his new skin fit, but ultimately he changes his life for the better. Like Jerry McGuire, we must face ourselves and the lives we have led and decide whether this is the future we desire. When we face our Ur-moments and decide to change, we must learn new behaviors that make our lives more meaningful and our relationships richer.

PART II
Affectional Communication

2

Getting Enough: Moving from Narcissism to Outward Focusing

I begin with the case study of Jonathan, examining what I call the affectional system. As with all the communication and developmental processes discussed in this book, the affectional system, like an iceberg, has a behavioral dimension, but also has a hidden developmental component. As we shall see, as with the other two communications systems that I believe are prerequisites for intimacy, ethical and authentic communication, much affectional communication occurs nonverbally. Intimate communication in adulthood requires an outward focus. Intimacy requires movement from what Jung called "forming the ego and getting established" to "finding a larger meaning outside the self."[1] The affectional system is the first yardstick necessary for adult intimacy. In the following chapter I tie our affectional behaviors to the developmental process that shapes them. Affectional communication implies having learned a set of skills that include attachment behaviors, such as proximity-seeking, a sense of commitment to the relationship, and profound feelings of loss or grief if the relationship is terminated. These behaviors are discussed in more detail in chapter 4. However, attachment behaviors alone are not sufficient for an adult relationship. We communicate our interpersonal needs for affection by learning to be both givers and receivers. If, as adults, we retain our childlike status as receivers and are unable to give emotional nurturance to others, then we have failed this critical passage for intimacy. The ability to give and receive affection is critical for healthy adult relationships. Affection demonstrates liking, a sense of being valued or important in a relationship.

Relational Currencies: How Affection Is Expressed

We may find ourselves with partners who express affection differently, or in different degrees. In such situations, we may have to work to find common ground. The behaviors that have meaning concerning the caring dimension are called *relational currencies.* They are actions and feelings that show appreciation and liking or the reverse, as the case may be. Positive relational currencies include cooking a favorite meal, sharing our experiences from the past and present, engaging in sports events, watching a movie or TV show together, loaning money, giving gifts, sending flowers, spending time together, or greeting one another with a hug or kiss. Whether verbal or nonverbal, these behaviors indicate a mutual exchange of affection. They make our interest clear and demonstrate that we value our partner's ideas, concerns, and contributions.

Affectional behaviors are ways of expressing love, but when couples come together they blend two systems, and their relational currencies may not coincide. What one partner values, the other may not. A bouquet of flowers, for example, may be viewed by one partner as a touching and thoughtful act, yet be seen by the other as a waste of money. In the film *Ordinary People,* the mother (Mary Tyler Moore) prepares her son's favorite breakfast. Despondent, he rejects her breakfast, thus rejecting her and her means of expressing affection. She takes his plate abruptly and puts the food down the garbage disposal. They have different relational currencies. Those with common currencies are able to exchange them freely, while those with different ones must find ways to convert their needs into commonly valued terms. Conversely, the way we show affection may create unhappiness, conflict, and disagreement. Couples report a greater sense of contentment when they negotiate and find mutually satisfying ways to communicate affectional needs and meanings.

Transcending the Self

Our affectional skills operate between two poles. At one pole lies our childlike behavior, where we focus on the self and exclude appropriate concerns for others. At the other are those communication skills that we associate with the reciprocity of a adult perspective or an outward focus, such as trust, empathy, commitment, the ability to affirm others, and hopefulness. These skills represent an ability to focus outside the self and a belief that we are lovable. When our style of communication suggests a fundamental inability to attend to others and to transcend the self, we call these behaviors *narcissism,* a core fear that we are unlovable.

Many believe that contemporary Western society suffers from the malaise of narcissism. Certainly the humor we find in the four main characters in the popular TV series *Seinfeld* is related to their uncanny ability to mimic the narcissistic traits that have become prevalent in modern society. Tom Wolfe characterized the 1980s as the "me decade."[2] Christopher Lasch has named the modern period "the Culture of Narcissism," in which individuals in love with the self find it impossible to be intimate with others.[3] Lasch sees narcissistic individuals as prone to use the terms *I, me,* and *my* less prone to have empathy for others, and more apt to be moodier, exhibitionistic, and lower in self-esteem. For many, he says, fantasies of omnipotence and immortality may substitute for intimacy. Similarly, Robert Bellah et al., in *Habits of the Heart,* connects narcissism with our cultural preoccupation with individualism.[4] Bellah agrees with Lasch that many in our society are unable to make meaningful commitments and unable to create intimacy in our lives. Kohut and Kernberg, "self-psychologists," have even identified a personality disorder that they call narcissistic.[5] A key trait in this disorder is social maladaptation.

It was Derber who first applied narcissism to communication. He coined the term "conversational narcissism" to designate the way that American conversationalists turned topics of ordinary conversations to themselves without showing sustained interest in others. Derber also attributed this pattern to our cultural emphasis on individualism, in encouraging self-interest and self-absorption.[6] Though features of the narcissistic personality and conversational narcissism may be valued and celebrated in our corporate culture, in interpersonal relationships, extremely self-focused behavior engenders negative responses from others. It does so because it violates a norm for reciprocity, a balance between give and take, both in the larger picture of the relationship and in the smaller picture of individual conversations.

Though varying, these viewpoints on narcissism agree on one point. Narcissism is a personality disorder and as so is permanently etched on individual personality. However, my research suggests something quite different. As we can see from the individual lives under study, narcissism is not fixed nor is a personality disorder but rather it is a social construct, that is, it is formed by our earlier relationships. This understanding of narcissism provides a hopeful note because with new types of relationships and self-understanding, we can change our earlier learned capacities to create satisfying relationships even in adulthood.

The narcissistic personality (within reason) may be appropriate for young adulthood when we are supposed to be discovering ourselves. Great works of art have been created and important mathematical and scientific discoveries have been make, during this self-involved, narcissistic period. The romance of forming relationships, the excitement of embarking on a career and the development of the self are the focus of young adulthood. By middle age many have begun to look for social connection and feel demands for commitment, responsibility, and perseverance, which no longer fit with the expansiveness and exhibitionism of narcissism.

Healthy versus Unhealthy Narcissism

My argument is not, however, that all narcissism in adulthood is unhealthy. Some narcissism, or love of the self, is important, since humans need a healthy narcissism or what we more commonly call self-esteem. An empathetically attuned parent who mirrors the infant's early feelings optimally develops healthy or normal narcissism. The quality of the emotional communication between the early caretaker and the child serves as the foundation of many communication skills associated with caring. Consistency in attention and caring leads to feelings of self-worth, confidence, and value. If we are properly nurtured as children, in adulthood we will be able to feel sufficiently emotionally sustained to give attention, affection, empathy, and other caring behaviors to others.

However, the infant who receives inadequate and inconsistent mirroring turns inward in despair, having failed to engage its first love, typically the mother. If these early behaviors continue as adults, we have difficulty providing reciprocity or mutuality in communication. When our behaviors suggest a sustained inability to attend to others, we call these behaviors abnormal narcissism.

Abnormal narcissism is extreme empathy failure, an inability to understand shades of meaning, as well as an inability to understand and express emotions in a mature way. Abnormal narcissists have such severe problems in empathy that maintaining close relationships is difficult. Often they are nonverbally impaired, missing vital cues in others' tones or gestures.

Unconscious personality features contribute to the loneliness felt by narcissists. Early childhood experiences result in such fragile and negative self-images that narcissists overreact to protect their tenuous sense of self, by seeming self-important or arrogant. Some psychologists have labeled this personality feature the "grandiose self" and connect it to a sense of overentitlement or overvaluation of the self, a feeling that while we deserve admiration and attention, others do not. This makes others feel uncared for and devalued.

Narcissists' negative self-images may result in aloofness which others interpret as disinterest. They may ward off others through interpersonal strategies that seem insensitive or not attuned to the situation. For example, they may self-disclose too frequently or too soon to new acquaintances. Or they may unleash a sudden rage in response to criticism. They have learned defective and self-centered ways of soothing and protecting their fragile sense of self from further injury. These may include rejecting strategies. To offset feelings of helplessness they may become preoccupied with fantasies of unlimited power and success. Some use deceit and manipulation to seek control over others. They have problems in maintaining the balance between give and take, triggered by their enormous neediness. Giving nourishment to a narcissist may feel like throwing food into a black hole. Their self-preoccupation is an effort to fill what feel like gaping holes. This may cause a sense of paranoia where innocuous and unrelated behaviors of others may be interpreted as about them. Narcissists receive, but seldom originate, caring behaviors that elicit love.

Certain features in conversation have been identified with narcissism. These include boasting, giving inappropriate and lengthy speeches about the self, refocusing the topic of the conversation on the self, using exaggerated and dramatic hand and body movements, speaking in a loud tone, "glazing over" or showing impatience when others speak, providing so little response to others that the conversation dies, asking questions only to demonstrate superior knowledge, and other forms of one-upping and attention getting behaviors. These behaviors reflect an inability to be genuinely interested in others and a compulsive need to hold the floor, by shifting the conversation toward themselves rather than offering supportive responses to others.[7] (Bette Midler parodies the narcissist in one of her movies: "Well, enough of me," she coyly remarks, "Let's talk about something else. What do you think of me?")

My first case study, Jonathan, has communication difficulties that block his ability to form a significant relationship in the first place. Jonathan's problems result, in part, from his inability to give and receive affection. As we shall see in later chapters, problems in the affectional system will also affect our capacity for ethical and authentic communication. In the following chapter, I examine Jonathan's personal narrative or myth, with an eye to what it communicates in regard to his affectional system.

3

Jonathan's Story: A Torn Net

Before turning to Jonathan, my first case study, it may be interesting for the reader to know how I found and selected those stories I decided to use in the book. I met Jonathan at a coffee hour following a Sunday church service at a Unitarian Church. As I got to know him better, I asked him if he would be willing to share the story of his life. Another case study was a member of an ongoing therapy group focused on interpersonal relationships. Other case studies in the book were found through referrals from interested friends and acquaintances, to whom I am greatly appreciative.

What I discovered was that finding singles who were still trying to form intimate attachments as adults was rather easy, as almost everyone, if they were not in this situation themselves, had friends and acquaintances who were. This may be, to some extent, more true for the urban culture in which I reside, but this phenomenon is not unique to urban life. I did not include all of those I interviewed as case studies in the book, but rather only those that I thought provided the clearest illustrations of the paradigms under discussion.

Jonathan is a forty-two-year-old never-married male who is struggling to put together the pieces of his life. He has had a difficult life, in which he has experienced poverty, an alcoholic mother, and the divorce of his parents, with only rare subsequent contacts with his father. He has a spotted job history of blue-collar jobs with high turnover. Most of his relationships, professional and personal, have not moved beyond a superficial level. Jonathan characterizes his parents as solitary and neither warm nor affectionate. His mother's alcoholism and self-focus subordinated Jonathan's needs to hers, a pattern that continues. Jonathan has yet to feel fulfillment from an intimate or committed relationship, and says he has great difficulty in expressing feelings. He has kept most of his women friends at arm's length. Although he has had sexual relationships, he has never felt the passion he expected or hoped for. He states that he has been waiting for that one perfect person who will magically change his life.

Jonathan's communication difficulties are tricky to see, since many of the skills necessary for intimacy are nonverbal and are reflected in his inability to create an emotional foundation for relationships. Without an underlying belief in the trustworthiness and good intentions of others, he mistrusts, rejects, misunderstands, and often projects his worst fears onto the relationships that he most desires. Jonathan's difficulties represent problems in the development of his affectional system and the capacity to use skills that exhibit mutuality, such as trust, empathy, commitment, affirming others, and self-monitoring. His communication skills lean toward narcissism. These skills, both nonverbal and verbal, are based upon the ability to turn attention and affection toward others and to care about them. In Jonathan's case they are arrested as a result of problems in early infant-mother relations. Jonathan's life history is an example of unresolved issues that have prevented an outward focus. I asked him to tell the story of his life, highlighting the most significant events and relationships. As with the other case studies in the book, I asked him to divide his life into chapters and to give each chapter a title.

The communication skills that show self-focusing, as compared to those which show caring or affection for others, lead in midlife in two different directions. The first path is one from which we never veer, and continues from the self-investment of childhood, with life revolving around self-worth, identity, and autonomy. The second path is one that we all seek, but do not always find. This path leads to investment in others, where our relationships with the world outside the self take on greater meaning as we seek connection. It is illuminating to examine Jonathan's narration in light of these skills. My narration follows Jonathan's own, using the chapter headings that he devised to give meaning to different periods of his life. These chapters develop a *Citizen Kane* theme of early childhood disconnection and a lifelong search for the sense of family he has lost. Jonathan divides his life story into five periods: "The Family," "Severance," "Abdication," "Arms and the Man," "The School of Boston."

The Family

Jonathan begins his story with a period that he characterizes as the peak of his life: the first eight years of his then intact family. McAdams calls peak experiences times of physical and mental strengthening when we realize our own power and our impact on others. This period is one that he calls " the family," a time when his mother, father, and Jonathan lived together prior to his parent's divorce. He fondly remembers his early childhood as one of relative stability and security, a feeling that he has never been able to recapture and which probably never existed even when his family was intact. A treasured memory is of his father in his state trooper's uniform and Smoky Bear hat, although his father held this job for only four years. If his story is a *Citizen Kane* search for reconnection, Jonathan's Rosebud symbol is his father's uniform. In fact, his father held a number of blue-collar jobs besides his four-year stint as a state trooper. Yet it is this image, much like Kane's childhood memory of his sled, Rosebud, according to Jonathan, that has become "seminal" in forming a bond and that has dogged Jonathan and informed his feelings about manhood. The uniform symbolizes his father, and he associates this "high point" with a time of security. The period is shattered at eight years of age by his parents' divorce. After this, Jonathan remembers his parents as remote and unapproachable. His mother was usually in an alcoholic daze and his father absent.

Jonathan felt that after this point something was lost, something he could not hold on to, and he remembers this with regret. Jonathan became emotionally fixated on the patrolman uniform that he associated with his father and began a lifelong obsession with jobs that required wearing a uniform in an attempt to recover that sense of security and protection. Both Jonathan and his brother have tried to recreate this through their choice of careers. His brother is a police captain and Jonathan has worked in a series of jobs such as police dispatcher, both active military duty and civilian jobs with the military, and security guard that have required him to wear a police-type uniform. For Jonathan, the uniform is a bond to his father, a way of staying close and being manly.

According to McAdams, the narrative tone of a story has its origin in infant attachment.[1] McAdams calls the narrative tone an indicator of our early relationship with our caregiver. The emotional communication between the caregiver and the child affirms (or denies) the infant's sense of agency, power, and goodness, as well as the basic attitudes about hope or despair that form our sense of the world before language. Secure attachment with a caregiver provides faith in the goodness of the world and hope for the future. Insecure attachment creates pessimism, a belief that the world is a capricious one where human beings do not get what they want. Optimists are more likely than pessimists to take positive steps to confront life's challenges and engage in more life-affirming strategies. Jonathan's pessimistic narrative tone reverberates with sadness and regret. We learn from our first interpersonal relationships a set of unconscious and nonverbal attitudes about the self. Jonathan's tone suggests a prerational and prelogical belief that his wishes, hopes, and dreams are not attainable. The world he depicts is capricious and unpredictable; it is a world over which he has no control.

He holds on to this period when his family was intact through his obsession with authority and discipline symbolized by jobs that require a uniform.

According to McAdams, before any story plots are within our cognitive grasp, we make sense of the world through emotionally charged symbols. The symbols, often preverbal and prelogical, animate our personal myths. Some images are modified or forgotten, while others survive into adulthood. Jonathan's early imagery of his family's togetherness, represented through the uniform he associates with his father, underwent dramatic rupture with his parent's divorce and his mother's decision to sell his childhood home in order to move in with her parents for financial reasons. His father's abandonment led to a lifelong rejection of him and his mother. When his father remarried he formed a new family and severed most emotional ties with his past. During this period, Jonathan replaced his father as the man of the family (with its Oedipal overtones) and abdicated any active role in life. His adolescence and young adulthood are filled with the images of uniforms. The fourth key period in his life he even calls "Arms and the Man," a period where he searched for lost security and family through the military. Even though Jonathan's family was probably never "together," we can see that much of this story is a fantasy of how he wishes it had been. It is therefore not surprising that uniforms and a military "family" cannot solve a problem that is unrealistically conceived in the first place.

In such a chaotic home, Jonathan, as a child, preferred games and activities that were organized and had exact patterns, not chaotic or anarchic. He did not like roughhousing, dirty jokes, crudeness, or spontaneity—the manly activities he was supposed to like. These differences made him feel that he did not belong with men or with "normal" children. He spent most of his youth with adults, except for his brother, who was seven years older and perceived as an adult by Jonathan. His brother adopted a protective attitude, becoming a substitute father, and Jonathan fondly displays a picture of the two brothers as children with the brother's arm resting protectively on Jonathan's shoulder. In the introduction, I defined the term *imagoes* as core personality traits and recurrent behaviors that stem from our internalized self-concepts. We see established a key imagoe for Jonathan—that of a misfit. He sees himself on the outside of life with his face pressed against a glass looking in. He desperately desires to belong, but is afraid to face the risk of rejection that occurs with feelings of affection. He has an on-going ambivalence about attachment.

The imagoe of the misfit pervades his life story. Jonathan felt he has had more in common with adults than with his own peers, and since he disdained the crudeness he associated with masculinity, he wondered if he would not have been better off as a woman. Women, he felt, were more civilized, less aggressive, and more responsive, qualities he associated with his own sensibilities. This clash of two different lifestyles—introspective/passive versus aggressive/active—he sees as a theme in his life. Certainly we see these extremes mirrored in his choice of manly occupations while at the same time he is passive in engaging life.

Jonathan's mother was formative in many ways, and he feels he is emotionally like her. He describes her as prejudiced, unable to plan a future, and excitable, in contrast to his father, who he remembers as quiet, able to plan a future, and firm. His mother was loud and prone to interrupt, making him feel his thoughts and activities had no value. Jonathan felt she lacked many maternal qualities. He describes her as "more like a big sister than a mother." Nor did he find her loudness inspiring. She did not cook or wear dresses, like most mothers. His grandmother he remembers as having more maternal qualities: she exuded a calmness, wore dresses, shared jokes, and was altogether an ideal companion.

Jonathan's mother struggled with alcoholism during most of his childhood and young adulthood. Her alcoholism and her divorce prevented her from showing Jonathan appropriate empathy. Empathy requires interpreting verbal and nonverbal communication by reading faces, gestures, and responses. The ability to empathize is based on understanding and expressing one's own emotions, an ability his mother lacked.

Her alcoholism and self-centeredness prevented her from responding to Jonathan's emotional needs, and as a result he has never felt valued. Yet she is his primary attachment. Her inconsistency and unresponsiveness resulted in what Jonathan refers to as a "torn net," to which he clings, because, as he puts its, "a torn net is better than no net." The image of a torn net implies Jonathan feels he is walking a tightrope through life without safety or protection. Jonathan's only safety net in life is his mother, despite her frailties. He seeks the protection, affection, and security from his mother that he feels was missing in his early years. This is not a home where emotional problems were dealt with openly or where feelings were discussed.

Severance

His parent's divorce ruptured the period he calls "the family." The next two chapters in his life he calls *Severance* and *Abdication*. These periods resonate with incidents that reinforce Jonathan's pessimism, resulting in his personal and social disconnection from personal and social responsibility.

The loss of his father and his home were difficult adjustments. Jonathan felt abandoned because his father had declared on leaving that the children were Jonathan's mother's problem and made few efforts to continue a fatherly relationship. Jonathan's estrangement was further highlighted when his father died. When the two families gathered around to hear his father's will read after the funeral, Jonathan felt deeply disappointed. Neither he nor his brother were mentioned, a final testament to his father's disinterest.

Abdication

In high school, Jonathan began another pattern that he has repeated throughout his life: he advanced to a position of responsibility, then walked away. Interested in politics, he was elected student body president. This honor gave Jonathan a budding sense of self-esteem. He began to speak openly against the Vietnam War hoping to shake things up. He dreamed of becoming a journalist or politician. He converted from conservative to liberal, like many young people at the time. Throughout his life, we see the traces of this imagoe developed here—that of promising but unfulfilled leader.

A traumatic event in high school served as a turning point after which he would forever shrink from responsibility. One day in speech class, Jonathan gave a playful speech on wearing condoms. The joke was taken poorly by the students and teacher in his conservative Bible-belt high school. After a female student screamed, the teacher broke her pencil and stormed off to the principal's office. Soon Jonathan found himself in the principal's office, where he was "fired" as student-body president. Under Jonathan's picture in the yearbook, the principal had printed the word "resigned." Although Jonathan felt this was vindictive, he felt too embarrassed to inform his family. He had repressed any expectations for sympathy or understanding. He expected nothing. Lacking a sense of control over his life, he had no skills to defend himself. Even we if interpret Jonathan's speech as provocative and self-destructive, such behavior is designed to test other's capacity to love, a behavior not atypical of those who fear abandonment from others.

The principal's behavior illustrates how the abuse of power can mangle lives. Consider what might have happened had students and teacher "gotten the joke." Resonating with a childhood of despair, disappointment and little positive reward, this incident reinforced Jonathan's sense of passivity, causing him to recede further from a sense of active power or autonomy.

This incident illustrates a pattern for him: resigning when faced with conflict. He passively fits into his environment rather than actively shapes his circumstances. It confirmed his feeling that others were untrustworthy and dangerous—leading to a pattern of rejecting before he was rejected.

A trusting person would have placed this event within a larger perspective, seeing it as a temporary setback or juvenile mistake (which probably best

describes what it was). The trusting person smoothes out momentary disturbances, life's ups and downs, and maintains an optimistic sense that things will
get better, that things will work out.

Those low in trust, like Jonathan, actively test for signs of caring and tend
to be vigilant in appraising situations as rife for betrayal. This vigilance leads
them to interpret ambiguous or neutral behaviors as negative.[2] They distort
and misinterpret relationships and events, then defend themselves by rejecting.
They reach conclusions that sever communication and thus an important
source of feedback. The low-trust person thus creates a self-fulfilling prophecy.

Throughout his life, Jonathan unconsciously connects with his absent
father by taking a series of blue-collar, military jobs, and student-teacher relationships in which he places himself in a childlike role and is supervised by a
parental figure. Most of these jobs, like his father-son relationship, end abruptly
in feelings of mistrust and betrayal. His choice of jobs continues his psychic
preoccupation with finding a father. He unconsciously seeks the protected
world of the dependent child, a developmental stage he has missed and repeats
the familiar feelings of loss and betrayal.

Jonathan responded to his forced resignation by becoming resigned himself.
From this time forward, he vows to abdicate any position of power. In this
respect his job history is consistent. Although this rationalization has protected
his wound, it is a pattern that has prevented him from moving forward in life.
Part of the problem is that he feels a good leader must be all-controlling and all-
knowledgeable and he cannot meet such perfect expectations. Examples of this
behavior are frequent in his life. When he was elected president of DeMolays (a
Masonic group for boys), he refused to accept despite the master counselor calling several times to encourage him. He has aborted at least two attempts to continue his schooling—one to get a Master's degree in history and one to get a
Master's degree in Library Science. He later turned down promotion to captain
of a private security guard unit, "because he did not want to take someone else's
job." His early imagoe of leader has never been fulfilled. What might have
become a positive ideal and goal has become replaced by the role of misfit.

According to McAdams, family life and culture provide the raw material that
we incorporate into our life stories through imagery and symbols.[3] These emotionally charged images are formed prior to our ability to form narratives but
they are remembered and incorporated during adolescence. Jonathan abdicated
active control over his destiny because incidents in his early family life and in high
school were too painful for his inadequate self-esteem. He backs away from all
responsibility, whether in the form of a relationship or a career. As he puts it, he
"kicks the bucket out from under himself," an image of hanging himself.

Jonathan decided that he was not to be like most people; he was superior and unique. So began another reactive defense. During high school he began a pattern of dress which continues: he always wears a suit, a full jacket and tie. He sees this as defining him as an adult and signaling his difference and superiority. Jonathan's "off duty" uniform of coat and tie he sees as a suit of armor offering protection. Dressing casually makes him feel vulnerable and unsafe. Feeling more at home out of society than in it, he has decided to reinforce his differences rather than similarities. The belief that he is unique and exceptional operates as a form of reaction formation allowing his fragile ego to survive but also reinforcing his isolation and protecting him from possible connection.

Many of his narrative events are stories of failed attempts at leadership or intimacy. Populating his story are authority figures: teachers, principals, and bosses, who betray him like his father did. He decided to shun a materialistic life and began a minimum-wage existence, taking hand-to-mouth jobs and living on cans of tuna fish, seeing this bare existence as a purer life. He has resisted making choices, whether in love or work, because he believes he is exceptional, brilliant, different, and apart from others.

Arms and the Man

The next period of Jonathan's life continued his interest in uniforms and hats. After high school he worked as a police dispatcher in order to save money for college. Jonathan proudly displays a picture of himself in dispatcher uniform and hat. In college he began dating, finding two girlfriends who accepted his intellectual way of talking. Christa was an exchange student from Germany and a born-again Christian. Jonathan joined a Bible study group to be near her. Although she was five years older than he, he was drawn to her because he saw her bohemian and hippie qualities as romantic and spiritual. He pursued her for two years and was hurt when she married someone else. He describes her as aloof and unfriendly. He also dated Lilith, who he met in a school play. He felt they were connected because both were trying to sort out what to do with their lives. Both relationships were nonsexual.

While Jonathan was in college, his mother continued her self-destruction through alcoholism and his brother moved to Topeka in order to get away from her. Jonathan's home life became characterized by fighting. Although he grew long hair to indicate his opposition to the establishment, at the same time, he had no vision of the future and no plans so he decided to join the army, the ultimate in establishment. Despite his dreams of being a West Point cadet, he became a postal clerk. His service began with a seven-week stay at Ft. Leonard

Wood, in Missouri. He had difficulty adjusting and did not feel he was as good a soldier as he should be. He was placed briefly in charge of a group but felt it was a disaster, one of the worst experiences of his life. He did not like being yelled at, was not comfortable with running and push-ups, and was not a good marksman. He felt he had failed. He saw himself as "placed with criminals and blacks." Yet, at the same time, he hated the ostracism and group mentality and sometimes befriended other ostracized men. When he became disoriented and sprained his ankle during an exercise, he felt so hungry and in such despair that he considered killing himself on his bayonet. Reprieve came when he did so poorly as a soldier that he was sent to Germany as a postal clerk, where he stayed for thirty months.

While in Germany he began a correspondence with Anne, a woman seven years his senior. She was a twice-divorced nurse who had had a brief affair with his brother. They met for a week in Paris, but Anne put limits on sex. Instead Jonathan went to a state house of prostitution, where he had sex for the first time at age twenty-two.

Although he left the army in July 1976 at twenty-four years of age, the army regimen continues in the present. He continues through his forties to live in single room, bunk-like settings without kitchens, bathrooms, or amenities.

Jonathan was discharged when his grandmother died, but he missed the funeral because the army was slow to process him out. Despondent, he went to Anne's for two days, where he slept with Anne for the first time. When he returned home, life had gone out of the house—his mother was drunk, his grandmother dead, and his brother "shacked up" with a girl in Topeka, Kansas. In contrast to the warm homecoming his brother had received on his return from service, Jonathan received nothing.

The School of Boston

During his middle twenties, Jonathan began to fantasize about Boston. He had spent a lot of time wondering what to do with his life, and now his plan became to move to Boston, which he saw as a city of high culture. He made a trip there, stayed for one week, then panicked and returned home to his mother, where he drifted for three months until finding a job with the army reserve. When the job ended, he lived off savings. This pattern of working for a few months and then living off his savings has followed him into his forties, with periodic trips to Boston, which have always ended in a retreat home.

This period was another turning point for Jonathan. He attempted to become more autonomous and to break away from the psychic realm of his childhood. Though his attempts were not ultimately successful, he did demonstrate an effort to effect change. This led to a cycle of taking jobs and leaving them, as he moved back and forth between home and Boston, much like a child who explores further and further but always returns to the mother to make sure she is still there.

Jonathan's life has been characterized by a lack of stable and intimate relationships. He tends to pick what he calls "castaways and nerds" as friends and describes one current friend as "a paranoid schizophrenic." These friendships are not deep, intense, or fulfilling. His association with women he calls "not really dating." He is waiting for something or someone to give his life direction. In a relationship, he feels stressed and tense, suspicious and shy, like his mother, who he did not feel was emotionally balanced.

He says he feels like he has dropped out of the world. He has resisted making choices or settling into any one thing, but continues to think himself exceptional, brilliant, and apart from the group. He tells himself he is happy in his solitude and introspection because he is purer and shuns the material life. An article in a magazine had a significant effect on him. The article stressed the ethics of not owning a car and provided a rationale for the life he had adopted anyway. He began to detest cars and to see his carless life as making him stronger. He also accepted his low wage jobs and his life in squalid, single bunkrooms as a reflection of the purer life he had chosen, where books and knowledge were more important than relationships and possessions.

At twenty-five, Jonathan planned to meet his father and have Christmas dinner, but did not have money for gas, so he spent Christmas alone. He felt too embarrassed to meet his father by bus and he had no telephone. When his brother banged on his apartment door with the police that Christmas, he hid. His brother left a note on his door and car windshield, but he did not read it. The next day he saw his father's obituary in the paper. His father's death was "a decisive event." It sent his mother into alcoholic relapse. Jonathan broke down and cried.

Helping him through this traumatic and lonely period was a woman he met while working as a clerk in the army record center. Although he felt superior to her culturally, Ella was affectionate, a quality he had trouble showing. He described himself as being insufferably stuffy during this period. Jonathan was grateful when she came to his father's funeral.

Although his father's death was hard for him, Jonathan feels that he hit an all-time low when he was twenty-eight. According to McAdams, nadir experiences are low points that have the potential to lead to self-redefinition. This occurred for Jonathan after a period of emotional and economic poverty when he realized he was living a very lonely, isolated, and pointless life. For the first time he decided to write, creating a third imagoe, leader, misfit, now famous writer. This demonstrated an ability to sublimate, to turn his unhappiness into something positive. Although he continued his single-cell style of existence, alone and solitary, he felt his time was now purposeful He survived on beans and baked potatoes, getting so big he could not wear his clothing. Days passed where he did not say a word to anyone. But, because he was writing he felt superior to those living a more materialistic life.

Finally Jonathan resolved to go to graduate school in history. He moved to the college town to live with his mother and entered the university. He stayed through the summer, sometimes getting a room in a hotel if he needed to finish a paper. During this period, he had a "dream" in which she came into his room in the middle of the night and urinated on the floor. The dream was so vivid, he does not know if it was a dream or reality.

The dream is an interesting one and certainly bears considering. We may understand it as Jonathan's belief in his mother's unconscious attempt to establish a sense of territoriality, much like a dog creates his territory, resulting in Jonathan feeling fenced within her psychic reality. If true (if she did actually pee in his bedroom), it shows a level of disorder in the boundary system with his mother and her inability to control her disheveled behaviors.

Jonathan met Gloria, his first major relationship, in the historical library while he was doing research. She later told him that she was immediately attracted to him, and had a coworker tell him to come back the next day. He was also attracted to her. Jonathan describes Gloria as cultural, interested in history (as he was), attractive, and tall. Yet she was extremely jealous. In particular, she was jealous of his brother's girlfriend, Monica, who she saw as a competitor. She had been jilted three or four times and was bitter. She made it clear that she did not want anything to do with the East Coast or his plans to move to Boston.

Jonathan remembers this summer as emotionally wrenching, trying to juggle his mother, school, and Gloria. Gloria complained that he was not affectionate enough, and Jonathan felt threatened by her fighting. Since he had had no experience with any sort of "normal" argument within a relationship, he had never learned to deal with conflict, and felt that any argument meant that the relationship was in trouble. He recognized this as an either/or mentality, but could not find a bridge, a way to communicate. If they argued, he felt that the relationship was over. This is the same pattern he sees in his childhood—if someone kidded him, he did not know how to fight back but could only withdraw, feeling oppressed; when his high school principal printed "resigned" under his yearbook photo, Jonathan vowed to passively resign from life.

His graduate career came to a halt when his advisor went to Germany and never returned. Jonathan took this personally and did not try to find another advisor. He viewed him as another father figure who had deserted him.

Meanwhile, his interactions with Gloria became more dramatic. She had loaned him money to move into a room. She insisted on getting back some of the money he had borrowed and threatened that she would make things such a big mess he would never hear the end of it. She complained that he did not use condoms when they had sex. One day when a random gunshot strayed through Gloria's windshield, she insisted he pay for it because, she said, had he not moved the car the accident would not have happened. On another occasion, when he wanted to watch a TV evangelist, she became angry and insisted that he pay attention to her.

Although it appears from his description that Gloria had serious problems of her own, he still remembers this as his first decent relationship. He was strongly attracted to her because of what he saw as her "cultural background," and considered marrying her.

When Gloria recommended he take a job at the state historical society, he did so, but she became angry at his lack of attention. It appears that what really bothered her was his admitted difficulty in expressing affection. One night she left a movie to sit in the car because he did not attend to her. He remembers her distinctly asking him one evening if he was serious and planned to marry her: "Are you serious about our relationship, or do you want to be pals, friends, buddies?" When he replied that he wished to be friends—obviously not the answer she wanted—she ordered him out. He had made her realize, she said, that she did not want to be with a man. Whatever her own problems, this was a natural attempt to clarify an ongoing relationship, which Jonathan interpreted as a threat because of his fear of closeness. He characterizes most of the women he has known as overly affectionate, jealous, and controlling, but whether this is real or his own projection is not known.

Although he agreed to serve as an usher at the state historical society banquet in order to please Gloria, he felt so threatened that he never went inside to join the party. He claimed it was his duty to guide people in, and stayed outside. His pattern of feeling on the outside looking in had become so engrained that it had now become a self-fulfilling prophecy. This upset Gloria so much that she insisted he would be in trouble for his strange behavior. His job was eliminated by budget cuts five months later, by which time he and Gloria had broken up. He took the break hard, and it took him several years to get over it. Since he had lost his job and his advisor, he decided to leave school. His mother was now sober and had begun to put her life back together. He was recalled to full-time duty in the army guard, his first decent job paying at a reasonable salary, and started to save enough to return to Boston.

He met Ruth, his next major relationship when he became active in a group opposed to the war in Central America. He became more radical, obsessing during this time with imperialism and nuclear war, continuing his pattern of political extremes. Ruth was a divorced Ph.D. student who had spent several years in Central America. As usual, she was older, thirty-seven to his thirty. She had been in an abusive relationship with her ex-husband, and her son was using drugs and had tried to commit suicide. She was brilliant, he says, but she had not been able to get her life together and lived on income her father sent her.

Their relationship worsened when she accused him of not caring enough and not paying enough attention to her. She believed Jonathan was dominated by his mother, and was conflicted about his military service because of her political views. She was extremely jealous, and if he glanced at another woman it led to a bitter fight. One night she insisted that they leave a movie when he failed to pay enough attention, saying, "I'm not your chauffeur" (they had used her car for transportation). When they attended a play together, she excused herself, and when she did not return he found her in the car, crying.

Another violent argument occurred when she brought him a plant and book as a gift but became infuriated by what she apparently saw as a lack of appreciation. She broke the plant, slapped him, and took back the book. At 3:00 A.M. she knocked on his door, demanding to know if he wanted to keep the relationship. At the end of her jealous episodes, she would storm off, then call him up at work or follow him there and demand to talk.

Despite the roller-coaster relationship, Ruth was hard for Jonathan to give up, but when his job with the guard ended, he decided it was then or never. He had to choose between Ruth and Boston. He had never told Ruth his plans for Boston, which he knew was dishonest, but this was just one more example of his communication problem. He feared that open and honest communication would threaten the relationship. Still he felt that his conflicts with Ruth were therapeutic, just as writing was therapeutic.

His choice of Ruth and Gloria, with their strong emotions and bitter feelings, suggests a basic blindness which he has yet to overcome. He is attracted to women who take the initiative, which he cannot.

Further, his inability to believe in a sense of continuity—in the day to day fabric of relationships—creates an environment where it is hard to grow interpersonally. He is bereft of a consistent source of nurturance and "safe" feedback. Therefore, he has little opportunity to reassess his faulty beliefs outside of stable relationships. His relationship choices have led to a diminished self-esteem and have replayed the instability of his experience.

Jonathan has trouble establishing a footing in the present and a view of the future. He is "waiting for someone to come along" to give his life a direction. Most of his girlfriends report needing more affirmation, affection, and attention than he can provide.

The adult need for kissing, smiling, and emotional caring have their origin in the shared gazing, smiling, touching, and babbling between infant and mother. For the adult, as for the infant, a positive response is required for a continued sense of well-being. Without the capacity for mutual affection, a gratifying sexual exchange is hampered.

In 1983, Jonathan broke his cycle. He moved to Boston and took his longest-lasting job as a security guard, staying in his firm for two-and-one-half years. He enjoyed his routine and was promoted from patrolman to sergeant and then to lieutenant, indicating once again that he was not without leadership virtues. A key problem he struggled with was his temper. He was easily frustrated and often became angry, resulting in temper tantrums where he would slam his first into something or break something. Although he still had trouble relating to people, he felt a sense of belonging for the first time. He had a new job in a new environment and was glad to be away from Ruth, a relationship that had become too painful.

During a visit home with his mother, she fell and broke her hip. He decided to stay and nurse her, and his care largely healed their animosity. This was aided by his mother's own progress. She had overcome her alcoholism and was enrolled in a job-training program that allowed her a measure of independence.

When he returned to his security guard job in Boston, he was asked to take over as captain but refused the position because he felt it would be a betrayal. He was asked to replace an alcoholic. Engaging again in an all or nothing strategy, he left the security firm and was unemployed for three months. He wrote a second novel, about a security guard.

Penniless, Jonathan decided to return to live with his mother, hoping to find a new career as a librarian. He believed he was outgrowing the mentality of his security guard work, where he was ordered around like a child. He felt distant from his brother, who was now married. Their distance was exhibited, Jonathan felt, when his brother fell asleep while Jonathan tried to converse with him. Jonathan stopped by the historical society to see Gloria and to talk about library science as a career. He took a job as a security guard while going to library school. However, when he found a job as an assistant in the medical library at the Veterans Administration he decided to abandon his education as a librarian because this new job was so good. When his job at the VA was eliminated, he took another security job and wrote his third novel. During a period of unemployment he decided to return to Boston to find security work.

In Boston, a big help for Jonathan has been his Scottish dancing, which has become integral to his social life. It provides the kind of structured activity he needs and makes it easier for him to relate to others. He has also become involved with a church, finding security there, and he spends much time listening to evangelists. He now feels happier and more socially adjusted, more grown up, and ready for responsibility. He has convinced himself that things happen for a divine purpose.

Jonathan feels he needs two more things to put down roots—to marry and to find a career—in order to become comfortable. He realizes his single-cell style of life is no longer viable. He would still like to be a librarian and says he is committed to giving it a try. He is also finding courage to circulate his writing. He has lived a private life, though he admits he has fantasies of a public one. He wishes not so much to be famous as to give something of himself. In addition to finding a stable career and marriage, he hopes to give service to the larger community and to God. He has returned to stay at his mother's house while he gives library science another try. He has a few friends there, and he feels he has left his life in Boston. He has taken work bagging groceries.

Commentary

Jonathan's story illustrates a number of points in our thesis, which we will discuss in detail as we go along, but a few general points need to be made here for future reference. In general, his life suggests a pattern of drifting, an inability to make long-term commitments in love and friendships, to secure an occupation, or to be able to give back. The theme of Jonathan's story is his search for love and protection. Implicit in this theme is a realization that he is waiting for someone to come along to give him the original wholeness that he seeks. Jonathan understands his life's plot as compensatory. In a sense his life has peaked early, and it's all been downhill since the period he calls "The Family." Unfortunately, he has cut off many of the expectations that many adults take for granted and that might lead to the stability he seeks. He is in a state of moratorium where he hesitates to make commitments in work or love. He keeps all options open. While a period of exploring or experimenting is common for adolescence or young adulthood, Jonathan has suspended this period indefinitely, creating a time lag. He thinks of himself as young, with his whole life ahead, in a period where many adults have made commitments and are planning for the second half of life.

Jonathan is extremely smart and possesses a great deal of knowledge concerning history, literature, plays, and music. He would make an excellent teacher. Yet, while these accomplishments might lead any of us to think well of ourselves, Jonathan uses his feelings of superiority to create an aloofness that allows him to deny his need for others. He offsets his feelings of helplessness through fantasies of power and success. Jonathan believes he is destined for greatness. At first he dreamed of being a great political leader. But when his dreams of public leadership were shattered in high school, he created a new identity—a famous and successful writer. Jonathan may have talent, but he has so far been able to achieve just enough success to provide justification, and has not achieved anything beyond promise.

Narcissists avoid intimate contact and tend to be lonely; they unconsciously ward off the efforts of others to be close. Maintaining relationships is difficult because they are vigilant for signs of rejection and sensitive to criticism. They have a kind of "best defense is a good offense" theory. Without a stable sense of self, they are reliant on others for their good opinions. Easily wounded, they act out with rage when hurt. As a result, their relationships are tenuous and they rob themselves of new sources of feedback to recreate themselves and correct earlier distortions. Any information that contradicts their grandiose sense of self is eliminated.

It is clear that Jonathan possesses intelligence and has a good deal of insight into his problems, yet this intellectual insight does him little good. As outsiders we see an obvious pattern which is likely to continue, but he has made progress nonetheless. He has received some positive response to his writing, yet his decision to return to live with his mother must be viewed as part of an early pattern and not ultimately liberating. Although he has a number of fantasies, he has not yet been able to actualize them, and he has no idea how to concretely build the future he desires.

Trust, empathy, commitment, affirming others, self-monitoring—all suggest a fully developed capacity for mutuality and an adult perspective. An adult perspective indicates hopefulness, what Erikson has called vitality, or an active engagement of life's problems and appropriate developmental concerns.[4] Self-focusing, failures in empathy and trust, and a delayed time perspective characterize the nonverbal communication of those whose capacity for intimacy has been poorly developed. Jonathan's communication skills suggest some degree of narcissism in his inability to fully attend to others and to commit to a relationship or job, and some degree of underactivity in getting his needs for intimacy met. Yet, as Jonathan's life is a testimony, all of these communication skills, no matter how perfect or imperfect, are products of the earliest set of social relationships. It is to this critical early stage between mother and child that I turn next.

4

Patching Our Torn Nets: A Stable Base and Consolidation of the Affectional Self

One of life's ironies is that we must be loved before we can learn to love. As we have seen, Jonathan's story suggests a lifelong search for a lost sense of protection and connection. Jonathan is developmentally arrested and has yet to surmount the critical early issues of attachment. Intimate communication—showing affection, being responsive, affirming others, making commitments, giving empathy, and accurately reading the nonverbal communication of others—is based upon an ability to focus outside the self. Without a proper emotional foundation, we are left so needy ourselves that we are unable to turn our attention outward. Although we can discern some progress over the course of his life, real intimacy seems out of Jonathan's grasp, despite his awareness of the problem. How can we explain his difficulty in finding connection or intimacy? To understand some of the issues involved, we turn to current theory on the significance of our first interpersonal relationship, that between mother and child.

Development of the Attachment System

Freud and most Freudians have emphasized infantile sexuality, the "Oedipal complex," as the key event in the development of children. Without denying the importance of the Oedipal events, developmental psychologists have focused in recent years on the equal importance of the infant's early relationship with the mother as critical to healthy development. This relationship occurs, or fails to occur, in the pre-Oedipal years, from birth to age two. This growing body of work, called attachment theory, has focused on mothering and the infant's dependency upon proper mothering for psychological growth. Much like imprinting, an important component of attachment behavior is proximity seeking and the beginning of the use of symbols.

Object Permanence and the Differentiation of the Self

The symbolic process begins with a transitional object that represents attachment to the primary caregiver—usually the mother. Teddy bears and security blankets are common substitutes for the mother as the child learns to be separate. The special object takes on the emotional feelings attached to the mother, enabling the child to take the mother's security along. The term *object* has a special meaning in psychoanalytic writing. Objects are both the things external to the self *and* our mental representation of them. The object, by means of this dual role, allows the infant to move from identification with the mother to consciousness of being outside and separate. The dawn of the "object world" coincides with the infant's gradual emergence from embeddedness, differentiating itself from the world, and the world from it. Object relations are an evolutionary activity and form the foundation of personality development.

At first the object is seen by the infant as transitory, a temporary substitute that magically appears and disappears, but gradually the infant endows the object with permanence and begins to build an independent, external world. This process is called by psychoanalysts "object permanence," and allows the child to separate from the mother. In Margaret Mahler's phrase, the child is "hatched out" from the maternal world in which it was embedded, much as the chick is hatched out of the protective egg.[1] This process of differentiation and integration begins a lifelong process of finding and losing, for the self is always "under construction."

Constructing the Emotional Self

"There is no more important communication between one human being and another than that which is expressed emotionally," writes John Bowlby. "There is no information more vital for constructing and reconstructing the working model of the self and others than information about how each feels about the other."[2] During the earliest years of our lives, before language, caregivers' expressions of affection and attention are the only means of communication we have. Their expression forms a preverbal foundation for our working model of the self.

Many have studied the quality of this early bonding between infant and mother, including Melanie Klein, W. R. Fairbairn, and the school of object relations.[3] More recently, self-psychology theorists such as Heinz Kohut and Otto F. Kernberg have used similar theory to develop their model of narcissistic personality disorders.[4] I choose here to follow the models of Winnicott and Bowlby.[5]

Both believe that the relationship of mother and child is the key to understanding human affectional development.

The Holding Environment, the Stable Base, and Attachment Theory

Winnicott and others have asserted the critical importance to the infant of the "holding environment." Stable routines combined with sustainment (holding) by the mother are seen as critical to ego development. Winnicott compares emotional growth to the growth of a plant. With care and water, an innate growth process unfolds. Yet this process occurs naturally only with the "good enough mother."[6]

Bowlby calls the holding environment the "stable base" and develops a theory of human development that he calls attachment theory.[7] Attachment theory regards the innate tendency to form intimate emotional bonds as basic to human nature. A feature of attachment behavior is the intensity of affection that accompanies it. Attachment behavior involves attaining and maintaining proximity to some other individual perceived as better able to cope with the world.[8] Although supplemented later by speech, nonverbal communication persists as the principle feature of intimate relationships throughout life.

For Bowlby, the capacity to make intimate affectional bonds is the foundation of effective personality functioning and mental health. This behavior is organized, he believes, by a control system similar to our physiological control system—that is, it operates at a level below consciousness. The attachment system maintains a person's relationship to an attachment figure between optimal limits of distance and accessibility. The basic components of this system consist of caregiving, careseeking, and exploration from a secure base. Limits of distance and accessibility are expressed though nonverbal communication. Our personal attachment system and attachment figures constructed during childhood form the working model of the self. These models become the central feature of personality functioning throughout life. Absent some dramatic or traumatic intervening experience, it is this system, established in infancy, that continues to monitor our personal limits of distance and accessibility as adults.

The Good-Enough Mother and Development of the True versus False Self

A "good-enough mother" nurtures the infant by responding consistently to its needs, permitting ego development and feelings of competence, so that the infant can explore its environment with the assurance that it can return to mother in times of distress. If all goes well, there is joy in growth, yet a sense of security between the mother and child.

What happens when the quality of mothering is not "good enough? According to Winnicott, if the holding environment is faulty (inconsistent or inadequate) the infant experiences anxiety, jealousy, and anger. If it is broken altogether, there is grief. A "not-good-enough mother" substitutes her own needs and fails to recognize the needs of the infant. If the mother cannot respond to or identify with the infant's needs, the child is forced to comply with *her* needs merely to survive.

What Winnicott calls a "false self organization" results.[9] For the infant, and later the adult, this creates feelings of unrealness, a sense of futility, a withdrawal from the world, and feelings of detachment from others. A false self must rely on external sources of affirmation and vitality in order to function. The person's emotions are under the control of outside forces, and reaction replaces spontaneity. Internal needs and ideas are replaced by the need to placate. Hypervigilence and concern with other people's reactions replace independence.

Many of these characteristics of the false self we have seen in Jonathan. Jonathan sees himself as living in a state of noncommunication or nonrelatedness. Even his clothing style, a full suit, acts as a suit of armor to protect him against vulnerability. He fears new experiences because his childhood attachment system, his relationship to his mother, is, in his own words, "a torn net." It is this system that continues to control his limits of distance and accessibility to others. His awareness of this can be seen in his periodic attempts to establish a life of his own in Boston, but the tear in his net is made obvious by his frequent returns home. If Jonathan were a two-year-old we could understand this easily. Yet in an adult this is clearly a sign of maladjustment.

Development of what Winnicott calls the "True Self," in contrast, results in feelings of aliveness, of existing as oneself and relating to objects as oneself, therefore creating the desire for new experiences—the desire to *learn*.[10] The infant learns that there *is* an external world apart from its own needs and desires. This leads to the development of the ego, the portion of the self that deals with reality. From a secure base, an infant can make sorties into the world, knowing that it will be welcomed when it returns, knowing that it *can* return if it feels threatened. It will be nourished physically, comforted if distressed, and reassured if frightened. Most of the time the role of the base is a waiting one, but it is nonetheless vital. Those who have the most stable bases make the most of their opportunities and are encouraged by their parents to become autonomous although aware that their parents are responsive and available. Jonathan continues, even into adulthood, to make sorties into the adult world, but feels a repeated need to return for reassurance. As he so aptly remarks, "a torn net is better than no net," yet his real question is "Is any net still there?"

Harlow, Ainsworth, and Attachment

Bowlby's views on attachment are indebted to the studies of a number of predecessors, including Harry Harlow and Mary Ainsworth.[11] Harlow examined infant attachment by studying rhesus monkeys. He constructed two surrogate mother monkeys, one of wire mesh and one of terry cloth, each with a feeding nipple. Even when the wire mesh mother was the one providing food, the infant monkeys became attached to the terry cloth mother. They cuddled it, ran to it when frightened, and used it as a base for explorations. This experiment challenged Freud's assumption that attachment between mother and child is based on feeding. Warmth, contact, and comfort are more critical than physical nourishment.

Bowlby's theories on attachment also rely on the research of Mary Ainsworth. Ainsworth's premise is that a responsive, available mother provides a secure base that results in an infant who can accept its own emotions and the emotions of others, the fundamental basis for caring ("I'm O.K., you're O.K."). She sees the attachment system as biological and fundamental to most species. Such a system has the practical evolutionary advantage of keeping the infant in close proximity to a caregiver that can provide food and protection. Other innate behaviors, such as crying, serve a similar purpose.

This system includes not only an outward manifestation but also an inner organization that is subject to developmental change. In other words, it also produces an internal sense of self. All the infant's physical instincts—crawling, walking, babbling, grasping, reaching—have intellectual and emotional concomitants that lead to recognition of the external world, abstract concepts, language, and the eventual separation of an external world from the internal one. The baby's inner representation of the principal caregiver as a separate object enables it to discriminate between self and world, but with this awareness comes distress when the caregiver is not present. There is thus a shuttling back and forth between exploration and security, exactly as we have seen with Jonathan. Like Bowlby, Ainsworth's premise is that a responsible and available mother provides a secure base and a set of affectional skills that are internalized and later used by the adult. When the process works, the growing child is able to spend increasing time and energy on its own exploration and development, with less and less need for return to base. A secure and predictable base leads to autonomy and independence. The childhood game of Prisoner's Base is a perfect representation of this going out and coming back.

Secure versus Insecure Styles of Attachment

Ainsworth studied mothers and children at home during the first year, measuring the mother's style of responding to the infant by observing feeding, crying, cuddling, eye contact, and smiling. At twelve months, infant and mother were taken to a laboratory room. The mother then left the room and the child's behavior was observed. Ainsworth divided the children's subsequent behavior into three categories. *Securely attached infants* had mothers who were responsive to feeding and smiling. These infants protested and cried when separated from their mothers, but greeted their return with pleasure and were easy to console. They were flexible, socially competent, curious, sympathetic, and assertive. *Avoidant infants* had mothers judged to be unresponsive and concerned more with their own needs than those of the child. These children gave an initial impression of independence, exploring the environment without using the mother as a base. They did not appear affected when she left, but when she returned they reacted by snubbing or avoiding her. They were sullen and oppositional and not inclined to seek help when injured or disappointed. Their pleas for attention had been consistently rejected and reaching out seemed useless. As adults, they often developed defenses based upon grandiose ideas about their own greatness and independence, achieving a rigid independence from others by becoming emotionally cut off. Many exhibited what we have called narcissistic communication.

The third category, *ambivalent infants,* had inconsistent mothers who were sometimes attentive and sometimes not. The children reacted by clinging and being fearful. They were anxious and agitated over separation. When the mother returned they arched their backs angrily yet at the same time sought contact. They remembered that their mother came through on occasion but, at the same time, tried to punish her for her times of unavailability.[12]

A secure child is able to communicate feeling because it feels it is safe to do so. Distorted communication patterns grow from the way that children learn from their mother to deal with negative feelings like anger, hurt, and resentment. Often "not good enough" mothers are unable to understand their own feelings and tend to overreact or not react at all. Insecure children learn to wall off negative feelings from consciousness, for fear their expression will lead to rejection. When the wall fails, they may be overwhelmed by their feelings, leading to tantrums and destructive behavior. This leads others to misinterpret the child's behavior as self-centered (what is usually called "spoiled") or rejecting. Both Bowlby and Ainsworth conclude that the child organizes his or her inner working model of the self on attachment figures and the environment they create.

These studies also suggest that women with disturbed childhoods tend to carry on the tradition by having fewer interactions with their infants. Those whose mothering was erratic, aberrant, critical, blaming, or simply absent grow up to be anxious about being deserted. They learn to regard emotional abuse or physical abuse as a part of the natural order and to expect little or nothing in the way of love. These studies indicate that children who have been abused are more likely to have been products of abnormal pregnancies or deliveries, to have been separated from the mother for forty-eight or more hours after birth, or to have suffered separations of other kinds. Both abused children and their mothers are more likely to have serious illnesses during the child's first year.[13]

Just as Piaget developed a model for cognitive development, Ainsworth offers an explanation for emotional and social development. Ainsworth's research was seminal in shifting the perception of developmental psychology. It was the first measure of emotional development, and revealed how experience shapes personality and the inner self. It suggests how this relates to adult personality and future relationships. Her research suggests how these early childhood patterns persist. By age two, children who were insecurely attached showed a lack of confidence and little enthusiasm for problem solving. At ages three to five, they were often problem kids with poor peer relationships and little flexibility, placing exaggerated emphasis on a few negative consequences of their actions. At six, many showed a sense of hopelessness.

Yet, on the positive side, most children proved amenable to later change through attachments to teachers and adults who provided alternative models of relatedness. Studies of resiliency demonstrate that having a surrogate "mother" in later life can compensate to some extent for earlier deprivation.[14] However, the alienating strategies developed by those with insecure attachment—narcissistic and grandiose defenses like Jonathan's armor—make finding alternative models difficult. To build a new model of the self with a new set of expectations requires patience and consistency by both those who give and receive care.

Extreme poverty, an unstable family life, early parental divorce, an absent and emotionally distant father, and a troubled and alcoholic mother—all of which suggest an extremely unstable base—have characterized Jonathan's life. His mother was not able to nurture enough to allow Jonathan's ego to develop a sense of active agency in his life. She was a "not good enough mother" whose own needs took precedence, and she failed to meet the needs of her infant.

Since his feelings and needs were not validated, a sense of futility resulted. Although Jonathan is now forty-two, his sense of time's passing is not in step with his years—he is still thinking in terms of what he will do "when he grows up." He has not developed age-appropriate concerns, although he is struggling in that direction. He has yet to develop a full sense of aliveness or vitality, because he must still give an undue amount of concern to his relationship with his mother and is still psychically and geographically connected to her. He has not yet been able to separate.

Although midlife can bring increased creativity, wisdom, and what Erikson calls an interest in establishing and guiding the next generation, those who have not moved beyond the self are likely to be deteriorating by middle adulthood.[15] Midlife raises the specter of lost opportunities, an awareness of failure, or at least of not having achieved innermost feelings and goals. Heightened awareness of our mortality and the limits of our accomplishments lead to feelings of envy and rage, and to defensive evaluation of others.

Jonathan admits that he has been reluctant to channel his life into any one direction, wanting to keep open all of his options. He has yet to commit to a relationship. He has yet to commit to a career. He has yet to commit to a place. He has yet to take a job that uses his academic skills or has a clear upward track to greater responsibility. He avoids responsibility, a pattern he established in high school. His minimalistic lifestyle further suggests that he has cut off the basic expectancies for adulthood.

However, there is evidence to suggest that Jonathan's level of intimacy and affection may be increasing. He calls his last chapter "The School Boston," indicating his awareness that there is much to be learned from this new chapter of his life. Bernice Neugarten thinks that the hallmark of middle age is complexity, being in control of a crowded life and involved in the world.[16] Jonathan is beginning to *want* something different for himself, but his crucial task is to separate from his mother. He is facing his Urmoment, that moment of anxiety when he must decide to change or remain the same. Freud suggested that all moments of separation and birth reproduce the painful feelings of that first separation from mother, a trauma that Jonathan has yet to face. Jonathan's financial and emotional poverty have imprisoned him, denying him the tools necessary to get help by seeking therapy or significant others for models.

Winnicott sees the mother-infant relationship as the model for psychotherapy. The therapist restores to the adult patient an environment in which development can resume. In this style of therapy, regression occurs so that verbal interpretation is secondary to maternal care. If the environmental failure has been severe, the patient will have developed a militant self-sufficiency, or what Winnicott calls a false self. Thus, attention to the situational aspect of the analysis, such as the punctuality and neutrality of the therapist, the regularity of sessions, and the contractual arrangement, are critical to providing a good enough holding environment, one that provides the consistency of care lacking from the earlier mother-infant relationship.[17]

A lack of attention to such details can lead to an unfavorable outcome for both patient and therapist. In one example, a forty-year-old male became angry and fearful when his therapist was late for his appointments. When he called his therapist in an emergency, the therapist did not return his calls. When he discussed the matter with the therapist later, the therapist told him not to call him in the future. This opened a rift in the relationship, which neither understood. The patient became less trusting and secure. When the therapist moved to a new office, the patient was not convinced that the therapist would continue to exist, so fearful was he of this base. The therapist took his fear and anger personally and began to attack the patient and accuse him of not believing in his good intentions. He ended a long-term group in which the patient participated, claiming that he had a shortage of male patients. The fights between the patient and therapist escalated. The therapist could no longer find a regular time in his schedule for the patient and finally told him he no longer wished to work with him. It is apparent that in this case the therapist, lacking either training or experience, failed to understand the issues with which the patient was dealing.

Those who suffer from failures of the holding environment live in fear of being rejected and become intensely angry, should they suspect anyone of deserting them. They may treat the therapist or a spouse to the same abuse and rejection with which they were treated as children, since unconsciously they fear what they perceive as the negative consequences of attachment. They may present a picture of themselves as emotionally self-sufficient and on no account beholden to anyone. Eventually they may experience despair over ever having a secure relationship with anyone. They have shut away their yearning for love and care.

Jonathan has insisted on maintaining a sense of his self-sufficiency. He works in low-wage, blue-collar jobs, which provide a sense of comfort and stability associated, however unrealistically, with his father, and which require little from him. Although much in his story suggests that he desperately needed and yearned for his father, he refused on a number of occasions to take the opportunity to get to know his father better. He did not have the skills necessary to talk about the relationship and about himself, or to ask for help when he needed it. It seems his father was similarly lacking, as is frequently the case. Just as mothers repeat the mistakes of their mothers, the entire family constellation typically exhibits a common problem. Jonathan has developed a vision of himself as destined for uniqueness, and feels that someone, or God, will come along to fix things. This magical belief sustains him through difficulties and is an effective coping mechanism psychologically, though not of much effect in the real world.

Winnicott stresses the importance of the therapist's noninterference so that the natural growth processes can reassert themselves. The knowledge that the attachment figure is available and responsive gives a strong and pervasive sense of security and encourages the patient to value and continue the relationship. The biological function closest to this is protection. In many ways, Jonathan's earliest memories of what he heartbreakingly calls "The Family" suggest that this was one of the few times in his life when he felt protected. After this "the family" fell apart and Jonathan suffered a number of losses for which he did not have the resources to cope. He calls three central periods in his life "Severance," "Abdication," and "Arms and the Man." These titles suggest the traumas he faced and the way in which he dealt with them. He found himself cut off and began to cut off others, turning to the imagined security of his childhood in his choice of work. The last period, "The School Boston," suggests an attempt to enter a new socialization process, but his uncertainty is still apparent.

Bowlby attempts to reconceptualize the defense processes, the heart of Freudian theory, by studying detachment. He considers the strange behavior of a young boy who, when hurt, shows no sign of seeking comfort. Attachment is temporarily or permanently deactivated, together with the whole range of feelings that normally accompany it. The emotionally detached child develops into what Winnicott calls the false self and what Kohut calls the narcissist. However, Bowlby observes, the information that such an adult blocks is far from the irrelevant and potentially distracting information that most adults typically exclude. What is shut off are the signals that would activate attachment behavior and enable the child/adult both to love and to have the experience of being loved. In other words, children develop a defensive numbing, or repression, in response to a mother who is negligent or rejecting. Later, the adult becomes afraid to become attached to anyone, for fear of further rejection.[18]

Following Ainsworth, Bowlby distinguishes between what he calls the "anxious resistant" attachment, in which a child is uncertain whether a parent will be available and an "anxious avoidant" attachment, in which the child has abandoned hope and expects to be rebuffed. Anxious resistant children and adults continue to have separation anxiety about intimacy and exploring the world. Anxious avoidants attempt to live their lives without love and support, pretending to be emotionally self-sufficient. Either may be diagnosed as narcissistic or having a false self. Many of the feelings that lead to a desire for a close and trusting relationship are blocked in these individuals. In therapy this fear of a trusting relationship is experienced as resistance. To find the True Self, the adult must recognize his or her attachment desire and feeling. Jonathan's behavior can be characterized as anxious resistant, in that he continues to make forays between his home base and a more adult life and has made several attempts at adult relationships.

Once a pattern develops, it persists, because the way a parent treats a child tends to continue unchanged, with the pattern eventually becoming a property of the child. Mothers with secure children demonstrate striking differences in their ability to communicate freely and openly, compared with mothers of insecure children, who restrict their communication. For a relationship between individuals to proceed or grow, both must be aware of and recognize the other's point of view and feelings, and both must adjust their behavior so that goals are aligned and negotiated. In this way models of the self become updated. Adults with attachment problems do not update their model of the self, but instead defensively exclude information that does not fit their early experiences. Jonathan is only beginning to realize that his idealistic fantasies may not develop by themselves and that his desire for both uniqueness and connection are inconsistent. He cannot have both and yet create the life he wants. Earlier he channeled this desire into fantasies of politics and a public life. After he pulled the rug from under himself by abdicating leadership responsibility, he then began to channel this desire into his writing. Although he has written plays and three novels, and apparently received positive response to at least one play, he has yet to publish. He has not developed the skills for self-promotion and is fearful of rejection. He has learned from his mother that any attempt to *demand* attention is likely to cause rejection, so he waits, just as he waits for her to be the mother he wants. Although we cannot assume that Jonathan's perceptions of his writing abilities are accurate, it is clear that he can test them only through the trial and error process that any author must pursue. Even the greatest writers have experienced initial rejection.

Attachment theory explains what Winnicott calls the key differences between those who develop a False Self Organization and those who develop the True Self.[19] It is the mother's ability to communicate freely, emotionally as well as cognitively, that distinguishes mentally healthy personalities. Studies show a strong correlation between how a mother treats her child and her relationship with her own mother/parent. Jonathan describes his mother as "more like a sister," meaning that she did not behave in a motherly fashion but was more like another child. He had a "dream" one night that she came into his room while he was sleeping and urinated all over his floor, something that might have really happened. Since she was alcoholic, this could be a real event that he has chosen to distance as a "dream," but whether dream or reality it indicates that he is unsure whether he is free from the territoriality of his mother's emotional realm. He still feels that her needs may intrude at any moment, and that he is unable to prevent or ignore it.

Failures in early development lead to difficulties in communication within relationships, in behaviors we call intimacy issues, such as trust, empathy, capacity for outward focusing, and nonrejecting or inclusive behaviors. Adults who have suffered from a failed holding environment have problems with reciprocity, or mutuality. Fearful of rejection, they may reject before they are rejected. They are vigilant for behavioral cues of the rejection they attempt to avoid. Adults, just like children, have a need for mirroring. Mirroring in psychoanalytical terms is the sense of self we achieve by looking at the self through the eyes of the primary caretaker or significant other. Encounters with this " looking glass self" confirm and reinforce our subjective self, serving as a test of our perceptions and contributing to an identity theme in the life process.

Empathy failures mean that attachment behaviors that permit mutuality have been disconnected. Jonathan protects himself from rejection by not expecting mutuality. Some individuals protect themselves by becoming detached, not developing either an emotional or a physical connection with others. Jonathan does this from time to time, withdrawing into his solitary room to write, yet he is aware that this is not satisfactory and will not fulfill his desire to engage and bond. He is aware that his sporadic job history is a way of seeking some bond with both father and mother—with his father symbolically and with the mother by return to the nest. Commitment to a real career might require that he refuse his mother's needs from time to time—he would have to make choices. He has never resigned himself to earning his own way and finishing the things he starts because he cannot conceive of himself as an adult, an individual separate from his mother. He has developed a set of protective filters that distort himself and others. The inevitable failures of his adult relationships have reinforced his sense of incompleteness.

Jonathan continues to live in one-room, squalid conditions, without even a bathroom or a kitchen, for much the same reason. He is only just beginning to realize that his lifestyle no longer fits his expanding sense of who he is. His low self-esteem has led him to a rationalized ideology about his "specialness" and prevents him from submitting his writing to the marketplace. Although this is the kind of attitude that might popularly be characterized as "egotism," it is in fact the exact opposite.

Jonathan's grandiosity has helped to protect him against the difficulties he has faced. His dream of being unique he has channeled into actions that serve to keep him isolated. He continues his poverty under the rationalization that he is shunning materialism, giving a vague glow of "selflessness" to what actually contributes little to a better world. The impact on tertiary children would be nil, should he choose to live in a moderately comfortable manner. Most of us would not see having a bathroom and kitchen as self-indulgent.

Jonathan's inability to love and to be angry with someone at the same time makes it impossible for him to negotiate a satisfying relationship. That would require that he see both parties as equal adults, able to make legitimate demands, relate empathetically, and support each other in the process. Moreover, it appears that he has sought out those who have problems of their own (he describes his friends as social misfits like himself), which of course makes intimacy doubly difficult.

Most of Jonathan's problems suggest failure in early mother-child attachment relations, and his self history supports the same conclusion. The problem for Jonathan, and for us, is to recognize and reconnect these problems to their original source rather than simply labeling him with "a personality disorder." A new and empathically attuned holding environment (therapy or an understanding other) may permit him to reach a fuller capacity to be intimate, to establish the mutual bonds of care and love.

While researchers have labored to describe narcissism and its behaviors, it is important to tease out its origins within the mother-child bond and its implications for intimate communication. Diagnosis may be a logical starting point in a medical model, but it may pose as many problems as it does answers for understanding individual behavior. Most real problems occur on the borderline of normal and abnormal behavior (terms of questionable value in any case), and diagnostic labeling distorts the picture by implying that Jonathan, or anyone, "has a condition" as he might "have a disease." Jonathan poses no problem for society, only for himself. What he "has" is a history, which is continuing and may or may not have a happy ending. Understanding that history is both his problem and ours.

The Reproductive and Caregiving Systems

We have examined in this chapter the development of the attachment system, a critical system which determines our capacity for, and style of, emotional attachments as adults, and underlies many of the communication skills, verbal and nonverbal, which show affection and caring. At some time in adolescence (a period that varies somewhat for each person) we begin a search for a partner. Our exact intent at the time also varies—some are already looking for a marriage partner, others for only a close and dependable friendship. Further development, according to Ainsworth, includes two other behavioral systems crucial for intimate relationships, the reproductive and the caregiving systems.

Ainsworth makes an important distinction between the affectional bonds of these three systems and those involved in other, more casual relationships. Affectional bonds differ in three important ways. First, they are long lasting (even outlasting the relationship—as divorced partners may continue in a different, yet still affectional bond). Second, they are an internal representation in the mind of the individual (rather than one outside the individual). Third, these bonds are unique rather than interchangeable. This uniqueness explains the desire to maintain closeness, the distress of separation, and the joy upon reunion.[21] Attachment is an affectional bond.

Adulthood requires the selection of new attachment figures. Our attachment to our parents, though it never ceases, even after their deaths, abates. The internal model of intimate relationships that we have constructed based upon our parents is now modified to include our experiences in close relationships, along with the influence of other attachment figures—siblings, relatives, teachers, priests, and therapists. All of these experiences modify our model of self, both through mirroring and through our own learning.

In addition to attachment behaviors, intimate relationships also involve a caregiving system. Marriage is a system that has evolved to see that our young ones are cared for, but it also provides caregiving for the partners. At times one partner takes on the role of being strong and wise while the other reciprocates by providing care, comfort, and reassurance. Attachment and caregiving bonds require proximity, and separation produces anxiety and grief over loss. The caregiving system differs from the attachment system in that the caregiving bond is mutual, while the attachment bond is one-way. The infant bases its security on the mother but not vice versa; a wife may be quite dependent upon her husband economically, yet participate equally in child rearing.

The reproductive bond is sexual. Pair bonding is not characteristic of all species, and we can mate without bonding, but sexual attraction is an important basis for beginning a relationship, even though relationships based on sexuality do not always endure. A longer relationship requires the support of the attachment and caregiving systems to sustain the bond when sexual interest has waned. Our attachment and caregiving bonds may persist even after breakup, and sexual attraction may reassert itself in the same relationship from time to time.

The advantage to the species in evolving these behavioral systems is the formation of groups to look after individual members. Infants must be socialized into these caregiving systems. Jane Goodall, in a *National Geographic* documentary, illustrates the problem among primates through a mother chimpanzee who does not properly socialize her infant into the group. When the mother dies, the group rejects the child. Caregiving systems reduce fear and wariness in individuals by providing them with trustworthy others.

Jonathan's childhood emotional experiences continue to shape his adult psychic reality. Fearful of abandonment, he refuses to pass through the door of adulthood and come to birth in the world. Refusing the adult summons, his adventures become negative, in part because he has given up the option of affirmative action. Refusal of adulthood means becoming fixed in an outdated system of ideals and goals. Only new birth, detachment, and transfiguration can conquer this psychic death. Jonathan's sorties to Boston are an attempt, but so far only an attempt. From a psychic viewpoint, these represent attempts to move beyond the infantile ego and its unconscious sphere of emotional relations. This attempt to move from an internal to an external world represents a radical transfer of emphasis. Joseph Campbell says, "the first work of the hero is to retreat from the world of secondary effects to the causal zone of the psyche where the difficulties reside, so that he or she can break though to undistorted direct experience."[22] This is what Jung calls the "archetypal image."[23] The second task of the hero is to return transfigured and teach the lesson learned. As Hero of our own life story we must undergo a similar transfiguration.

PART III
Ethical Communication

5

Do the Right Thing: Moving from Victimization to Responsibility

The next chapters, through the life stories of Adam and Laura, examine another need critical to adult intimacy that I call, following Schultz, the control system.[1] Adler called this the degree of activity versus passivity. Control differs from the desire for emotional closeness or affection, the subject of the first section, in adding an element of power relations. In doing so, it includes our ability to handle conflict and stress, critical to intimate relationships. As R. D. Laing observes, "Neither love nor madness can be separated from our desire to seize control of those with whom we are intimate."[2] Intimacy, he concludes, is about the politics of power. People in close relationships struggle to define the other's identity, and may deny each other's perceptions of reality. Typically, all interpersonal conflict includes a struggle for power. As communications researcher David Johnson has remarked, "Absence of conflict in a relationship is not a sign of intimate communication but rather a sign of a lack of one."[3] Although as adults we need to assert our needs in order to have them met, many adults continue to use a child's ego state, expecting others or the world to meet their needs automatically without their expressing them.

These unmet and unexpressed needs become a source of conflict. Many relationship struggles are about working out a balance between the dominance needs of each partner. Who makes the decisions? Who drives? Who cooks? Who pays the bills? To some extent the dynamics of a relationship are dependent on cultural norms. It was once assumed that the man worked and paid the bills, while the woman cooked, kept house, and provided primary care to the children. Today the cultural norm is toward equality of roles. In any case, there are dozens of particulars to be negotiated, and each may require the working out of dominance or submission. Ultimately the arrangements must be mutually satisfying on the average, though disagreement may remain over certain issues. Sometimes it is a matter of "agreeing to disagree," and if the relationship is good "on balance" some particulars may never be resolved. This is another way of saying that no two persons ever achieve a perfect relationship, nor should they expect to.

Because conflicts are normal and unavoidable in relationships of any depth, our challenge in any relationship is to manage conflict effectively. Just like our capacity to express affection, unproductive conflict styles reflect a preoccupation with self and a disregard for others. As we have seen, in narcissistic communication neither person recognizes the other as unique. This also affects how we deal with conflict. In not valuing the other, each damages the long-term health of the relationship, establishing a climate characterized by defensiveness. Defensiveness results in such conflict strategies as physical attack, name calling, avoidance, gunnysacking (storing old grievances up and bringing them out all at once in an explosive manner), hitting below the belt (using information given to us in confidence to hit others where they are most vulnerable), sarcasm, and ridicule. It also results in self-summarizing, repeating what we say over and over while ignoring the other's communication. We may also resort to such tactics as mind reading, or interpreting the intentions of others (often wrongly), fleeing, and even termination. These are the famous fight or flight strategies.

In most interactions, we are actually safer when we lower our defenses rather than engage them. Often our rules for conflict, whether openly expressed or unexpressed, whether polite and diplomatic or rude and heated, are learned from our families. We each get a childhood script for conflict.

Mature versus Immature Defenses

Beneath the family style of conflict expression, however, lie more unconscious processes that determine our personal capacity for ethical communication. By ethical communication, I mean to suggest the ability to choose what George Vaillant calls mature ego defense mechanisms over immature ones.[4] Central to how we express who we are is the type of defense mechanism we choose. Mature self-defense mechanisms allow us to turn passive into active, signaling a shift from unconscious awareness to consciousness and the ability to take responsibility for our expression. These mechanisms allow us to delay immediate gratification and resist impulsive and aggressive actions. The task of a successful defense is to resolve conflict, but it must do so in a way that allows continued growth and development in both our self and our relationships. In an 1894 essay, Freud suggested that feelings could be separated from ideas, their owner, and their objects.[5] This insight paved the way for our understanding of what we call the self-defense mechanisms and how they modify both internal and external reality.

Following Freud, Vaillant agrees that we live in a mental universe in which conflicts are oriented by a discordant tug between four lodestars: our desires, consciousness, relationships, and reality. Conflict arises when there is change in one of the four lodestars, in order to compensate for anxiety or depression.[6] The ego—the integrating principle in our nervous system—stalls for time until we can bear the feelings of depression and anxiety by distorting or ignoring one or more of these lodestars. Mature coping mechanisms allow all components to be present. A successful or mature defense resolves conflict without sacrificing or modifying one of these four loci. Vaillant links mature defenses to development of trust, autonomy, and initiative, allowing us better control over our impulses, and the ability to plan ahead in a resourceful way.

Immature defenses involve denial of one or more of these four loci, which include projection, hypochondria, passive aggression (which he also calls masochism), acting out, disassociation, and fantasy.[7] These defenses rely on primitive idealization of self and other, such as splitting others into all good or all bad, turning hate and anger against the self because the true object is too dangerous, and projecting denied personality characteristics, known as projective identification, onto others so as to place blame outside the self.

Immature mechanisms share many characteristics. They are irritating to others while benign to the user. They make the observer, not the user, suffer. They tend to get under people's skins. They are more obtrusive. They tend to perform legerdemain with relationships, since they involve self-deception. Many involve all-or-nothing solutions. Vaillant feels it is the immature defense that is at the core of much of humanity's self-inflicted suffering. Current self-psychologists identify many with character disorders as using this class of defenses. Those with immature defenses are "hoisted on their own petards."

Vailliant correlates the immature defense with self-centeredness, passivity, and dependency. In particular, he associates these defenses with impaired psychological functioning, since they perpetuate in adult life a merger of boundaries between self and other that I have earlier associated with the infant and mother. In an unconscious effort to preserve the set of relationships established in this early period, these defenses alter mental representations in the present by dividing others and self into all good or all bad, and using projections that confuse current relationships with earlier ones. Unlike the mature ego, the immature one is inflexible and unable to bend with internal or external stress. It does not provide a sense of emotional continuity, and interferes with the ability to form and maintain relationships.

Vaillant cites an intermediate class of defenses that he calls the neurotic ones. The neurotic defenses are more self-aware and amenable to interpretation and adaptation. In other words, they imply an element of choice and awareness. They include repression, reaction formation, isolation or intellectualization, and displacement.[8] These defenses go largely unnoticed by others but alter the inner life of those who use them.

At the other end of the spectrum are mature defenses, which involve synthesis. As Vaillant suggests, straw is spun into gold and despair into poetry. Because all four lodestars are allowed to be conscious, they seem more voluntary. They integrate sources of conflict, diverting energy from a primitive emotion or instinct into a culturally higher one. These defenses include altruism, suppression, anticipation, humor, and sublimation.[9]

Mature defenses are adaptive, creating loving interaction. Developed through the early set of interactions and through identification with role models, they lead to health and resiliency. Here we learn to respond to life's difficulties with autonomy or initiative rather than with resignation, despair, and passivity. These mental mechanisms suggest we have turned agency in our lives from passive to active, which is central to a firm sense of identity.

Our ability to select mature over immature defenses has a dramatic impact on our relationships. When we have armed ourselves with mature defenses we are less likely to respond to life's blows with bitterness or prejudice, or by blaming others, projecting our insecurities onto others, denying reality, being unable to tolerate frustration, and chronically complaining. Immature responses become a feedback loop in which we can become caught. Failing to consider their impact on others, these defenses often result in the very set of negative relationships from which we are seeking to escape.

The mature ego, by contrast, allows us to feel fully, though our feelings need not be acted upon. Experience is integrated as active rather than inactive, centered rather than shunted to the periphery, selective rather than overwhelmed, aware rather than confounded. This increases our capacity to moderate change and take risks. A strong self allows us to tolerate swings of self-esteem in response to victory or defeat, success or failure. These swings can endanger a precarious sense of self, leading to distortion and passivity.

Other psychologists, such as Robert Kroeber, have made similar distinctions between what they call coping mechanisms and self-defense mechanisms.[10] What Vailliant calls mature defenses and Kroeber calls coping mechanisms are associated with the capacity of our ego to use cognition, reasoning, concept formation, language, memory, and intelligence. Secondary process thinking—a later, more logical overlay of our earlier primitive imagistic thinking (which

Freud calls the primary process)—occurs when the individual pays more attention to reality regulation. A better grip on reality equips us with the ability to sustain disturbing negative experiences without distorting them. When we use mature defenses, or coping behaviors, we have more flexibility, a clearer sense of purpose, and more future-oriented (rather than past-oriented) behaviors, all critical to relationships.

By contrast, immature defenses create more rigidity and compulsivity. First conceptualized by Sigmund and Anna Freud, our defense mechanisms, or what they sometimes called repression, are the ego's way of handling our sexual and aggressive drives.[11] A mature ego is strong enough to withstand these drives, while a weak ego falls back on more childlike means of defending the self. In modern usage these defenses not only encompass psychic repression—pushing something from the conscious to the unconscious mind—as they were used by the Freuds, but also a myriad of other defense mechanisms. In immature defenses, the ego operates to remove disturbing elements from consciousness. Immature defenses also use more of our primary process, our primitive, associative style of thinking, which includes magical thinking.

The Growth of the Ego

Acquisition of language, unlike any other process, is responsible for the growth of the ego. A healthy ego allows us to differentiate our internal and external environments. We learn to think abstractly, to separate thoughts from actions, to separate internal projections from external reality, to tolerate ambiguity, and to distinguish fact from inference. Ego strength is revealed in our staying power in pursuit of life-enriching goals, whether in love, work, friendship, or citizenship. It reflects competence in our ability as an adult to complete tasks. We learn we can influence the environment and meet our needs, and each success adds to a growing repertoire of competent behaviors. Those who have not been able to develop a healthy ego lack the ability to control their base instincts and to effect change in their environment. Successive failures in asserting control over others or the environment may lead some to suffer a radical loss of hope and a regression to compulsive and impulsive behaviors, which only insure more failures. Just as the ability to perform physical tasks requires a step-by-step movement toward competency, so, too, the psychic self must grow incrementally.

Our choice of self-defense mechanisms determines, put simply, our ability to handle conflict or solve problems. Problem solving, a synthesizing function, is an asset of a strong ego and involves analyzing situations and alternatives and developing coping strategies based on feedback from the environment. Why we are able to choose an effective response from a hierarchy of responses is tied to our level of ego functioning.

A high functioning ego enables us to establish an equilibrium that maintains centrality and wholeness and allows more mature and adaptive behaviors. We become more resilient. Conflict strategies employed by those with mature defenses can be helpful in resolving relationship issues. Functional fights generally involve discussing, listening, identifying, and agreeing on issues. The result is typically a compromise or mutually negotiated decision.

A low functioning ego, on the other hand, feels vulnerable and relies upon immature defense mechanisms to mount a counterattack to any perceived threat. Typical of dysfunctional fighting is that neither side can clearly state its position or feelings. Neither can hear or express the feelings of the other. Physical violence and verbal abuse ultimately mean there can be no resolution, since the issues become tied to a wounded self, one whose boundary system is damaged, as we shall explore in the last section of the book. The maturation of our defense system is tied to the resolution of a developmental stage which Freud calls the phallic stage, one that has become identified with the Oedipus complex, explored further in chapter 8.

The Signature of Our Fighting

Aggressive or controlling people get what they want. They also attempt to control the lives of others, ignoring the others' concerns and denying their rights. In engaging in these types of behaviors, we may be perceived by others as abusive, rude, or dominating, all characteristics that create difficulty in relationships.

Those who lack confidence in themselves and their ability to influence their stories engage in submissive behavior. The payoffs for submissive behavior are many. It allows us to avoid conflict. It allows us to avoid leadership. Yet the price of being nice also takes its toll. In our desire for approval from others, those lacking in confidence do not get to call the shots. We "go along to get along." If we do state our needs, we do so in an apologizing and diffident manner, so that we are not taken seriously, and may add qualifying phases such as "it really doesn't matter to me," "do whatever you want to do," or "I don't care." We may use nonverbals, such as a shrug of the shoulders, a soft, hesitant voice, or other factors that undercut our space and invite others to take advantage, and we may do other things that make our relationships lopsided. Though praised for their selflessness, ultimately submissive people grow to resent those for whom they sacrifice and to find their relationships dissatisfying and lacking in intimacy.

The submissive person lives an unlived life. When one submits, one avoids responsibility. Often those who narrate submissive life stories feel that life is happening to them rather than being lived by their own initiative. This leaves them feeling that these individuals, like Jonathan, have abdicated, having failed to develop a sense of control or efficacy.

Our next two case studies, Adam and Laura, each spin a personal myth that emphasizes their struggle to take control of or responsibility for their lives. The control issues for both can be traced to a critical childhood stage, the Oedipal stage, when many elements necessary for the next stage of intimacy development are being consolidated.

The balance point between aggression and submission is assertion—when we stand up for our own rights and needs while not abusing or dominating others. We express our ideas and concerns in direct and appropriate ways. We take responsibility for living our own lives and getting our own needs met. We like ourselves. While pain is sometimes associated with honest and caring confrontations, being assertive means allowing ourselves to be vulnerable in expressing who we are. An active adult is one who monitors his or her cognitive processes and strategies in order to achieve this healthy balance. The unaware person is often guided by unconscious strategies that are habitual and not monitored, and thus do not take account of others. Adam and Laura are individuals still struggling to separate or individuate, and thereby to create a sense of active identity or control.

Intimacy in adulthood requires that we have successfully mastered this developmental passage from immature to mature defenses. This shift dramatically affects our ability to fight fairly, what I call ethical communication. It is often remarked that it is not what happens to us but how we react that gives each of us our signature—whether we choose to absorb or deflect, confront or displace, clarify or distort. Typically, as we have seen, this is determined by the mechanisms that we select to protect or defend the self.

As we shall see, our next case study, Adam, chooses techniques that absorb and distort. He has trouble maintaining a firm sense of delineation. He tends to be hypnotically drawn to cult families with dominant father figures, and picks partners who reproduce an earlier set of Oedipal relations. He chooses women who have an illness and a religious connection so he can assume an earlier role of caretaker for his grandmother. His grandmother's death and his association of women with sex and death further his fear of sexuality. This pattern has prevented him from finding a marriage or relationship where love and sex can come together. His repetition of this pattern is an attempt to regain the original wholeness of his lost relationship to his grandmother and attributes to his partner the magical power to make him whole. When his wives fail to meet this need, he perceives them as withholding, failing to realize that by continuing to engage in this archaic power struggle he has structured his life so as to avoid intimacy. In addition, Adam remains in a state of psychosocial moratorium professionally, living the life of a perpetual graduate student.

As a rule of thumb, we pick partners at the same level of self-differentiation as ourselves. If we are more highly differentiated ourselves, the lower will be the emotional fusion in the relationships we select. The less individuated and differentiated we are, the more uncomfortable the emotional fusion. If we have not developed the ability to see the other as separate, with their own needs and emotions, then we may project onto them unwanted parts of ourselves.

Our third case study, Laura, similarly, is still struggling to establish an active identity outside her family's "magnetic field." Laura chooses different defenses than those that we see used by Adam. In selecting more mature defenses she is able to confront her feelings, grieve her losses, and actively clarify and take charge of her life. She, like Adam, has experienced difficulties in the world of work, having felt that her father sabotaged her attempts to launch. Like Adam, she has entered her adulthood transferring an earlier feeling of passivity and incompetence in her home and education in her work endeavors.

However, by her mid-thirties Laura has reached a turning point where she is consolidating a firmer sense of self. Laura has been able to extricate herself from her early set of relations largely though the kismet of a supportive partner.[12] Unlike Adam, she does not replay early relationship patterns. In fact, seeing her mother as a slave in a loveless marriage and herself as the " third rape case" between her mother and her father, she has reacted against what she sees as an unhappy model by choosing a lesbian relationship.

Our choice of partners for relationships can provide us with an avenue to escape the past by taking responsibility for our own issues and consciously attempting to live in the present, or, conversely, we can continue to repeat patterns, and in doing so victimize ourselves. Mature relationships require that we take responsibility for our own unresolved primal issues, rather than project and blame them on a partner who fails to fulfill them. It is a choice, between anxiety, in the Freudian sense of clinging to an object, and letting it go and mourning it.[13] While Adam still compulsively clings to his past, Laura had been able to mourn her past and is letting it go in order to make different choices. It is a choice that psychologist Karen Horney characterizes as offering "dread or hope."[14]

Alfred Adler linked the degree of activity in resolving life's problems to the degree of social interest, seeing social usefulness as a primary measure of maturity.[15] Mature people learn to subordinate their own needs for the greater social good. Social interest, the opposite of self-interest, is the ability to show empathy for all humanity and the willingness to contribute to the welfare of others. The maladjusted, he said, seek a life with only a private meaning and are preoccupied with self-interest and self-protection. He saw neurosis as the logical development of an individual who is comparatively inactive and filled with a personal striving for superiority and is therefore retarded in social interest.[16] Neurotics develop faulty lifestyles due to childhood affliction, pampering, or rejection, and so miss out on the fundamental values of human life.

Adler was one of the first to point out that people's lives are motivated by fictional goals, guiding images that give purpose or direction.[17] We see Adler's idea of fictional goals expressed in each of our case studies. Jonathan's fictional goal is to wait for someone to come along to help him get untangled from the "torn net" of his family. Similarly, each of my next two case studies have their own fictional goals. Adam is trying to escape a "glass prison" where all his moves are visible to his warden father. Laura is trying to find her own orbit outside the magnetic field of her family's pull. While each shows some positive activity toward growth, each also is tied to a conceptualization from the past.

We travel through life guided by an inner life plot—partly a creation of family, partly an internalization of broader social norms, partly a function of our imagination and our own capacity for insight into ourselves. The more control we exercise over our expression through a healthy ego that appropriately monitors between external and internal reality, the more we assume responsibility for getting our own needs met and meeting the needs of others. We become the actors or the heroes of our stories. Otherwise, we find ourselves becoming sidelined, a bit player in our own lives. This leaves many with the unsatisfying feeling that somehow their lives have gotten off track.

In these chapters we examine turning points in life stories, what we have called Urmoments, and our concern has been with those that occur in midlife. Although we are constantly adjusting to changes in our self and our environment, midlife is a time that may require especially difficult adjustments. At midlife we become aware of our mortality and our success or failure in many long-term goals, such as career, attachments to others, and social position. Not many of us have been as successful in these areas as we had hoped or planned, and we must now accept our limits and redirect our goals. This process is an overlooked aspect of adult development which is usually discussed in terms of "crisis," suggesting that it is somehow abnormal, when in fact it is simply a part of our ongoing need to redefine and redirect ourselves. As is apparent from our case histories, whatever problems are present in our lives have been present for a long time, in most cases since birth. What creates the Urmoment is not the sudden appearance of a new problem, but rather that midlife has made a person aware of that problem and intensified the desire to find a solution.

We cannot know if either Adam or Laura will completely succeed in achieving the intimacy they seek, but in no case is change likely to come easily. On the other hand, each seems to have taken the first small step of recognizing that they need to change, which is perhaps the most hopeful thing to be said. We shall, as with Jonathan, attempt to understand the kind of relationships they have developed and examine the kinds of characters who populate each life myth. As with Jonathan, I will follow the narrative thread of plot, symbols, and themes they themselves have created in order to see how each gives meaning or order to his or her life. We will begin with Adam.

6

Adam's Story: The Glass Prison

Adam is a forty-two-year-old, thrice-married male. He does freelance editing and writing and is currently finishing a Ph.D. in philosophy at a major university in the Northeast. His attempts at regular jobs in business have not succeeded. Neither have his brother's, who though trained as a lawyer has now become financially dependent on their father. Adam is one of two sons of a prominent workaholic surgeon. His depressed mother, suffering from breast cancer, became addicted to Phenobarbital shortly after Adam was born and grew agoraphobic, confining herself to her room during much of Adam's childhood. His elderly fundamentalist grandmother (matriarchal) oversaw the upbringing of Adam and his brother, and "screamed the doom of Cain and Abel" whenever Adam and his brother fought. His domineering and dictatorial father worked long hours and was seldom home.

As a young adult, Adam has had several traumatic experiences. He joined the Moonies after graduating from college. More traumatic for Adam was that his father had him kidnapped, virtually imprisoning him for the next year, while he was deprogrammed with the help of drugs and a therapist. Adam was able to turn these traumatic events into a best-selling memoir about his life with the Moonies. However, this incident resonated deeply with Adam as he feels imprisonment is a theme in his life. He also became involved, briefly, with a group of Satanists. The trauma of these events led to a series of psychotic breaks, for which he has been hospitalized.

He has been married three times and tends to marry women with both some form of illness and a religious connection. He characterizes all of his marriages as sexless. His present wife is manic-depressive. He admits that he has yet to have a relationship where love and sex have come together. Adam divides his life into five chronological periods: The Lost Phase: Who Is Mama and Where Is Mama (0–3); The Death of My Soul (6–10); Grades 6–12; The College Years, and Post College.

The Lost Phase (0–3): Who is Mama and where is Mama?

In a separate article written for publication that Adam shared with me, he says, "he grew up in a vicious greenhouse, the kind of place that was sufficiently remote from predators, famine, and disease." This greenhouse was like a "glass prison" where he "felt unprotected," and "invisible" except when needed.

His earliest memory is of himself at two years of age. He is sitting on the floor in a playroom, moving a crayon across a piece of wood. His mother asks him if he can write his name. He remembers scribbling in an effort to please his mother. It is, he says, one of the earliest and most positive memories of his mother. He links his obsession with writing to the early imprint of this moment.

The theme of writing became associated with peak experiences throughout his life. A number of these experience came together to culminate in his successful publication of a book with a commercial publisher and the resulting lecture tour. This represented the integration of a number of happy earlier experiences focused around writing, such as his memory of a summer in journalism camp during high school, his discovery of his love of poetry, and his identification with the Jewish intellectual tradition in high school. The Writer became a key imagoe for Adam—spinning the negative experiences of his life into positive ones.

Like Jonathan, Adam's narrative tone is characterized by a joylessness and lacks assertiveness. He feels massively depleted of self-esteem and vitality. His sense of "loss and of being lost" (Who's Mama and Where's Mama) suggest a struggle to develop an early autonomous sense of self. Adam's narrative indicates that the mother-child mirroring necessary for feelings of trust and safety was absent. Shortly after his birth, his mother was diagnosed with breast cancer and lay drugged, sleeping, or watching TV in a separate part of a big house. Although his grandmother became his *de facto* mother, he nevertheless remembers feeling alone and terrified, ignored and abandoned as he wandered around the family's big house.

As he puts it, he learns to be good, but seldom himself. Similar to Jonathan, a lack of stable mirroring and a precarious sense of self lead to feeling endangered or overwhelmed. What psychologists have called a false self is dependent on the approval of others rather than learning to rely on one's own inner moorings. Adam's prison continues in adulthood with his desperate need for a sense of belonging and approval, which leads him to be drawn to charismatic leaders and groups. Trust and recognition, based on the relationship between mother and child, are paramount for forming later intimate relationships. The ability to trust is a big step in the processes connected with identity, since it forms the basis for self-esteem. Erikson considers it the cornerstone of personality.[1]

Adam's early failures at trust are significant. He not only feels abandoned and rejected by his mother, but just as significant he learns to fear his father and brother. This fear leads to a defense mechanism that is prominent in Adam's story that of projection, assigning unacceptable parts of our self to others. To protect his fragile sense of self, Adam uses a number of immature defenses that suggest his inability to delineate a sense of identity. Such defenses as projection, and its extension paranoia, where one fears love as much as hate, suggest a merging of boundaries where what is self and what is other become unclear. Both suggest fear of harm by those one is close to as well as intimacy with strangers— a pattern in Adam's life. Many of the details of Adam's story, such as the psychotic episodes and types of drugs, suggest that medically he has been diagnosed with schizophrenia, though he never identifies himself with this label.

The theme for Adam's life story and the reason for my classification as an Oedipal story is the domination by his father. If his mother was critical in her absence, his father loomed large in his presence. The Oedipal phase is crucial to identity formation in determining to what extent certain moral elements, such as conscience, commitment, and object constancy, are internalized. It typically involves a love-hate affair with the parents. Resolution of these elements is a pre-condition for identification. When the intense love-hate feelings experienced by the Oedipal child have not been appropriately integrated into the ability to tolerate ambiguity, then fragmentation rather than wholeness results. Integration results in an important shift in direction—from immature defenses to mature ones—from passive to active. This involves the ability to control one's impulses rather than acting them out instinctually.

Adam characterizes his father as a psychopath who shaped him by saying "just remember I could destroy you." His father, a surgeon, who though he spent little time at home, nevertheless, proceeded to psychically control Adam's family life and indeed his life story. Throughout his journey toward selfhood, Adam encountered again and again hypnotic male leaders who attempted to destroy him and hold him against his own will; his persecutors all bare a striking resemblance to his father. His willpower was barely strong enough to escape destruction in many of the stories he narrates. Adam's childhood existence, as he interprets it, was provisional upon his functioning as passively as possible. He lived in a glass prison. This continued in college where his parents overruled his sense of personal power by insisting he end a sexual relationship with women at a neighboring college, calling him a psychopath and threatening to send him to a psychiatrist.

After college, Adam continued his search for an independent self by involving himself in a number of situations that tested him and repeated the theme of losing control and being held against his will. This included joining the Moonies, his kidnapping, deprogramming, drugging by his father, his attraction to a group of Satanists whose power over him scared him, and his institutionalization in mental hospitals. Adam seems drawn to flesh out his precarious sense of self by merging or fusing with others rather than through internal completeness. Immature defenses alter mental representations in the present by continuing to divide them into all good or all bad, as Adam seems to, or by combining and projecting them with other representations. Adam's defenses have allowed him to continue to build a world where he faces the same enemy, his father, and the same lover, his grandmother. As Adam has traveled through his life, his choice of mentors and role models has not been random but rather consistent with a father figure who "hypnotically" overpowered the willpower of his family members and a fundamentalist grandmother whose illness served to fulfill his role of caretaker, where he felt needed.

Oddly, a key memory Adam recalls as an adult is of his father's use of hypnosis on the family. As a surgeon, his father had become familiar with hypnosis as form of anesthesia for his surgery practice. When Adam, his brother, and his mother struggled with weight problems, he decided to employ it in an effort to help them lose weight. To this day, Adam feels that his mom and his brother remain completely helpless. Although he received a law degree and worked as a lawyer on Capitol Hill, his brother convinced his father to take over his mortgage and his expenses after his divorce. Adam believes he has become, like his mother, totally dependent. His captive mother has remained an invalid throughout their marriage, assuming no responsibility either in typical housewife duties or in work outside the home

The image of a glass prison is an interesting one. Like the evil Dr. Rappaccini in the Hawthorne short story, "Rappaccini's Daughter," Adam sees his father as a gardener/surgeon who tends flowers/patients but uses his pathological/hypnotic power to hold them against their will as prisoners. The image of glass is one of exposure, vulnerability, and lack of protection from his father's power. Here is symbolized his fear of love and intimacy.

Another key character in Adam's story is that of a clubfooted older brother (the lawyer), Woody, who was born with only one arm and one leg and was prone to attacking him because he had two good legs. Adam's father, so the family story goes, was exposed to radiation as a resident because there was no money for lead aprons. His father believed that this exposure was the cause of

Woody's congenital deformities. Years later this belief was confirmed when his father ran into another resident who also had given birth to a child born with only one arm and one leg.

According to family lore, Woody's first words toward Adam when his mother brought him home from the hospital, and which set the tone for their subsequent relationship, were, "throw him in the garbage can." Thus began a sibling rivalry which has continued to this day. Throughout his youth, Adam's brother resented his two good legs and retaliated by teasing and hitting him, to the point that Adam felt unsafe at home during much of his childhood.

This relationship culminated as adults in one final confrontation that effectively severed the relationship. Adam has not seen Woody for ten years, since Woody threw Adam out of his car for suggesting that Woody date women with handicaps. Woody had been commiserating with Adam concerning his desire to find a romantic relationship. Adam felt that Woody might have been rejected due to his deformity. The fact that there has been no resolution of this on-going sibling rivalry suggests that the Oedipal complex has not yet been fully resolved for either brother. He has yet to see his brother as a separate, functioning adult apart from the sphere of their earlier fearful relationships. They continue these early difficulties caught up in the same web of childhood psychic relations.

Six to Ten Years Old: The Death of My Soul

When Adam was in the second grade, he and his brother were sent to a private school, largely out of deference to Woody's self consciousness concerning his handicap. Here Adam found sustenance through his schoolwork and poetry, and a safe harbor from his home life, where he felt physically terrorized by his older brother, verbally abused by his father (who threatened to destroy him if he misbehaved or to send him to military school), and abandoned by his vegetative mother.

During this period, Adam created another imagoe that became a central theme to his later three marriages—that of caretaker. At eight, his grandmother also developed cancer and became bedridden. Adam got the job of taking care of her. When he was twelve, his grandmother died, a traumatic event which Adam calls the "death of his soul." His grandmother was the one positive connection who provided him with a sense of self. In an effort to deal with his sorrow, he attempted to bond with his mother through Weight Watchers but was only able to achieve a very guarded relationship.

Grades 6–12

In high school, Adam made an important friend, a young Jewish intellectual who introduced him to the Jewish intellectual tradition and informed him with a positive imago for manhood—that of intellectual. Another positive high school experience was his summer in journalism camp where he was able to hone his writing skills and get a taste of independence.

During this period he remembers many fights between his parents. His mother became emotionally vegetative, even to the point of hiring a man-servant to oversee her responsibilities while she lay in bed all day, watching TV and sleeping. Having no skills, she was completely dependent on her husband's financial and emotional good will. She was so ill-informed about motherhood that, according to Adam, she would have been no less prepared had "aliens dropped he and his brother from the mother ship." Emotionally debilitated and depressed, she became agoraphobic, surrendering active control of her life. According to Adam she had no friends, no life and merely ate and survived. Very unhappily married, she had chosen her husband as a last resort over the horror of old-maid hood.

By comparison, his father was at least functional although a "workaholic" and a "psychopath." Adam jokes, his father was "able to put his pathology to good use." In addition to continuing his surgical practice, he took a job later in life as Medical Supervisor to three prisons. His father became the warden in real life that Adam had imagined he was in his family.

The College Years

During his college year, Adam began a period of identity, what Erikson calls a moratorium. Erikson believes that failures occur because we can become stuck in one of two ways: we fail to experiment or we fail to make commitments in work and love. (See chapter 12 on boundary systems and identity.) For Erikson, identity resolution is a requirement for a committed intimate relationship. Adam's intellectual achievements led him to Yale University.

At Yale, Adam studied philosophy and psychology continuing his love of ideas and intellectual pursuits. A key experience during this period was his relationship with his roommate, a bi-sexual, who fell in love with him and became emotionally dependent upon him. This attachment became so strong that at one point his roommate became incensed when Adam returned later than expected from vacation, and began to hit him. Adam was so intimidated that he moved out of the apartment and lived in a professor's office until he graduated.

At Yale, Adam experimented with a number of ultra-state experiences, such as marijuana, hyperventilation, self-hypnosis, and what he characterized as semi-psychotic experiences, a symptom of avoiding the anger and loss he felt over his upbringing. During this time, he fell under the spell of another student, Philip, whose charisma had inspired a number of followers. Adam believed that Philip could read people's minds and influence things from a distance. Adam found Philip's sessions energizing ones in which members of the cult stayed up all night, they were so bursting with energy. This theme of finding energy in a magnetic father figure to fill his own depleted source became a pattern for Adam. Adam found the cult's spiritual experiences both scary and exciting. Drawn to these semi-religious experiences, he saw them as a way to heal his misery. Adam's feelings soon became mixed as he changed his initial fascination for Phillip to fear. Apparently, other group members shared Adam's concern that Phillip's powers were evil. Realizing that he was able to maintain his power over individual members only by keeping them isolated and mistrustful, the group decided to challenge him. Adam felt their unity broke his power like a spell. This experience whetted Adam's appetite, and he decided to seek out a guru in California. The episode with Philip was the first of three in which Adam used projection and paranoia as a defense. His need for belonging and approval were so strong that it led him to trust too much, and then to a lack of trust. Whether these groups were indeed as dangerous as Adam believes them to have been or whether he continues to project onto them his fear and obsession with his all-powerful father is unclear.

Post College

After hitchhiking to California, Adam had what he dryly characterizes as either a religious experience or a psychiatric or literary insight, when he awakened one morning to a voice that told him, "It is time to get up and join your mission." A short time later he was invited by a "creative social worker" to dinner. This is the beginning of Adam's induction into the Moonies. After the initial dinner, he came back to spend the weekend and decided to join them on a farm. After a few weeks, he agreed to commit his life to this idealistic group, whom he saw as having the spiritual and family dimension that he was seeking.

As a group, the Moonies were unfamiliar during this time period. Cult affiliation represents an extraordinarily dramatic action, which profoundly declares that members do not share their family's values or identities. It represents an attempt at rupture. The time Adam spent with the Moonies provided an ideological rationale for an occupational, personal, and sexual moratorium, a period postponing an adult resolution of identity.

The Oedipal stage represents a break from the family of origin and permission to create one's own life. Since Adam has had a difficult time breaking from the magnetic pull of his father, his attempts at breaks have been dramatic ones, and have included altered states and cult-like experiences, such as the Moonies, drugs, Satanists, and finally psychotic episodes. In selecting these experiences Adam has replicated his early association of his father as a prison warden, in addition to an earlier set of emotional relations, which he has characterized as drugged, sleeping, numbed out, and hypnotic. Through projection, he has continued to reproduce the emotional realm with which he is familiar.

A turning point for Adam came when his father kidnapped him from the Moonies and attempted to deprogram him using a professional deprogrammer with techniques Adam found intimidating. When his father visited Adam in California, he invited Adam to dinner. As he left the resaurant, what Adam describes as "professional thugs" pushed him into the waiting car. He was imprisoned, locked in a hotel room, drugged (with heavy doses of haldol and melloreal), and guarded by what he calls professional thugs, to prevent his running away. His father was the mastermind behind the whole scheme. Adam feels he suffered a serious trauma as a result of the kidnapping, a trauma that has cost him several years of his life. Since the kidnapping, he has felt "numbed out" and "dead." This experience left him with a great deal of rage, both toward his father and toward the psychiatrist who deprogrammed him, whom, Adam believed, had cut some sort of a deal with his father. He blamed the psychiatrist for putting him on drugs rather than helping him to escape from his family and get his own life.

Adam turned his experience with the Moonies and his imprisonment by his father into a best-selling book. The success of the book brought on a lecture-circuit tour that allowed Adam to talk about his experience and net an income. Here Adam was able to turn an unhappy experience into art, a process known as sublimation, to make unacceptable feelings acceptable, although, truth be told, his success did not occur without accompanying denial and repression. Interestingly enough, this early book was a renunciation of the Moonies; it was only later that he decided to renounce his father's kidnapping and deprogramming. This suggests that Adam now has more awareness of his pattern of the all-powerful father than he did during this time period.

The next major event in Adam's life was his first marriage to Sharon, a woman he met at a friend's wedding and married eighteen months later. If, as Erikson suggests, the test of a firm identity is our ability to commit and sustain relationships, this marriage, the first of three, reflects Adam's identity confusion. Those who fail to resolve their identity are never able to develop a close relationship in terms of passion or intimacy. Sharon suffers from debilitating migraines, which worsen throughout the marriage. His selection of mates who are ill allows him to continue his earlier caretaker role, learned from his mother and grandmother. In his marriages, Adam's disavowed qualities, which proved too threatening, are defensively projected onto and experienced as part of the partner. The use of others as part of one's own psychic organization interferes with the resolution of conflict and the development of a greater internal structure. This inhibits individual growth and interpersonal relatedness. If couples remain open to learning new things and the defenses do not rigidify, self-development can continue. However, if these mechanisms become paralyzed and destructive, the couple creates a relationship with an unconscious sense of security but little gratification.

Despite his three marriages, there is an overall rigidity in Adam's patterns of relationship. Adam chooses partner's based on his inner model; and, one may theorize, pressures them to conform. Adam selects women who are ill and who become withdrawn, unavailable, or critical. Subsequently, he must tolerate an unusual amount of deprivation in order to create a fit. This deprivation— the feeling of emotional aloneness—mirrors that of his early years with depriving and critical parents. Because of his incompleteness, he recreates an archaic merger based on his childhood archetype. His first wife, Sharon, and he soon "grow sick of each other." Adam feels it was not a "fruitful" marriage (literally as well as figuratively) as his wife decided to have an abortion due to her migraines, without consulting him.

In order to avoid his unhappy marriage, Adam spends more time with a colleague at the journal where he now works. Harry, as he soon finds out, was a member of a group of Satanists begun by Alistair Crowley. Harry introduces him to the group's godfather, who he calls the "most evil guy in the world." A significant memory for Adam was his narrow escape from what he interprets to be a mystical rite of sacrifice. At a group meeting one evening, he sensed that he was to be inducted when he was placed in a chair around which a triangle or rectangle was drawn. Adam had the feeling that something was going to happen and he was in intimate danger. He feels the group might have done anything from play pin-the-tail-on-the-donkey to shove a knife through his heart. He thought the leader had tremendous hypnotic power; and, fearing for his life, he bolted from the room.

Adam was so overcome with fear that he would be sucked in by a power beyond his control, he suffered a psychotic break. He found himself standing in front of a church, screaming at God, pumped up on thorazine, an anti-pyschotic drug. Catatonic, afraid to move and talk, he was taken to a psychiatric hospital. This began a series of institutionalization in psychiatric hospitals, at the request of his father, which he characterizes as like prisons. He found his parallel universe scary, and in between stays at the hospital had fantasies of talking to angels on the subway.

While hospitalized, Adams fantasized about his earlier attraction to his grandmother and sensed that when he masturbated both God and his grandmother are watching him. He dreamed of his fanatical Bible-thumbing grandmother warning him that he would go to hell. In his fantasy, he remembered putting his fists up and trying to protect his grandmother telling his father not to bother his grandmother. He remembered telling his father that he failed his grandmother and let her die when he should have protected her. His grandmother's death connects sickness, death, and women in his mind.

Another memory that furthers this connection is his relationship with an older women nurse in a hospice for which he volunteered. The nurse, whose father was dying, killed her father with an injection. This again connected women, sex, and death for Adam.

Adam had three psychotic episodes during his thirties for which he was hospitalized. During his second hospital stay, he met his second wife, and they became engaged six weeks later. Adam now feels that this marriage was a stupid mistake, as he and his wife Nina were opposites. She worked as an administrator for a Christian "arts" group. However, her epilepsy did not manifest itself until after the marriage. As her epileptic attacks increased, she became moody and withdrawn. The result was that the marriage became increasingly traumatic for Adam. When she began hitting him and verbally abusing him, his therapist suggested another hospitalization. Nina who helped Adam through the trauma of other hospital stays, kicked him out. They separated and divorced.

A short time after his second marriage ended, he met Donna through a Bible study group. They married two-and-a-half years later. This marriage has lasted, to date, although Donna has been diagnosed as manic depressive. Adam knew she suffered from this prior to the marriage. She, like Adam, goes into her own reality. Another key problem is the lack of a sexual relationship in their marriage. After marriage this aspect of their relationship worsened, and Adam and Donna now sleep apart. Adam feels this is a barrier to intimacy, as she is afraid to let him in.

Adam recognizes his pattern of choosing sick women who have a religious connection, modeled on his grandmother. He feels he has yet to produce a successful love relationship. Part of this he attributes to residual guilt from the Moonies, who considered sex the greatest sin.

Adam is now forty-two. For the most part, he has maintained a moratorium in terms of his career and has yet, after three marriages, to create one where sex and love can come together. Lacking a full identity, for Adam his marriages represent a narcissistic mirroring of his earlier primal relationships.

In extreme instances of moratorium, according to Erikson, disturbances of time appear where individuals no longer consider time to be a dimension. At forty-two, Adam is still completing his Ph.D., though he does work part-time as an editor. Severe identity confusion can be accompanied by a failure at workmanship. Though intelligent, Adam has still not taken hold of his capacity and continues to revive his Oedipal struggle, where one parent is the goal. He continues to attempt to rebuild a shaky childhood identification. Erikson believes that work goals enhance the ego, helping to turn passivity into activity.

Whether or not he has made headway in his intimate relations seems inconclusive. Certainly the third marriage seems to reflect the same emotional cloth of his earlier Oedipal pattern, which combines women, fear of sexuality, and death. If inappropriate defensive structures are not developed to cover the damaged self, behaviors such as psychosis can result. Adam has had three psychotic episodes, a defense he uses when he is overwhelmed or fearful of control by others. Psychoses are a form of dissociation or denial whereby we distort identity or external reality to fit an internal reality. Like dissociation, the stressed individual focuses on an inner over outer reality. Unlike psychosis, disassociation is more voluntary since it can be evoked through such states as religious ecstasy and hypnosis.

Even in adulthood, Adams projects two key patterns from his early set of childhood relations. First he continues to replay the early terror of his father's seemingly all powerfulness. However, Adam is more self-aware concerning this pattern and has made a bit of headway with his choice of all-powerful relationships. Second is the Oedipal love for his devout fundamentalist grandmother. This continues to form his choice of relationships even through his third and current marriage. Freud believed we choose to repeat patterns in the hopes of mastery.

Adam has yet to finish his graduate work, but he feels that the last few years have been good. He feels a deeper sense of self and is better able to protect himself from his family. He values his own experience and enjoys his life more. When he recently joined a trauma recovery group with a renowned, charismatic leader, he decided to leave, trusting his own experience and perception that the leader was cruel and harmful. This suggests that he is now able to anticipate and act when he senses the reoccurrence of his earlier patterns, reflecting conscious insight and awareness. He has decided to join another group with a more benign leader. While he is still drawn to "mindfuckers," he feels he now trusts his own intelligence more. As he puts it, "hitching a ride to other stars is less seductive as he establishes a sense of his own inner power."

Adam's future goals are to continue writing and to have a major impact. He would like to have a loving sexual relationship with Donna. Adam is also now aware of this pattern though he seemingly is still in its grips. He would like to solidify his spiritual path, which he sees as a stream in his life.

Adam's task is to develop a firmer sense of his own identity, where he has active control. Interestingly, his chapter title ends at post college. He, at forty-two, is still struggling to enter the adult world. Some say that when snakes shed their old skins to make new ones there is pain and discomfort. The attempt to find a new life is difficult for Adam. He struggles to shed an earlier family identity and to be wary of reproducing his father's and grandmother's psychical realms. Important to note is that this is an identity that has never made him happy, yet there is difficulty in any attempt to live consciously and not reproduce the past. It is easier to continue to employ the defense mechanisms we have learned no matter how dysfunctional we may find our relationships. A healthy sense of identity is experienced as optimal well-being, a feeling that we are at home in our bodies and that we know where we are going. Crisis in identity may be experienced as psychotic episodes, such as Adam's, that self-perpetuate, consuming the psychic energy needed to create a sense of wholeness and leading to a deeper sense of isolation. However, most of us would agree that a sense of aliveness is at the core of ownership of the self. Adam's self has thus far been subject to the plans of others. He has trusted too much and found himself betrayed. This has often led to paranoia, where conspiring parties waited to take advantage of him. Adam's paranoia has resulted in a loss of initiation, since he has not developed internal guides to help him set a course. Without plans of his own, he fears being overwhelmed by the plans of others. To develop a sense of health requires reestablishing healthy skepticism along with a sense of initiation. A fluidity of defenses is necessary in order to overcome a sense of victimization and choose a course of action and self-expansion. This will allow the ego to expand and grow and not be drawn back into repeated infantile patterns of conflict yet to be resolved.

7

Laura's Story: "Magnetic Field"

Next we turn to Laura, who, like Adam, is having a problem taking control of her life. She, like Adam, struggles to separate her adult life from her father's influence. Rather than seeing herself as a prisoner, the central metaphor for Laura's journey is a magnetic field from which she has found it necessary to take a rocket ship in order to escape. She feels the magnetic pull of her father was so great that she had to catapult beyond this force field or else risk being pulled back.

Laura is attempting to separate from her family and establish a separate and active identity. She holds her father responsible for what she calls "failed launchings." Laura is a thirty-seven-year-old female who is in a committed, twelve-year relationship with another female. She is the youngest of three children of Italian immigrant parents whose marriage was arranged and "like slavery." Her father's need for control created a world ("the castle on the hill") experienced by Laura as an upwardly mobile, middle-class existence where accumulation was valued over relationships, a world isolated and disconnected from the rest of society. Her home was filled with silences; tension, and stewing anger, with occasional explosions between her parents. In this world, Laura viewed herself as the "third rape case," since, in her mind, she could only imagine her father forcing himself sexually on her mother, thereby giving birth to her two older siblings, and she being the "third rape case." In adolescence she rebelled by becoming sexually active with boys at age fifteen, after rehearsing sex play with a girlfriend at twelve. A turning point for Laura was her parents' discovery of her high school diary, which recorded her sexual experiences and desires and her rage at her father. This precipitated a depression and a downward spiral. As a young adult, she moved to Boston and began a lesbian relationship, although she still defines herself as bisexual. This relationship has been a fulfilling one that has stimulated her emotional growth and allowed her to separate from her family and begin a career. Her father's death when she was twenty-nine, following a partial reconciliation, was a relief. She is currently working toward a Ph.D. in counseling psychology. Her most influential male relationships were with two young men who happened to be brothers, the more serious one lasting four years. Laura divides her life story into the following chapters: "Isolation," Launching," Spinning My Wheels," and "Rocketship: Breaking the Magnetic Field."

Isolation

Laura begins her life story with the story of her grandparents' accomplishments. Her grandfather worked for a senator and was written up in the *New York Times,* while her grandmother was a feminist and started a woman's bank. Laura's own struggle is about her attempts to gain competency in the world of work.

Laura, thirty-seven, has two older siblings, a sister, forty-three, and a brother, forty-five, from both of whom she is estranged as an adult. She thinks her birth order as youngest was critical, in that she was used by her parents as a problem child in an attempt to avoid their own unhappy marriage, which she describes as like two dying people. She views her father as controlling his wife and squashing his children, devastating any attempts at independence; and her mother, she describes as incredibly passive, angry, and selfish. Laura says that her mother looked after the kids in an obligatory way but never took an interest in any of them or what they did. Neither parent fostered the children's positive sense of self. Laura remembers that they grew up with lots of negative verbal and nonverbal messages that they were inferior, which contributed to her lifelong low self-esteem.

An important early memory for Laura is of her parent's relationship. Her parent's marriage had been arranged. In Laura's view it was a loveless relationship, and for Laura it became an important symbol of the institution of marriage as "something women definitely don't want to be in." According to Laura, there was an "indentured quality to it, similar to slavery." She notes that her mother was completely dependent on her father financially, controlling her with an allowance. This control extended to other areas. Laura cites an instance of her angry father pulling the wires on the family car so that her mother could not go anywhere. She views the marriage as undemonstrative and full of tension.

Her father would not allow her mother to practice her Catholicism, which she experienced as a significant loss. As a result, the children were raised without religion, in a world where it felt taboo.

The dominant images from this period have to do with isolation, silence, and lack of color. Laura likens her home to a morgue or funeral home. Her narrative tone is pessimistic, befitting an unhappy childhood where she was unable to fulfill her wishes. However, one critical difference from Adam's story is that Laura has been able to transform her personal myth from one in which she was a victim into one in which she is a survivor. The survivor becomes the central imagoe in her story. She has been able to turn passive into active. This means her story will be more integrative, because she has been able to create a self that is purposeful, giving her life meaning. Thus her tone shifts from Kansas to Oz, from black and white to color, from negative to positive as she becomes an active agent in her life.

When she was eight, her family moved to what Laura characterizes as her father's "castle on the hill." It was her father's dream house, which he planned and built himself, a gigantic house that was "like Texas." Yet to Laura it was the epitome of the saying "all dressed up and nowhere to go." Laura felt it was ready for a party, but the party never happened. Its very spaciousness, to Laura, created a paradoxical sense of isolation and disconnection.

Laura associates isolation with not only "her father's castle on the hill" but the absence of friends and companionship that she associates with her parents' life. No one came to chat or for coffee, not even repair people, since her father was a "do-it-yourselfer" to the extreme. Her parents had no friends. Laura found humor in her father's line of work, painting white lines on the streets, which he called the White Line Company. His slogan was "Your Silent Policemen," which she feels epitomized his linear thinking and rigid approach to life.

Laura sees their household as revolving around the television, the one focal point that tied the family together. According to Laura, everyone was in his or her own world, watching television. The children were encouraged to watch it, be quiet, and stay out of their parents' way. Laura learned to minimize herself in this environment. Growing up in a home with little positive interaction between parents, lots of silence and tension, and brewing anger, Laura felt lonely. She remembers her parents vacillating between periods of not talking to each other for weeks at a time, times of silent tension, and periods where they would explode verbally. The threat of explosion pervaded an otherwise "sealed up" atmosphere. Her parents failed to resolve the underlying tension and unhappiness. Neither parent could communicate feelings or resolve the conflicts in a way that led to reconciliation and growth.

Laura became sexually active at age fifteen. She now thinks that this was too young, and feels its says a lot about the emotional deprivation in her home. Desperate for someone to like her, she turned to sexual intimacy. She had a steady boyfriend throughout high school, whom she viewed as worldly in contrast to herself. At the same time, however, Laura admits simultaneously having an "incestuous" relationship with her boyfriend's older brother, which she describes as a great sexual relationship. She found it open and liberating. But the five-year age gap between them seemed enormous at the time and created a sense of distance. She felt that his role was to introduce her to life after she had grown up in such a "lifeless" house. These relationships, which lasted until she was twenty-two, were her most significant ones until her current partner, Margo. Like most teenagers she sought romantic attention realizing that her desperate need for love made her sexually reckless and out of control. She now feels that the combination of being a pretty teenager, an inability to say "no," and not having a sense of self was a bad combination which led to her getting sexually involved too early. Laura's actions, she admits, in part, were to get back at her parents and in part an attempt to find the love she craved.

She was aware at this time of feminist leanings and wondered what it would be like to share her life with a woman, though she never really thought of it as lesbianism. She had had her first lesbian sexual experience when she was twelve and remembered it as very appealing, though she did not actively pursue this course until her early adulthood.

Depressive phases last as long as it takes us to assert ourselves. Self-assertion is a sign that initiative is at work and that we are less dependent on self-defense mechanisms of projection. The key for both Adam and Laura has been to lure healthy narcissism back to the ego by reframing the self in a more positive light and by seeing oneself as valuable. As we rebuild ourselves, we build new relationships. This allows us to replace our paranoid feelings with friends. Such processes as negotiation, assertiveness, aspiration, and initiative make the old paranoid processes unnecessary.

Launching

The dominant theme for the next period of Laura's life is failed or poor launches. The image of a launch is of moving away from a port or dock where one has been anchored. A successful launch for Laura was one in which she would be able to propel or drive herself in life rather than being pulled back into the magnetic field of her family. This is similar to the image of a baby bird flying from the nest or a baby animal learning to walk. To use her metaphor, Laura needed to find her own orbit. This would become a central theme in her life story.

Laura feels that all of her attempts to launch were thwarted or sabotaged by her father, while her mother lay passively on the sidelines, not knowing how to help her gain the skills she needed. She feels that the length of time it has taken her "to get on her feet" as an adult is a result of this. She credits herself with a deep sense of persistence and perseverance, triggered by her desperation to survive in spite of the desperation of her home life. Laura feels that her depression and family woes held her back, causing her to be an underachiever.

A key childhood event on this theme was her first job. This was one of her earliest attempts to launch herself, and the attempt was thwarted by her father. This incident, she feels, is worth a chapter in a book. In an effort to connect with her father, who had a "hardware store in his basement," Laura got a job working at a hardware store. The first day, her father took her to work. The boss, who was too busy to orient his new employees, gave them a few dollars and told them to go next door and get a coke for about twenty minutes. Laura's father became irate and had a fit, screaming, "Who do you think you are, taking advantage of these kids?" Laura was fired before she had even begun her first day. These types of incidents chipped away at her, and suggest that her father employed a pattern of inappropriately displacing his deep-seated anger. His inability to control his temper continued a pattern of acting out. In this case it was not only self-defeating but also hurtful to his daughter.

Laura reacted to this environment with a lot of pent up anger of her own. A milestone event for Laura was her parent's discovery of her journal while she was away on a trip. Her mother had discovered it hidden under the mattress in her room. In it she had recorded what she describes as "primitive descriptions of what an asshole her father was." She had also documented her sexual escapades with her boyfriend. She later realized that she was acting out her rage through sex, which she also used to satisfy her neediness and loneliness. The discovery of the journal was the beginning of the end of a very long spiral. Laura felt here efforts to be independent were once again sabotaged and her relationship with her father was destroyed. Based on this, her parents decided to send her to a psychiatrist for a brief period. Given that her parents never talked about anything, she felt it odd that they would send her to a therapist. This incident precipitated a depression and became for Laura a low point because her parents isolated her even further by forbidding her to see her boyfriend and "grounding" her for the entire summer.

Grounded for the summer, Laura planned a great escape to Cape Cod. She left a letter and a phone number detailing where she would be. The letter explained how she wanted to be a good daughter but had found it too difficult. She and a friend convinced the police at Port Authority bus terminal that they where not run-a-ways. By the time she got to the Cape, her father had arranged for someone to meet her who insisted she call home. She did call her father but refused to come home immediately. This is early evidence that Laura is able to assert herself against her father. Laura has a budding ability to act to change her environment rather than allow herself to be victimized.

Rather than attempt to heal the breach between them, Laura's father hardly spoke to her for a year withdrawing in anger. For Laura, this felt like a death sentence. She became so depressed and humiliated that she asked to be pulled from public school and placed in private school. Her parents obliged but Laura characterizes this change as traumatic because she was held back a year, to sophomore level by the principal. She could not relate to the other girls, who seemed more sheltered. She felt older and different.

To her credit, Laura did take active control of the situation and begged the principal to advance her to senior level the following year. She demonstrated an early ability to problem solve. She resolved the problem by discussing it with the principal. The switch from public to private school, she admits, created a botched, inconsistent and depression-laden high school career.

Spinning My Wheels

Despite her trouble, she went to college, which she admits "meant nothing more than a ticket out of the house." It meant nothing to her academically or job-wise, as she did not have a sense of the future. She felt even more a failure when she got pregnant and decided to have an abortion. Despite some academic success, Laura's father insisted that she was "spinning her wheels." She did not know what she wanted to major in, so he "pulled the plug" on school.

This was another key experience in which her father undermined her attempts to launch. Not knowing what she wanted to do at that time was age appropriate. This was to Laura another major sabotage. Not only did her father prevent her from sailing, he pulled the plug, draining the water out of her attempts. These sabotages left Laura depressed and without energy, much as Adam felt in our second case study. Laura did not have the emotional strength at that time to be independent of her father's will. In retrospect she realizes that she could have gotten a job and gone to school part time, but she did not have the strength or ability to challenge him. She had never really made a decision on her own. She had been taught to be dependent.

She returned home and took a series of demeaning menial jobs, although something inside her told her that she should be doing more. Yet she had no idea how to pursue this. She had gotten snagged developmentally during the adolescent phase of her life. It would take her many years to "regain her foot-ing." She considered these incidents a devastating setback for her budding sense of self. Her father's sabotages were the acts of a desperate man, trying to keep his "problem child" as the focus of a failing and flailing marriage. By projecting their marital woes onto their last child, her parents were able to continue to deny the lack of glue in their own troubled marriage. Unconsciously they used Laura as their last attempt to bond as a couple.

Around that time, Laura decided to seek therapy for the first time. This she credits with instilling in her a belief that things could be different. With the help of her therapist, she expanded her thinking, returned to college, and graduated. She credits her own perseverance as a key factor in this accomplishment. She knew she had to finish in order to show herself she could do it. Laura thus has shown an ability to seek help from a professional and to develop a plan to accomplish her goal. Her success shows her tenacity as a survivor.

Rocket Ship: Breaking the Magnetic Field

The next chapter of her life Laura calls "rocket ship." She views her move to Boston as a key event. A gut feeling told her that it was time to leave. She calls this move a rocket ship because for years after that, whenever she visited home, she sensed an overpowering pull. So she began thinking of her home as a magnetic field. She imagined that the only way to get out was to take a rocket ship and go beyond the field, to catapult herself, because she saw no way of leaving with any graduation. She notes that this image of the rocket ship taking her beyond the magnetic force field of her family did not occur to her until adulthood. Of the next twelve years of her life, the first five were the hardest, because she began to grieve for what she had missed. She cried a lot during these years but got in touch with part of herself. The move to Boston was a turning point for Laura as she began to assume active agency in her life story. The key coping strategy Laura used during this period of her life was catharsis. Laura was sufficiently in touch with her feelings. She was able to express her grief and mourn her childhood losses. She was able to face and accept the situation both cognitively and emotionally. Her repertoire of coping skills had increased.

Certainly another key turning point during this period was her decision to look up Margo, a friend of hers from college. Although she knew Margo was a lesbian, she did not consciously plan to get involved in a long-term relationship. Margo and Laura became lovers when Laura was twenty-five. They have been together ever since. Laura's relationship with Margo seems critical in rebuilding her sense of self through a loving relationship. Laura's choice of a lesbian partner suggests a determined effort not to repeat the despair of her parents' marriage. Her relationship is carefully crafted to provide the joy, color, and life that she felt was missing in her childhood.

Laura believes her decision to be lesbian is not foreclosed but rather is sexually fluid. She is still attracted to men and could live either way. She does not identify with the lesbian label, as sometimes she feels straight and sometimes not. But because people need a category or label, she gives them this one. Sometimes she feels like her twelve years with Margo have caused her to miss the whole dating scene, and she wonders if she would be with a woman if she were not with Margo. Yet, for the most part, she is where she wants to be. She also realizes that if she wants something more, she is free to pursue it. Yet she has not acted on this because she is satisfied with her relationship.

Laura credits Margo with helping her enormously. With her emotional support, she stopped feeling lost and depressed and learned to do things differently. She has made dramatic changes as a result of her newfound ability to problem solve. In comparing her relationship to that of her parents, she feels it is Technicolor to their black and white. Her relationship is based on respect. She and Margo have fun and laugh every day. They are childlike and kid around a lot. Compared to the colorless, funereal atmosphere of her childhood home, she finds her current situation both colorful and fun.

Laura admits that she has not directly told her mother about being a lesbian, even to this day. Since her family never really talked about anything, she does not find this unusual. She assumes that her mother has deduced this from the fact that they own a house together and there is only one bedroom. She has told her mother that she does not date men and does not plan to get married.

Laura does not necessarily attribute her lesbianism to her parents. Her mother, she admits, was not a great role model. She was not caring, supportive, or nurturing. Yet none of these attributes necessarily led to Laura's sexual orientation. Furthermore, she feels that if having a tyrannical, controlling father contributed to lesbianism, there would be a lot more lesbians in the world, since she does not feel that she was the only one with a bad relationship with her father.

Another turning point for Laura occurred on one of her obligatory visits home. She bought a new outfit so she could get praise from her father. Looking pretty was one area where she got attention, although she admits that this was a mixed blessing because it also made her feel like her father's adornment. On gong to bed that night, she accidentally overheard a conversation between her mother and father in which her father implied that her new outfit looked whorish, her new car was a bad decision, and her friends were lacking. "She's never going to be anybody. She's got big problems," he remarked. Laura felt completely denigrated. In the course of two minutes, he put down how she dressed, her friends, her decision making, and her prospects for the future.

This was powerful, but at the same time it was validating, because this was what she had really always believed that he thought of her. Characterizing herself as a crumbled heap on the other side of the door, she called Margo to come and get her. The next morning she confronted her father with the comments she had overheard. He responded by walking out of the room. Sobbing, Laura left with Margo, but even as she left, she hugged her father and told him she loved him. At this he started crying, because this was the first time she had said this.

With the help of her therapist, Laura later insisted that he apologize, but instead her father told her he had meant what he said. Laura considers this moment a milestone because for the first time she realized how troubled her father was. When she realized how immature his behavior was and how disturbed he was, it burst her bubble, her picture of who her father was. This was good for her because it snapped her into a different perspective, allowing her to move away from self-blame and bad feelings. Laura was then able to put her father's failings where they were due—on him, rather than on her. She had, to this point, turned her anger against herself, using a strategy of passive aggression, and had continued her childhood pattern of minimization of her self. This had, in particular, affected her professionally, where she was afraid to talk to her teachers or be noticed for fear of criticism. Having internalized her father's strict and self-punishing ethics, she had continued in adulthood to believe herself incompetent and unsuccessful. Now she was able to place the blame on the appropriate object—her father.

Another key character from this period is her therapist, whom she has seen for ten years and whom she credits with helping her find a sense of self. This suggests using cognitive coping strategies to get in touch with her emotions and attach them to the appropriate objects. She now feels good about herself; She feels she is on track. She is in school, she has formed a relationship, and she feels hopeful about the future. She has kept moving. The image of movement is a big contrast to the stuckness of her earlier attempts to find her own orbit.

A further turning point for Laura was the death of her father, of lung cancer, when she was twenty-nine. Laura had attempted to mend the relationship about five or six years prior to his illness. She had tried to repair some of the damage and had found a sense of resolution. She had learned to connect with him in a different way and felt that by the time he died they had had some meaningful conversations. She was able to be altruistic, giving to her father even when she realized he was unable to give back.

Laura feels that her father willed his own death, due to depression. He did not feel he had anything to live for. After she was able to launch, she feels her parents "were like two dying people." Their relationship worsened after her departure. They began to sleep separately, and her father spent more time out of the house. There was a great distance between them. An example she cites was the way her mother cared for her dying father. She shut him in the TV-room and closed the door, leaving his orange juice outside the door as for a dog. Laura remembers that this is also how she had cared for her—feeding her and keeping her at a distance. Her mother, afraid to engage, was unable to reconcile emotionally and intellectually with her husband.

Laura's father's death led to a feeling of relief, and some happiness as well as sadness. She remembers crying at his funeral and saying to her aunt, "I don't have one good memory." Yet she also felt a relief not to be criticized anymore. The message she had received from him was that no one could do anything right unless it was done his way. In some ways, she feels her life has become fuller. Laura jokes that in death he is literally in a mausoleum. She had seen him as larger than life in his influence. After his death she realized that his large persona hid another reality, a fear of his insignificance. To help her with the grieving process, Laura has made two collages that she characterizes as funny and irreverent. She has been able to turn negative into positive through humor and creativity. Laura's story is filled with the humor of irony, which she uses to mitigate the distressing effects of her life. This is a mature defense that allows Laura to get in touch with her feelings.

In some ways, Laura feels that her relationship with her father has continued. She has many transference fantasies about older men in her schooling. She still yearns for a father figure. The transference is so intense that she is attempting to work on it in therapy so that she can re-experience having a father in a more satisfying way. Relearning, she feels, will help her sense of self so that she will not feel like a moron. This suggests recognition that she is prone, like Adam, to superimpose her childhood reality on the present through projection.

After her father died, Laura began graduate school, and she is in training now to be a therapist. She is still working to overcome the buttons she finds pushed from old wounds, especially when she feels jolted by other, more positive, experiences. Realizing she has been recapitulating all of the losses, she has worked in therapy to avoid being triggered by the awareness of what she has missed with her parents and siblings.

Laura now feels that she is truly separate from her family and is no longer trying to save them. She is no longer involved with her sister, who has problems with rage, and her brother, who has problems with depression. The death and illness of a close friend and relative has made her and Margo more aware of living in the moment. Laura and Margo go out of their way to have fun every day, and this she sees as the opposite of her family lifestyle, enduring death. Laura uses anticipation, preparing emotionally today for the future she desires.

Future

For the future, Laura wants to live life simply. She wants to stop yearning for things. She feels her journey has been about experiencing loss and getting in touch with what she has missed. She has successfully mourned and feels less needy. Laura's story suggests a midlife reconciliation and a putting to rest of many of the issues that she has felt conflicted by since childhood. There is a hopeful tone in the last half of her story, suggesting that she has made peace with her past and is now free to enjoy the future.

The flip side is that she has gotten in touch with what she has. She wants to focus on this and be happy with what she has achieved. She wants to learn to give more to others and share what she has, as well as to let people know who she is. She has been cautious in the past, since she has been unwilling to risk others not liking her. She feels strong enough in her sense of self to be able to take this risk now.

Her professional decision to complete her doctorate in psychology is a further indicator of her perseverance, a key quality that has infused her life story, and this also is an attempt to rework her botched high school and college experience. As she gets older life becomes more interesting, because she has a history to look back upon. Complexity and movement are all signs of a healthy adulthood. Although there remains some prejudice against same-sex relationships, it is clear that Margo has been an important source of strength for Laura. Given her father's and mother's problems, it is understandable that she is wary of men and marriage, although at thirty-seven, this is not impossible.

8

Escaping Our Magnetic Fields and Glass Prisons: The Oedipal Complex and Consolidating the Ethical Self

We turn now to the process most critical in determining our ability to choose mature over immature defenses and conflict strategies: the Oedipal phase of human development. During this phase, which occurs between the ages of three and six, we differentiate self from others, learn to be male or female, and internalize a conscience. Without resolution, many of our Oedipal struggles follow us into adulthood.

The Oedipal phase and its resolution, sometimes called the Oedipal Complex, was the nodal point of human development for Freud and his followers. Although Freud's theories have been largely discredited as a science of psychology, they continue to offer a useful model for understanding family dynamics. Freud saw the Oedipal period as a time when major emotional, cognitive, and affective shifts occur, leading ideally to the organization of the personality into a more or less stable form. As the ego becomes more integrated, we develop a firmer grasp on what is external and what is internal and acquire what Freud called the superego (literally *over* ego) to guide us in issues of conscience and morality.[1] The superego develops, Freud believed, as a result of praise and criticism by our parents whose beliefs, values, and attitudes become internalized into a self-observing function, what Victoria Hamilton has called a "watching agency."[2] This agency measures our ego, or self-concept, against our ideal self.

The Structure of Personality

Freud divided the mind into three components. The first inborn component of the psyche to develop is the id, the pleasure-seeking principle. The second is the ego, the reality principle, which distinguishes between fantasy and reality, between internal and external worlds. The ego also mediates between the super-ego, the last component of personality to develop, and the id, attempting to sat-isfy our wants and needs within social and realistic limits. An especially important component of this mediation is learning to delay gratification. This involves being able to plan ahead and delay immediate desires for the benefit of long-term gains. The ego thus becomes the basis of our defense system as we attempt to balance three psychic worlds: impulse, reality, and conscience.

It is important to bear in mind that these are not actual structures. If we open the skull we can see the brain, but not the mind, just as one can open a com-puter and see the circuit boards but not the software being used. Freudian terms are metaphors that we can use to talk about personality, but they are not bio-logical facts.

The ego, our sense of self, becomes gradually differentiated from the id, our primitive imaginistic and instinctual drives, as we become increasingly aware of the external world. Much of this separation occurs between birth and three years of age. When the ego is inadequately or improperly developed, it has dis-torted or resisted one of our three psychic worlds—impulse, reality, or con-science—resulting later in what Erikson calls identity diffusion,[3] a lack of differentiation between self and others, between internal and external worlds. This failure creates difficulty in initiating and asserting active agency. Without some distinction between self and world, sanity is not possible. Here, the groundwork is laid for the later consolidation of the superego as an internal-ized, relatively stable, autonomous agency. With the development of the super-ego, internal controls replace external constraints to protect against harm and to assure approval initially by the parents and later by society.

Object Constancy and Continuity in Relationships

The ability to make clear and stable distinctions between ourselves and others, between internal reality and external reality, known as *object constancy* by psy-chologists, is critical for a healthy ego system. The achievement of object con-stancy means that whatever our internal feelings or desires, we are able to maintain a realistic and balanced view. Without object constancy, the state of our needs may distort our perceptions. If I am angry with someone, I may per-ceive him or her as an immediate threat and be unable to recognize that this may be only a passing condition. Thus, in terms of intimate relationships, the person who lacks object constancy tends to see others in black and white terms. With object constancy, a person can be angry with particular issues or events, while still recognizing the overall value of the relationship. It permits a person to recognize both gratifying and frustrating aspects of self and others and thus make realistic choices.

With ego development comes advances in memory, cognition, language, self observation, and the mature defense or coping strategies. "Coming to selfhood," as Jung calls it, is a life-long goal, a continuing process whereby the individual integrates opposing desires and forces into the overall unity that we call personality.[4] Although personality must be relatively stable for others as well as we ourselves to have a sense of who we are from day to day, it is not a permanent achievement but rather an evolving concept.

Rehatching the Self

Piaget has said that the self emerges from a shifting balance that necessarily produces anxiety and depression. As we emerge from an older self toward a new self that we have not yet sufficiently differentiated, we have difficulty recognizing "that which was me is not me."[5] We are "hatched," to use Margaret Mahler's words, over and over again.[6] Development involves a succession of negotiated balances that organize experience in different ways. This evolutionary activity is the fundamental growth process of personality. Adam and Laura, for example, have shown different kinds of depression and reactions. Laura recognizes her sadness at the loss of childhood and family, but nevertheless moves forward to consolidate a new, more independent self that provides greater compensation. Adam is still enmeshed in his family dynamics and not yet willing to make whatever break is necessary to move on toward his own goals. He is still fighting old battles.

The Oedipal Imprint

Freud also proposes that it is through the analogy of the Oedipus story that we become sex typed and develop our models for identification with the same sex and for opposite sex attraction. In both Adam's and Laura's stories, the father continues to impact the formation of adult identity. All children inculcate parental values into their personalities, but Adam and Laura, both with strong, controlling fathers, have obviously done so to excess. Weak mothers, who provide neither nurture nor balance in their development, also limited both. Each needs to achieve gratifying self-experiences apart from the father in order to abandon infantile aims and achieve emancipation from his or her status as parental objects.

Freud was the first to understand that children are born with sexual urges and that the mother and father are the first sex objects. Not only is our emotional/sexual relationship with our parents our first, it is apparently the most permanent, leaving an imprint for future human relationships etched on the psyche. Freud thought this importance stemmed from the fact that our development at mother's breast is the longest of all animals, although later research has called this into question. In any case, it is the unity of mother and child that most see as the basis for our notions of bliss, truth, and beauty—in other words, perfection. Freud based the Oedipal complex on the child's unconscious desire to possess the opposite sex parent, a developmental stage that he saw as occurring between the ages of three and six. Oedipus was the character in Greek tragedy who killed his father and married his mother, and thus lends his name to the idea.

Freud believed we continue these issues through latency, the time roughly from the age of six through puberty. These issues are resolved by identifying with the same-sex parent to lessen our fear of aggression, and by internalizing standards of moral conduct, which protect us against our aggression. We then repress our feelings of attraction toward opposite sex parents and identify with the same-sex parent, internalizing a system of self-control. Put another way, we learn to behave in acceptable ways. During this phase there is a shift from oral eroticism, to anal eroticism, and finally to genital eroticism, as we shift from needs gratification to object constancy and become sexually mature.[7] This shift is a prerequisite for development. If unsuccessful, we carry residual needs into adolescence and adulthood. Freud's ideas on this matter work out better for males than for females, although most theorists agree that there is some similar process in each sex.

The Shift from Intrapersonal to Interpersonal Relations

The Oedipal stage sees a fundamental shift from autoerotic stimulation, oral and anal, to genital sex, which requires an object, another person. Thus we turn outward from self and parents toward other people, some of whom will be actual sex objects and others friends, mentors, or co-workers. Some see this development as the specific wish of the child to share with another person the kind of relationship it perceived to be shared by the parents. Thus the task of this stage is finding an appropriate love object to make this possible. This requires mature object choices and learning to value others.

The way parents handle their feelings is critical to the Oedipal phase because they lay down the pattern. When parents fail, the child internalizes a distorted pattern for later relationships. We have seen this clearly in all of the case studies so far. Jonathan is looking for a supportive mother so that he can explore his own virtues and leave home. Both Adam and Laura are working to free themselves from an over-controlling father.

Freud believed that the Oedipus Complex and its unconscious sphere of relations are internalized and survive in the structure of the personality. If a person fails to find an object outside the self, later relationships may be used as part of a person's intrapsychic structure and function as a repository for unacceptable parts of the self and/or to create essential human ties. Successful resolutions leave the person free of unconscious manifestation. Adam recreates his earlier psychic relationships and is still unable to bring love and sex together. Desire has failed to turn outward. The personal has failed to move from the intrapersonal to the interpersonal. Laura, on the other hand, has chosen a different model from the one she witnessed growing up and is, to a considerable degree, reacting against it. The choice has helped her to establish a different type of feedback, where she is able to nourish her self-esteem. Further, she has made peace with her father, achieving an emotional synthesis, which Adam has yet to achieve

The intense love relationships formed during this period between child and parents are complicated by sibling rivalries, hostilities, and emerging identification. Though lay people tend to think only of the sexual aspects, at the core the essence of the Oedipus Complex is competition or rivalry between siblings and between child and parent for the attention of the opposite-sex parent. The feelings are universal and intense.

Greenberg suggests that the intricacy of the Oedipal Complex becomes impressive when we recognize the vast array of human motives, affects, and capacities that the child feels. He or she feels powerful emotions, with wild oscillations between love and hate directed toward one person and torn loyalties between the two people that are most important. The child is excluded from what seems to be the most desirable relationship, that of the parents, resulting in self-contempt, jealousy, and fear of retaliation.[8] Culturally, the Oedipal Complex and its resolution work to inculcate the incest taboo, in that the sexualized feelings between parent and child, though felt, are forbidden to be acted upon if the child is to move beyond the sphere of psychic relations of the original family. If unresolved, as with all stages, the Oedipal issues continue through later life stages.

In the case studies of Adam and Laura, we see their attempts throughout adolescence and early adulthood to separate and their simultaneous struggle with an incestuous attraction to the family sphere of relations. Adam calls his struggle a "glass prison" from which he cannot escape, and Laura imagines having had to take a rocket ship to escape the magnetic force field of her family.

The core of this complex is the need for, but resistance, to consciousness. It is only as Adam and Laura consciously begin to understand their mythic patterns that turning points occur and permit change.

During this period, a child's relationship with one parent strongly influences the relationship with the other parent. As compensation for this unattainable rivalry, the ego and superego are integrated as one negotiates relationships with each parent and learns basic standards of permitted behavior.

The consolidation creates a system of moral constraints, and permits the postponement of goals that once seemed urgent in order to pursue more realistic ones. In this system, the father plays a role in modulating the intensity of the interaction between the child and the mother, helping to resolve conflicts and providing the same kind of secure base once provided by the mother. Although Freud has come under attack because he thought that the mature superego was developed only in the male, the developmental process he cited is important for both genders. Developmental theorists such as Carol Gilligan believe that the male superego develops in directions that are harsher, more absolute, and more punitive, than that of females.[9]

A child's early struggle with extreme and irrational feelings toward the parent may result in what Freud called the family romance. Freud wrote in "Family Romances" that children struggle with love/hate by imaging themselves to have been adopted and that their "real" parents were of noble birth.[10] Creating a second set of parents helps children to cope with the their ambivalent feelings. The second parent who appears so frequently in children's literature, often in the form of a wicked stepmother or witch, Freud believed to be an unconscious expression of this early fantasy and unacceptable feelings of hatred toward the parent.

Typically Oedipal wishes involve being chosen and loved over rivals, thus leading to rivalry and competition between siblings to identify with aspects of the parents. Growing up requires coming to terms with this ambivalence. Successful resolution allows the wishes and fears of this experience to move off the center stage of consciousness. A stable emotional relationship with a caregiver teaches one to feel secure. Successful Oedipal resolution teaches a number of complex skills: to feel that we have some control over internal emotional and external physical environment; that we are able to compete successfully by finding a niche; that we feel comfortable, to some degree, with a sense of masculinity or femininity; and that we are able to let go of early primal relationships to make more fruitful commitments to others. In the stories of Jonathan, Adam, and Laura, we see exemplified the negative aspects of ambivalence, intractable blocks that preclude choice and paralyze action.

Oedipal struggles continue when we divide our worlds and our relationships into black or white, good or evil, life or death. Splitting our view of the world into polar opposites creates a distortion, even if it makes for a good western or science fiction movie. While there must be a division between good and bad objects, between love and hate, this division must not be so compartmentalized as to leave us unaware that both exist in the same person. Those who pass successfully through the Oedipal struggle learn to tolerate ambiguity in relationships. As adults they have the capacity for creative integration, rather than viewing situations as either/or or win/lose. The increasing consolidation of the psychic structure permits the person to recognize and accept a variety of wishes in the context of well-being and self-esteem.

Resolution also results in increased cognitive maturity, allowing one to pursue goals with a sense of personal agency. Adolescence should permit the loosening and final dissolution of parental dependencies. If this does not occur, a person may continue to rely on primitive defenses (denial, projection, or even psychosis) rather than mature ones.

Jonathan has failed to develop a firm sense of his sexual identity and still wonders if he would have been better off as a woman. He has not been able to commit to an independent life and still has difficulty envisioning a future as an adult. He has not developed autonomy nor self-discipline. He has not developed a sense of active agency and intentionality. He tends to see decisions as either/or—he must be a perfect leader or he will be nothing, he must not only live frugally, but must deny himself even the most basic conveniences. For him, relationships must be nonconflictual or else they are bad.

Important to psychological maturity is the development of a realistic time perspective in terms of the life process. If we continue to view ourselves as adolescents, denying our adulthood, forever young, we must engage in considerable self-delusion. This can lead to increased despair when we wake up in our fifties and realize many of life's opportunities have passed us by.

Most research has focused on the forbidden and repressed in the Oedipal crisis, but what is allowed is equally as important. In a successful negotiation of the Oedipal crisis, the child is able to maintain permanent and satisfying relationships in the family, despite the realization that he must lose his parent as the direct object of desire. In opening the door to relationships outside the family, the Oedipal process repositions the primary family as a gateway rather than a barrier. It opens a pathway to individuation.[11] The loss of Jonathan's father resulted in his becoming a substitute spouse, a parent-child at an early age. From an Oedipal viewpoint, he had won his mother and killed and replaced his father, the fantasy of the Oedipal child. His parent's divorce and his mother's

alcoholism have made individuation difficult in that he has not been given permission to exist apart from the family. We see this same struggle in the studies
of Adam and Laura. Laura is very much aware of her family's "magnetic pull."
Adam's awareness is dawning.

Self-differentiation is crucial to healthy relationships. The lower the degree
of self-differentiation in a two-person system, the higher the emotional fusion
that occurs and vice versa, the higher the degree of self-differentiation, the
lower the emotional fusion. In other words, the lower the level of separateness,
the more uncomfortable the emotional fusion and the more conflict in a relationship. Neither recognizes the other as separate with their own needs and
emotions; and therefore, there is a failed empathic connection. What earlier I
have called a false self relies on external sources of affirmation and vitality in
order to function and uses others to complete the self. When self-esteem is low,
others typically influence our feelings unduly about the self. Reaction replaces
agency. Hypervigilence replaces self-reliance. Fantasy continues not only as a
major psychic determinant of childhood but as a force in the psychic reality of
the adult. Thus Jonathan dreams of becoming a great writer, but has not
accomplished this. A true self is more highly differentiated, which requires that
we learn to be more active, to validate ourselves, and to create the reality we
desire.

One critical area affected by the degree of Oedipal resolution is our
achievement in the arena of work. The ability to work satisfactorily involves the
ability to sublimate, to plan for the future, to control emotions in a positive
way, and to postpone gratification. Breakdowns in work and schooling often
reflect Oedipal conflict. Successful resolution of the Oedipal experience means
that the child has considerable ego development and is able to form and pursue structured goals with a sense of personal agency. The child learns to defer
gratification when he or she realizes there is an external world, apart from his
or her own needs and wishes, and accepts active strategies to deal with it.

The Good-Enough Father

Much has been written about the not-good-enough mother, but what about the
not-good-enough father? The father is critical to the Oedipal situation. If he is
depressed, withdrawn, critical, nonresponsive, or not available, the child then
experiences a failure in the capacity to see him- or herself as a sexual being, in
that the child identifies with his or her own sex and is attracted to the opposite.
The Oedipal experience is the first triangulated relationship in which the child
learns to transcend the immediate situation. It replaces the family romance

with visions of growing up, marrying, and having children. This requires that the child imagine the effect of his or her actions across time and space. Thus the Oedipal experience is not only one with real parents, but it is a force in the psychic reality of the adult. Some children have no vision of themselves in adult sex roles. They do not rehearse marrying and having babies during childhood, so these roles fail to become a part of their psychic makeup. The child has not internalized a sense of personal agency and thereby has been denied an important source of satisfaction. We go through the complicated motions of baking a cake because we can envision the result. If we have no visions to sustain us, we have little motive for the tasks required to attain them.

A good-enough father helps to extricate the child from the maternal orbit, facilitating a sense of reality, self-constancy, and sexual identity, thus helping to secure object constancy and a healthy identity. With triadic involvement comes an increased capacity for differentiating between internal and external reality and an ability to better tolerate anxiety. In each of our case studies we have seen clear failures in the basic triad. Jonathan's father is missing; Laura and Adam have tyrannical fathers. All of the mothers are weak in crucial ways—sick, alcoholic, unavailable, and apparently uninterested. Subsequently, each will have problematic imprints for basic relationship patterns.

The Oedipal period involves a vast array of human motives, effects, and capacities as the child feels a wild oscillation of love and hatred toward the two persons most important to him/her. Yet this period also leads to development of self as a separate individual. Ideally, that self emerges with an active sense of self-esteem, a sense of right and wrong, a sense of confidence in his or her ability to cope with the world, and a template for future relationships.

The onset of Oedipal development is tied to interpersonal transactions in the child's experience and is affected significantly by the parent's attitudes, both conscious and unconscious. The Oedipal resolution marks the end of infancy and is part of the process of becoming human, as the ego and superego are strengthened and consolidated. In expressing the often-unresolvable coexistence of love and hate, growing up means coming to terms with ambivalence. Moving forward requires repressing wishes, desires, and fears, later to be reenacted at the appropriate moment.

The Capacity to Commit

Erikson defined intimacy as the capacity to commit oneself to concrete affiliations and partnerships and to develop the *ethical strength* to abide by such commitments even though they may call for significant compromise.[12] Ego strength is revealed in our staying power, whether in love, work, friendship, or citizenship. Competence is the exercise of dexterity and intelligence in the completion of tasks that require planning and commitment. It means learning that we can influence the environment to meet our needs. Failure to achieve a level of competence means that we are subject to control by our instincts or our environment and allows passivity to play a more significant role in our lives.

Both Adam and Jonathan exhibit a pattern of failures in competence, which suggests a lack of ego integration. Adam wants love and sex to come together in his relationship but he has a great deal of baggage to overcome. Jonathan has yet to find a real relationship or vocation and must make the decision to grow up. The prognosis is not good for either. Laura has found a happy relationship, but it is a same-sex relationship and she is somewhat ambivalent about whether this is what she really wants. Since all these subjects are in their late thirties and early forties, they do not have much time left in which to make decisions and implement them. It is their awareness of the ticking clock that brings them to discuss their issues.

If intimacy is not achieved, people such as Jonathan may repeatedly withdraw from close relations, resulting in a deep sense of isolation. Adam may go from marriage to marriage, as he has before, without finding the satisfaction he wants. Laura has overcome much and finds her present life rewarding, but she is still aware of unresolved issues with her father, and with men.

Besides conflicts over genital love and rivalry during the Oedipal period, we always retain oral and anal conflicts as well. In order to resolve the Oedipal Complex and establish a firm personality with a sense of identity, the child has to work through oral-separation conflicts, guilt feelings, and separation anxiety to integrate oral, anal, and Oedipal guilt into a modulated and integrated superego. The result, Freud believed, is the development of an internalized, relatively stable and autonomous agency that replaces the external restraints of parenting. This requires and provokes ego advances in memory, cognition, language, and self-observation—the qualities we generally lump as "abstract thinking."

Rather than facilitating ego advances, traumatic experiences in childhood lead to fixation, a replay of conflict from earlier years. Adam chooses projection, paranoia, and psychoses. Jonathan takes refuge in regression to his humble dwellings and his fantasies of becoming a great writer. Laura has worked through many of her problems, but remains uncertain of her sexual identity and still feels her father's control, even from the mausoleum. All show retaliatory efforts toward significant others for stirring up anger and feelings of deprivation, but only Laura has shown success in not revisiting these feelings in her adulthood.

The Road to Adult Sexuality

Following the Oedipal stage, Freud postulated that children go through a period of latency during which they learn their sexual role though feelings and acts directed toward the same sex, a period he saw as a largely homosexual one. This is the period when boys and girls play separately and sometimes express disgust for the other sex. This is followed by the genital phase as sexual behavior is re-directed toward appropriate love objects and psychically the former child becomes an adult, relinquishing the passivity of childhood. Key to a vital adulthood is learning to work, to postpone gratification, and to share with others in a loving, caring way.

Adult sexuality means that the individual assumes an active role in dealing with life's problems. Relational maturity presupposes a capacity to turn attachment outward and a healthy level of individuation. Prior to this time desire is largely narcissistic, directed toward the self and others of the same sex.

However framed, the events that occur during the Oedipal stage are key to the development of a psychic structure, which permits mature relationships with others. Oedipal resolution involves the acceptance of limits and the loss of a powerful and exciting, if illusory, love relationship.

Plato thought the journey of love an ethical one. Love that enabled us to grow beyond ourselves, he believed, ennobled us, but love that did not move us to accomplish good deeds in our family, community, society, and culture, inhibited our growth. Love pursued only as worship of the self resulted in a withdrawal from larger pursuits.

Both Adam and Laura are struggling to overcome the unconscious sphere of psychic relations that they formed in childhood and that threaten their adulthood. Both struggle with a father who has prevented their launching. Escaping his psychic prison of his father had proven difficult for Adam who is replaying the family romance. Laura has taken a rocket ship beyond the magnetic field of her father's control and has created a life in which she is no longer a psychic victim of her past.

We turn to the last passageway necessary to understand intimacy as a part of adult transition. This passageway builds upon the work of the first two periods but adds its own challenge. The challenge of developing a stable but flexible self-concept rooted within an appropriate boundary system.

PART IV
Authentic Communication

9

What We May Be: Moving from too Closed or too Open to Healthy Boundaries

Our next communication passageway critical for mastery of intimacy in adulthood is the *inclusion* (or exclusion) system, which determines how open or closed we are to sending and receiving information about ourselves. Schultz defines inclusion as feeling known, acknowledged, and recognized, or the degree to which we reveal our identity and individuality to others. Unlike affection, inclusion does not assume strong emotional attachment. Unlike control, it is concerned with recognition rather than dominance. Whether we are open or closed in letting others know who we are is based on observable communication behaviors. Communication researchers call this self-disclosure, an indicator of how *authentic* we are in our relationships. Our position on the inclusion/exclusion scale determines, in part, our inclination to be close or distant.

Those who have little sense of belonging or community exhibit what we call exclusion. Their behaviors keep them separate from both potential partners and social groups in general. Skills that create community or relationships are inclusion skills or behaviors. A lack of inclusion skills causes others to see a person as uninterested or rejecting, and they may respond by showing little or only fleeting interest in that person. Most of these behaviors, excepting the true oaf or boor, are below the level of ordinary consciousness for both the sender and receiver. They are the subtle clues that we give off by our posture, tone of voice, level of attention, or phrasing of sentences.

Exclusion behavior stems from a sense of worthlessness, while inclusion behavior grows from feeling worthwhile. Yet, once again, we must beware the extremes. Those who are too high in inclusion may be seen as extroverted attention seekers, even desperate—like the salesperson who seems to work *too* hard at being liked—while the snob or know-it-all represents extreme exclusion. The ideal is a balance between separateness and being with others.

Our next two case studies, Beatrice and Ian, exemplify people whose restrictive self-concepts effectively defend against the intimacy they desire. A key difference in their narratives is that Beatrice has been able to effect a conversion in identity, while Ian is still struggling to do so. Beatrice and Ian illustrate the third yardstick that I believe is necessary for intimacy, authentic communication. We are authentic when we are able to let someone know our private self, to let down our public mask. Authentic communication is tied to self-disclosure. We all know those individuals who find it difficult to get close to others beyond a superficial chat or cocktail conversation. They hide who they really are behind a fearful and restrictive self-concept, which serves to protect them from harm but also cuts off important sources of feedback and keeps interpersonal relationships at a distance. They are what I call (following Ernest Hartmann)[1] the thick-boundaried. Jonathan is a good example of the thick-boundaried, keeping relationships at bay and even using a dressing style that serves to defend his sense of self from others.

On the other end of the scale are those who are too open and disclose too much, who seem to be easy to get to know but also are vulnerable and unprotected. These thin-boundaried people fearlessly plunge into relationships without testing the water, often leading to inappropriate ones, since their sense of judgment is often impaired as well. Rather than the restrictive self-concept of the thick-boundaried, which keeps others at a distance, they use others to define who they are, having little sense of themselves. As we shall see, Adam's three marriages, for example, seem more like an attempt to define who he is by seeking out relationships in an effort to repair damage from his childhood. The thin-boundaried have difficulty separating what is other from what is self. Authentic communication, I believe, is tied to our boundary system, a developmental process explored in chapter 12. In Beatrice and Ian's life stories, we examine two individuals who are trying to shed earlier attempts to define themselves, much like snakes shed their skins, in order to move into new and more resilient identities. This is a healthy movement. These new identities allow them to better monitor distance between themselves and others, and give them as adults the intimacy that they seek.

The ability to let others know who we are requires a firm but flexible sense of boundaries and a sense of personal identity, a process begun in adolescence—both of which are explored in the next chapter. Adolescence is a time of biological, sexual, and cognitive change, when we learn to think about who we are and who we might be. This period begins our search for identity by consolidating our personal stories and integrating such factors as narrative tone, imagery, symbols, motives, imagoes, and themes into an overall tapestry. The formation and reformation of identity and our attempts to unweave and reweave this tapestry become the central psychosocial task of our adult years. We attempt to realize an integrative life story by creating a sense of self that is purposeful and meaningful. McAdams says adolescence is the departure point for our myth of identity. Beatrice and Ian's stories are examined as attempts to reweave an earlier self-concept or identity that has prevented them from finding the intimacy that they seek.

How we reveal who we are and the degree to which we reveal ourselves communicates to others our capacity to be intimate. Our self-concept can be either a positive or a negative force in shaping how we communicate with others. It determines whether we are good relaters or poor ones. In order to let others close we must be willing to permit them to see who we are. True intimacy requires a sense of identity resolution or stability.

The Open or Closed Self

The beliefs we hold about the self are one of the most powerful forces shaping our communication, more powerful, in some cases, than even the biological drive to live—for suicide is based on a negative self-concept. Self-concept is our filter, defending and protecting our ideas about ourselves against those who would define us differently. These beliefs about self are protected, even if they are outdated or inaccurate. So fundamental is our need to have some sense of self that even a negative sense of self seems better than none at all. Morris Rosenberg describes our self-concept as a collective term that includes three different components: the Perceived Self, how we view ourselves, the Desired Self, how we would like others to view us, and the Presenting Self, the self we show to others.[2]

The *perceived self*, or self-image, includes the qualities and characteristics that we see as defining us. It is the set of relatively stable cognitively held beliefs about the self, our firm convictions about who we are. If asked to make a list of the most common phrases or words used to describe ourselves to others, some of us would choose social roles (daughter, student, or employee), some physical characteristics (short, tall, overweight, or blond), some intellectual characteristics (curious, clever, or dumb), some moods (energetic, enthusiastic, depressed), some behaviors (shy, outgoing, funny), some belief systems (Christian, Jew, vegetarian, capitalist), and even some skills (jogger, artist, gardener, homemaker). Self-concept reflects how we see ourselves, as compared to personality, which has more to do with how others see us.

The *desired self* is an idealized image that we use to measure ourselves. This ideal image borrows qualities from people we admire in family and culture, along with abstract notions of traits and virtues we would like to have, or feel we should have. The greater the gap between our perceived self and our ideal self, the lower our self-esteem or self-approval. Self-esteem is the credit or debit balance between the perceived self and the desired self, and is therefore the emotional component of self-concept. It is our evaluation of net worth—how we feel about our self now, and, to some extent, how we feel about the direction in which we are moving. Freud understood guilt as based on our judgment of an unacceptable disparity between actual and ideal. There are two obvious solutions to such guilt: we may reevaluate our perceived self and try to change, or we may modify our ideal self so as to bring it more in line with actuality. Since there is always some disparity between perceived and ideal self, this depends in part upon basic attitudes of optimism or pessimism, the sense of safety and security we have discussed earlier.

The superego, or conscience, functions primarily on the basis of feared punishment, but the ego ideal is a goal. The superego and the ego ideal are the stick and the carrot of self-concept. Laura has struggled to change her view of herself as incompetent and dependent, a view developed as a result of her father's sabotages of her attempts to launch. Once she ejected herself from the family orbit she was able to develop in the direction of her ego ideal, being separate, independent, and competent. She has closed the gap between her ideal self and her perceived self, and is happier.

A healthy ideal image is associated with some degree of commitment, the effort we are willing to expend to attain our goals. A person may dream of him—or herself—as a famous writer but if that person makes only desultory effort to attain this, like Jonathan, this is only a fantasy. Adam, by contrast, has taken action and published a successful book. Laura also has taken active steps to move from victim to survivor. Our next two case studies are Beatrice and Ian. Beatrice has acquired faith in her direction of movement and committed to a marriage, so that, while still not satisfied, she has a positive sense of self and a feeling of support from others. Ian recognizes that his notion of loving as pure and total devotion is unrealistic and thus is bringing his ego ideal more in line with possibility.

The third component of self-concept, according to Rosenberg, is the presenting self, sometimes called *face,* which undergoes the greatest change during adolescence as we try on different possibilities. We may deliberately present ourselves in order to manipulate others, as in job interviews, or we may unconsciously reveal ourselves through tone, posture, and perhaps those famous "Freudian slips." We most often act like the person we perceive ourselves to be, though of course we are all capable of putting on a face. Yet, deliberate acting is not easily sustainable over the long term, and research shows there is a positive correlation between self-concept and behavioral consistency.

If we are reasonably happy with who we are, we have little need to pretend. If we are not happy with who we are, we continue to try out possibilities, as we did in adolescence. Ideally we integrate all our faces and achieve constancy of behavior. Those who have not integrated their explorations may remain, like adolescents, sensitive, shy, easily embarrassed, and too eager to be approved of, because they have not developed an internal self and they continue to rely on external cues. Self-concept is a self-fulfilling prophecy because our beliefs determine our actions, especially at the level of unconscious, which most affects communications. These subliminal actions influence the expectations of others. If we expect someone to be mean to us, we invite him or her to be mean, and even if that person's behavior is neutral, we may interpret it as mean.

Although we must think of ourselves as stable, a healthy self-concept must be flexible. Too consistent a self-concept can be a drawback rather than an asset. Too strong of a filter may ignore information that runs counter to our beliefs. When we receive information that challenges our self-perception, we may deny the facts rather than change the self—even if the new image is favorable. Change is always annoying, if not painful, and we have as many doubts about our virtues as our faults, so we tend to prefer the comfortable present over the uncomfortable possibility of change.

This means that our self-concept can be our enemy by denying us vital information we need to feel better about ourselves. The better we feel about ourselves, the more easily we form and maintain interpersonal relationships. The higher our self-esteem, the more accepting we are of others and ourselves. Those with lower self-esteem have a difficult time with intimacy, often picking partners who reinforce their negativity and judging others by their own insecurities. For example, a person who is insecure about his or her intelligence may be hypercritical of intelligence in others. If concerned about aging, a person may be judgmental about the aging of others. Learning to accept and love the self is the foundation for a healthy relationship.

Bowlby defines self-esteem as the belief that we are lovable.[3] It requires mastery over the interpretative side of life rather than the material one. People who are good relaters have developed friendship skills and feel satisfied with their relationships. They are characterized by self-reliance, self-esteem, a sense of mastery, social competence, and coherence. Poor relaters are insecure, helpless, and frustrated in relationships. They are incompetent at interpreting information in a realistic and balanced way, and are thus anxious in interpersonal relationships.

It is possible to exit the conveyer belt that leads from lack of self-esteem to isolation and depression if secure attachments can be found in adolescence or adulthood with a marital partner, mentor, or therapist. One woman, at fifty-one, found herself suddenly optimistic despite an unhappy history. When her father died at age seven, she was sent to an orphanage. In her late teens she got pregnant and married a spouse who proved unfaithful and abusive. They were divorced. Finally, in her forties, she met the right man. "We can talk and talk about everything. I used to expect everything to go wrong and it did. I used to be a terrible pessimist. I'm not anymore."

Our self-concept is usually different in some degree from others' perceptions of us and, within reason, this is normal. We tend to distort our self-concept, putting ourselves in an excessively favorable or unfavorable light. Yet a seriously unrealistic self-concept is a distorted filter that preserves obsolete information and distorts feedback. We may hold ourselves to standards that we find difficult to meet. We may judge others (and ourselves) more harshly than required. Like the mirror of the anorexic, self-concept shapes fact to belief. Similarly, we may use our beliefs about the self as a shield to protect us from feedback that would make us more attractive and available to others.

It sometimes takes a powerful force to change our self-appraisal. Some features of self-concept, like eye color, height, or hair color, may seem objective, but it is the importance or interpretation we assign to them that matters, whether positive or negative. Changing our self-concepts often requires new sources of feedback. If we continue in the same environment, we repeat our earlier mistakes. This is why AA-type groups encourage their members to form new relationships that can provide a different set of reinforcements. Jonathan, constantly drawn back to his mother, is denied the feedback that might allow his self-concept to grow. Adam's projections keep his early family system intact. Laura, in selecting a supportive partner and a helpful therapist, has been able to revise an earlier negative self to a positive one. Beatrice has met with success in transforming an earlier sense of self as a result of the influence of her church, while Ian is still struggling to do so. We can see in each case study that change comes with difficulty and even trauma.

Chris Argyris, a Harvard researcher, makes an interesting distinction based on these differences, which he labels "theories in use" versus "espoused theories."[4] A theory in use how we act, whereas an espoused theory is how we believe we act. By comparing how people act with what they say they believe Argyris was able to demonstrate in a study of managers that in many cases their behavior was not consistent with what they espoused.[5] This suggests that managers whose behavior did not match with their espoused beliefs were filtering feedback to distort their perception.

Another way of phrasing this is to say that these managers had an ideal self-concept of themselves as managers, which was inconsistent with their behavior.

This was in part a defense mechanism, denial, which enabled them to ignore behavior that conflicted with their self-image. The more congruent our theories in use are with our espoused beliefs, the more realistic we are about ourselves. We are human, and our behavior seldom measures up to our goals. We can recognize and accept this, working to improve, or we can deny and distort reality in order to avoid the pain of change.

Interaction and feedback from our environments, as we can see now, importantly shape self-concept. However if this were all there were to it, there would be no possibility of change. When we change environments and social conditions, we have the opportunity to reshape who we are, and sometimes we must do so. The former "party guy" who takes on the role of parent may reshape his self-image—as most parents do—but this is a powerful motivation, reinforced by biology, supported by culture and spouse, and personally desired. We do not always have that kind of support.

The Development of Self-Concept: The Reflected Appraisal of Others

Self-concept is not present at birth. It is not until six or seven months of age that a child begins to understand its body as separate and begins to develop a concept of self. The child quickly begins to expand on this rudimentary understanding of self as he or she responds to social, psychological, and emotional feedback. Our sense of self is formed largely through social interaction. As children we have slight opportunity to select those around us. If we are ignored, threatened, or treated inconsistently, we must cope as best we can, and one means of coping is to form a concept of self as different from others. As adults we can select, to some extent, those who will provide us with rewards and feedback in order to reinforce positive feelings about the self.

Our view of self stems from the appraisals of others.[6] We can each remember some special person who enhanced our self-concept by acting in a way that made us feel accepted and valued. For example, an older brother might take the time to read a story to a younger sister. Although the sister might be too young to grasp the story, she can grasp the emotional importance of his belief in her intelligence and worth. We also remember those who have diminished our self-esteem, even if we were too young to remember details. These generalized beliefs about the self are what Cooley called the Looking Glass Self, a self that is formed by our reflection in the mirror of others.[7]

Fitt's review of parental influence on self-concept found that parents with healthy self-concepts tend to have children with healthy ones.[8] Conversely, parents with negative self-concepts tend to impose these on their children. Yet children who grow up in homes with negative self-concepts tend, like the plant in a dark corner, to seek the light. They seek outside sources of self-esteem in neighbors, teachers, and friends who offer new interpretation and hope. Just as we have physical mechanisms that urge us to live, so we have psychic mechanisms that push us to form the best self-concept that we can. Another, more negative, way of putting this is to say that we all avoid pain and unhappiness.

The early years of life are filled with messages that shape our self-concept, since we have little sense of who we are except for the feedback we receive. If asked for a list of adjectives describing the self, many adjectives come from these interactions with significant others—parents, siblings, relatives, neighbors, and teachers. Later in life we expand these beliefs about the self to include employers and fellow workers, to lovers and friends. Although we have an increasing amount of choice, we still see ourselves reflected in the mirror of others, and if we have what Erikson has called "a tenuous sense of self," we are more at the mercy of that reflection. The inability to achieve an identity results in a feeling of inner fragmentation; little or no sense of where life is headed, a difficulty in gaining the support needed from others. Erikson saw identity as a sense of mastery or competence. The individual with a positive self-concept may be happier, but even a negative identity is better than none at all. Thus we have the teenage "rebel" who defines self as the opposite of what significant others desire. Later sources of self-concept are the roles we assume as a child, parent, student, and teacher. McAdams calls such central roles in our life stories *imagoes*, formed by our role models.[9] When we refuse to make decisions about career or romantic commitment in order to postpone the demands of adulthood, we place ourselves in a state of psychosocial moratorium, awaiting a magic day when we will "grow up."

These early beliefs about the self-reflected from outside sources determine our narrative tone. Some of us develop selves that exude optimism and hope; others develop selves filled with pessimism and resignation. Learned early in life, they become a self-fulfilling prophecy and shape our self-esteem, our net worth.

Social Comparison and Self-Concept

We also form our ideas of ourselves through social comparison with others. We compare ourselves to others, determining whether we are superior or inferior, or whether we are the same or different. A primary sense of comparison comes from our family, in particular our birth order, which is examined in more detail in the next chapter. Grade school children see those born in another country or a distant state as different. The same is true for skin color, sex, class, and an exhaustive list of other attributes. Our reference groups offer comparisons that shape identity—whether we see ourselves as part of a majority or a minority, and how we feel about this difference. Media and culture also provide models against which we measure and define the self. We have more choice of reference groups as we get older. Beatrice, for example, has found her church group to be an effective source of reference.

Research on midlife has found that those with a healthy sense of self-esteem make their comparisons downward rather than upward, counting their blessings rather than ruing their losses or the unfairness of life.[10] They may seek jobs where their sense of self is not threatened, choosing to be a big fish in a small pond rather than a small fish in a big one. This process is part of the urge to find the best self one can.

Observability: How We Self-Disclose

Self-disclosure is the manner and degree that we use to reveal our ideas about who we are to others. The ability to self-disclose can mean the difference between the dark solitary confinement of isolation and the lighted meeting place of intimacy. We can be reserved or difficult to get to know, or too open risking injury to our self-esteem. Self-disclosure has both rewards and dangers. The rewards include greater self-knowledge; better coping skills as we adjust our self-concept through feedback; better integration of our emotions (rather than hiding behind defensive behavior); and energy release, as many feel a kind of catharsis in talking about the self. While openness deepens relationships, we also risk the danger of rejection or criticism. Though self-disclosure may be risky, it is crucial to finding out who we are and to building relationships.

Perhaps the strongest barrier to intimacy is fear. A person may fear the vulnerability that accompanies self-disclosure, or fear that he or she may appear foolish, may be criticized, or may not be accepted. Exposure is difficult for those with low levels of trust, whose past experiences have taught them to expect attack and abandonment. Intimacy also may be feared because it means responsibilities, commitment, and self-discipline. Success may be feared because it heightens expectations and therefore risk and responsibility. When we reveal our personal thoughts and feelings, we emerge from the shadows of role, status, or history and are seen as unique.

Self-Disclosure: Balancing Expression and Protection

Since the 1960s, communication researchers have focused on the importance of candor and self-disclosure in interpersonal relationships, but William Rawlins has pointed out that the "open school of communication" needs serious qualification.[13] The open school has emphasized self-disclosure as critical to intimacy. The goal of self-disclosure is to reveal more about ourselves to others and to receive more feedback from others.

Yet, according to Rawlins's research, in most intimate relationships communication serves not only expressive but also a protective function. It may be equally important for individuals to develop skills at restraining remarks and withholding private information. Rawlins sees expression and protection as strategies in managing relationships. Those who are too open—who say whatever is on their minds, without regard for the feelings of others—have not developed an appropriate strategy for intimacy (as everybody knows without need of theory). Equally important with disclosure is monitoring our statements and estimating their positive impact. In a study of conversations between pairs of friends Rawlins found that unchecked expression was rare because of the anticipated consequences. Since friendships are of lower emotional intensity than intimate relationships, there was less likelihood of "blurting out" information or feelings that might have negative consequences. Intimate relationships create the conditions for openness, but simultaneously create need for closure. Unchecked candor may hurt feelings—a hurt felt more intensely where trust has been offered and risks taken on the other's behalf. Intimacy presupposes that we will not divulge shared confidences and will exercise restraint in broaching sensitive topics. So, Rawlins argues, protection of self and others is as important to intimacy as disclosure.

Rules for Self-Disclosure

What this means in practical terms is learning to disclose within implicit rules. Research shows that disclosure usually occurs gradually. This enables reactions and feelings to be weighed as we go along so that information can be modified or withheld. It is basically a matter of judging how much the other person can take.

People differ in their view of what constitutes significant self-disclosure. Those with thin boundaries, with an undeveloped sense of self, may open up quickly and deeply, while those with thick boundaries may reveal little at any one time. Some may never reveal their innermost doubts and fears, while others may couch their disclosures in careful phases that permit immediate withdrawal at any lack of acceptance. These differences also have a gender and cultural base. For example, females are typically more disclosing than males. The British are known for their reserve.

Another important consideration is the level of trust in the relationship. Disclosure early in a relationship is always less full than it will become at a later stage, and this is both a fact and a rule. Some people have vested interests in outcomes, so we must choose our confidantes with this in mind. Single friends may have a vested interest in maintaining our singleness, and married friends in promoting marriage.

Self-disclosure must also respect mutuality. A pattern of one-way revelations puts the relationship off balance, making the partner feel vulnerable and perhaps overloaded with information or feelings. We all know the experience of someone at a party who tells us their whole life story, including personal details we do not especially wish to hear. The effect is to make us feel uneasy. It creates the expectation, sometimes almost a demand, that we will reciprocate. Even if this expectation is not there, the person doing the revealing is violating the rule of balance in conversation.

Many of the protective tactics necessary to self-disclosure are apparent in the model of active listening. Active listening is listening to both the content and the nonverbal or relational dimensions of the message. It is listening fully, but without passing judgment. When we listen without judgment the speaker feels attended to, accepted, and protected. This encourages the speaker to reveal further information about him- or herself. The listener has created a safe harbor in which the speaker can talk without fear of being hurt. More than this, the listener responds to the relational dimension of the message as well as the content. Such comments as "You sound down today," or "You must have been proud of that," make the speaker feel understood at a deeper level than content. This is empathy, the deep and subjective understanding of another's struggle. Through empathy we enter the subjective world of the other and communicate concern and understanding. Empathy facilitates exploration of the self. It is a potent factor in learning and self-directed change because it develops the power for self-revelation.

A final concept researchers use to understand the self is that of rigidity or fluidity. The rigid person defines self and others in strict and mutually exclusive terms. One is friend or foe; events are black or white. The fluid person has less strict notions, seeing shades of gray rather than black and white. As with most of our concepts, neither extreme is the optimal position. We need some rigidity in order to have a consistent sense of self, to maintain a set of values, to have a position toward the rest of the world. Yet we must reserve the option for shift and change, or else we cannot grow and learn.

Next we turn to Beatrice and Ian who struggle with revising self concepts that have proven too restrictive and rigid. The goal at midlife is to develop new sources of information about the self in order to provide new and different feedback. Without new feedback, the self concept acts like a filter ignoring information that runs counter to archaic childhood beliefs about the self and preventing growth.

10

Beatrice's Story: "Conversion"

We will begin our exploration of the boundary system and authentic communication with Beatrice, whose story I call "conversion." Beatrice, in reaction to her upbringing, has excluded key qualities from her sense of self that she must include in order to find the life she seeks. In expanding her sense of self, she has been able to turn her life around. In the following chapter we will turn to Ian, whose self-concept must be similarly expanded in order to allow him to safely experience a different type of love than the type of devotion he fears. Beatrice, now fifty, has made headway in transforming the identity first integrated during adolescence. Her story strikes an optimistic note at midlife. She has moved from defining herself negatively, in reaction to early traumas, to a positive and active identity, which she credits to "God's finally getting her attention." Conversely, Ian, at thirty-eight, is still struggling to reintegrate and reframe a different model for intimacy. As he puts it, his categories are beginning to shift.

Beatrice is a Caucasian computer programmer who married late in life to an AfricanAmerican man thirteen years her senior. They have been married for six years. Beatrice has suffered a number of traumas, including the death of her sister from diabetes; the suicide of her father, despondent over his retirement; a gang rape while in her twenties; and a mysterious illness from which she still suffers. She had significant relationships with three men before meeting her current husband: one with a boyfriend she met in college, one with a married man, and one with an alcoholic cross-dresser. She was baptized on her fortieth birthday into what she describes as a "nondenominational fundamentalist Christian religion that goes by the Bible." She divides her life into two parts— before and after her baptism.

Before Baptism

The imagoe that dominates Beatrice's early story is that of a rebel, one who goes against. She defines her self-concept negatively, in reaction. Unlike Adam, in chapter 6, her goal is to relax control rather than to attempt to assert control. Beatrice's conversion or transition occurred when she relaxed her boundary system sufficiently to include those qualities and needs that she had shut out. Through her church she found an accepting and compatible group which made possible a loving relationship and marriage. Even though she and her husband are different in many ways, their commitment enables them to keep working and the church continues to support them in doing so. She and her husband share a spiritual sense that they are engaged in a holy task.

Beatrice's pattern of rebellion was shaped by her early childhood experiences, particularly her birth order as the eldest of two siblings. She begins her narrative with her younger sister's death at forty-two from diabetes, just as Beatrice was to be married. Her sister had been critical in shaping her early sense of identity. As she puts it, her sister was indoors and dolls while Beatrice was outdoors and tomboy; her sister was people-oriented and reflective, Beatrice was action-oriented and reactive. Defining oneself in opposition to one's siblings is typical for those close in age, according to Frank Sulloway's *Born to Rebel.*[1] After being diagnosed with diabetes, her sister became more comfortable in the family because the parent's expectations were reinforced. Beatrice became the chore girl for her invalid sister. Beatrice became the instrumental one, while her sister became the expressive one. She cites a number of examples that reinforce these differences.

Beatrice felt out of step with her family and wondered if she had been switched in the hospital at birth, a common idea that we have seen with both earlier with Adam and later with Ian. Feelings of alienation and anger characterize her early narrative tone. As a firstborn, she would be the one to rebel. Sulloway notes that in families where sister dyads exists, the firstborn becomes the nonconforming one and the laterborns more conforming, reversing the traditional notion that the firstborn becomes conservative and closed to experience as a result of efforts to seek parental approval. In the absence of a brother, Sulloway believes, sisters assign themselves instrumental (masculine) and expressive (feminine) niches.[2] Being displaced as the sole object of her mother's attention, the firstborn shifts her principal identification to the father, which encourages instrumental traits. Beatrice's way of achieving a sense of identity was by rebelling. She opposed or rejected the roles modeled by her parents, whom she characterizes as materialistic and hypocritical. While her parents' roles seemed dangerous, opposing roles seemed to offer life and strength. A reactive choice of identity represents an attempt to gain mastery and characterize what Erikson calls a totalistic orientation, an all or nothing viewpoint.[3] Yet by defining him- or herself in opposition, the child, and later the adult, cuts off in early life the possibility of moderation or synthesis. For example, Beatrice "drifted apart" from her sister when her sister refused Beatrice's offer of alternative medicine for her diabetes. The situation was not helped by her sister's dramatic method of rejecting her help—flushing the herbs down the toilet. Beatrice insists that her sister's refusal to listen to her was a major factor in her death.

Beatrice defines herself similarly in relation to her parents. Since they ate frozen vegetables, she will eat only fresh organic ones. They were not socially active, so she entertains and cooks for friends. Her Mother nagged others to do things for her, so she does everything for herself. Her father wore suits to the dinner table, so she appears in her underwear. Since she sees her father as anti-sex, anti-love, Republican, materialistic, a workaholic, and prejudiced, she is sexual, antimaterialistic, anti-nine-to-five, and Democratic, and married to an African American.

A characteristic of rigidity is its obsessive commitment to mutual exclusivity. A mental object belongs to one class and to no more than one category. This is similar to an on-off switch for an electric light, in contrast to the shades of a dimmer. The rigid mind allows no contact between mental entities, in many cases fearing things out of place, which challenge these boundaries. The too-fluid mind sees a gradual extension of dimension with no absolutes, similar to daydreaming and sleeping.

Beatrice remembers a high school experience which became formative. She noticed that adults avoided shaking hands with a new assistant minister who had only stumps for hands. She decided that the best way to avoid such hypocrisy was to stop going to church. She took this further by deciding she would not get married, because married women who went to church were the most hypocritical of the lot.

Two themes in her narrative emerge that become important parts of her later "conversion": religion and marriage. Certainly her parent's marriage (at least as seen by Beatrice) did not seem to be a healthy model for a relationship. Beatrice sees their parent's marriage as distant and adversarial, filled with game playing. She thinks her father married only to advance his career in an era where single men were seen as questionable. She remembers her father as disdaining love and sex and has no memory of her father telling her mother that he valued or loved her.

Beatrice's earliest memory is of her father's meanness and cruelty. She now believes that his meanness may have been due to his alcoholism. Beatrice feels that her parents' evening ritual of having martinis before dinner made him even nastier. Even today, Beatrice hates the tinkling of ice cubes. If this were marriage, Beatrice decided, she did not want any part of it, an attitude we saw earlier in Laura's story. Beatrice's father, a workaholic, spent a good deal of his time traveling for his business. Unable to face the prospect of a failing business, an unhappy marriage, and his upcoming retirement, her father committed suicide by hanging himself with his own necktie.

Neither did Beatrice remember her mother as admirable. If she had to live with her mother, Beatrice comments, she would kill herself too. "She comes across as the sweetest thing in the world but in her own way she is mean and nasty and gossipy, looking for the worst part of everything." She is what Beatrice hates, a hypocrite. Fitts found that parents impose their own concepts, whether positive or negative, on their children.[4] From what we can decipher of Beatrice's upbringing, we can conclude that her parents imposed their own negative self-concepts on Beatrice and her sister.

Beatrice identifies more with her father than with her mother, the masculine role predicted by Sulloway. She is amused by her tendency to pick men friends like her mother and women friends like her father. Her women friends share her father's verbal repartee and critical attitudes. Her men friends, like her mother, have trouble taking charge and getting things done. She cites an example of a boyfriend who wouldn't let her get her car fixed because he was going to fix it but never did. This reminds her of her mother, who will frantically call her about preparing her taxes at the last minute. Beatrice cannot abide frantic or last-minute plans, a dislike which she attributes to a condition she diagnoses as hypoglycemia. Her mother is easygoing and lackadaisical, but things never quite happen for her, according to Beatrice. Erikson calls Beatrice's all or nothing rejection of her parents a totalistic orientation and understands it as a means of treading water until necessary healing can occur.[5]

A negative identity is not sufficient to mark the end of adolescence, according to Erikson. Certainly we can see this in Beatrice's story. Only when she has turned her identity from negative to positive did she signal a readiness for intimacy in adulthood. Erikson feels that intimacy requires a firm sense of identity or ego integration. This requires the weakening of a harsh or overstrict superego so that we can learn to forgo repetition and accept the self and others. Instead of rejecting or protecting threatening parts of our identity, we integrate them to achieve wholeness.[6] We do this through our ability to receive feedback. Feedback is the means for allowing our self-concept to be more open; and, as we are more open, we receive more feedback. One of the means that Beatrice has used to achieve this is her church. She, in effect, turns over aspects of her superego to her church group, and their approval enables her to be more personally open, in much the same way that supporting parents might have done much earlier.

Another important theme in Beatrice's story is represented by a reoccurring childhood dream. Looking back, Beatrice now believes that she has had a number of callings from God, which she has ignored. In her childhood dream, she is on a white horse in a dark thicket or forest, trying to find her way out and following a white light. She never succeeds, but always wakens before she can find her way out. The dream represents a part of her that is on a spiritual quest, trying to find truth or God. At fifteen she remembers awakening one morning to hear the question, "Are you going to do it?" She answered "no." She also cites a tarot reading where her childhood card was a woman, with her hand over her face, running into a wall. She has blinded herself and continues to run into a wall in terms of spiritual awakening. She has failed to turn herself, she now believes, toward the message God was sending. God has been trying to get her attention but she has failed to listen. Beatrice has now sublimated her rigid self into religious conviction. She can now allow God, working through her church groups, to guide her direction.

Another significant theme that begins in high school is her struggle with hypoglycemia. To this she attributes her alienation from the nine-to-five work world and her trouble functioning during "regular" hours. It accounts also for her special diet, so different from that of her parents.

In high school, she became part of a group of girl intellectuals. She saw herself as the lowest in terms of aspirations in the group. While the others set their sights on Radcliffe and Wellesley, she set hers on veterinary school. This followed her regular practice of "going against the grain." Using social comparison theory, we can see that she defined herself against her peers, just as she did with her parents. On her first day at college she met a student who presaged her future by informing her that he took six years to get his degree. She would take seven years. She interprets this chance meeting as preparing her for a hard struggle, one in which she would change majors from veterinary school to journalism. The delay in her schooling occurred because she essentially had to start over from scratch. She cites two factors that contributed to her delay in graduating from college. Affairs with boyfriends caused her to miss classes, sometimes for long periods, and her perfectionism made it difficult for her to turn in papers. This delay, she feels, set the tone for her life. She was no longer part of the normal world because she had not finished college in four years, and she had no job. She wasn't materialistic but was very sexual. She now interprets these events from a spiritual viewpoint: In Beatrice's words "sometimes the wrong context can make a person feel out of hand." The wrong context also meant viewing men as sex objects and expecting little of them. Now reinterpreting these same events through a spiritual lens, she believes, that God was trying to get her attention.

At college, she met her first significant boyfriend, with whom she lived for four years. She decided not to marry him because he did not believe in God, did not finish college, had trouble staying in a job, was not sexually faithful, and smoked. She feels that her involvement in this relationship provided further proof that her priorities were out of whack. As she describes it, her modus operandi during this period was to go to bed with a man first, then date later.

After college, Beatrice moved to another state to work as a newspaper reporter. She disliked the increasing bureaucracy of the newspaper business, which she describes as moving from a frontier phase to becoming civilized by replacing entrepreneurial journalists with corporate managers. She was now twenty-five. Since newspapers were hardly in a "frontier phase" when she began this career, it is likely that what disturbed her was the "normalness" of regular work.

A key event from her newspaper period was her rape. One day on her way home from work, she was jumped from behind by three men that she believes almost killed her. She was raped by all three men but attributes their letting her go to her treating them as normal people. The worst part of the experience, she allows, was not knowing what the men would ultimately do to her. If she had known for sure that they only planned on raping her, she says, then she would have been able to tell herself, "Fine, tell me when you're done. I'll take a nap or something." Not knowing their intentions made this event even more traumatic for her. Having no support in dealing with this event, she returned to work the next day, even though "she couldn't open her mouth wide and had to eat with a straw." Her colleagues at the newspaper wanted to put the story on the front page but she insisted that the news be relegated to a small article toward the end of the paper in order to protect herself and her family. Her subsequent interrogation by the police, and the newspaper's handling of the story, caused her to question her own ethical motives as a journalist. She wondered whether her personal code of ethics would be strong enough to override the importance of a story. She believes the rape had little influence on her experience so she has never sought out counseling. In fact, her anger becomes directed not at the rapists but at society for alienating them to the point that they would do this.

Although Beatrice denies significant after effects of this traumatic event, her next three relationships become increasing chaotic, suggesting some damage to the ego system. One means of defense is seeking out men who guarantee protection or safety from true intimacy. Following her rape, Beatrice engaged in a series of relationships that indicated difficulty in judgment. Current studies understand rape as creating post-traumatic stress syndrome, one symptom of which is difficulty with trust. Those with damaged egos have difficulty knowing who it is appropriate to trust since they lose faith in their ability to determine this. Beatrice reports that for some time afterward she could not tolerate anyone standing behind her. Although an entirely understandable reaction, this was indicative of her loss of trust.

She minimizes the event, claiming that, even now, she sees the rape "spiritually." Three or four years ago, Beatrice had a feeling come over her that some or all of her rapists had gotten baptized. She hopes that someday they will meet again and give each other one big hug. She has forgiven them and seeks reconciliation rather than alienation. It is fairly clear from her narrative and its tone, together with this wistful fantasy, that Beatrice has not dealt fully with the rape.

Her next three relationships were with an impotent man (for two years), a married man (for six years), and an alcoholic cross-dresser. She expected little from them except sex, keeping the relationships to a physical level rather than risking emotional involvement. One suspects that her choices were unconsciously connected to the aftermath of her rape. In particular she describes her last boyfriend as "the pits." Although he was heterosexual, he dressed in women's clothing in order to achieve sexual excitement. He worked as a bouncer in a strip joint, where she fraternized with the strippers "like nothing was wrong." When she gave him a nightshirt for Christmas and he gave her a gown, they ended up switching. His problems, together with her worsening health and her father's suicide, became an Ur-moment that forced Beatrice to examine her behavior in order to find a different future. Beatrice's identity task has been to heal a traumatized boundary system to a point where she is able to decide who to let in and who to keep out. The lower our self-esteem, the more likely we are to choose partners who reinforce our sense of unworthiness and negativity, much in the same way that a man with a poor self-image will avoid a beautiful woman on the assumption that she could never be interested in him. In hindsight Beatrice feels that God gave her the worst boyfriend possible so she would change her life.

Once she put her faith in her church, she was able to establish different standards and expectations for relationships. She learned to expect love and respect from others. She changed her self-concept and her expectations of a relationship, and in doing so, her destiny. Beatrice now feels that one gift she possesses is her ability to get people to open up to her. She attributes this ability to what she sees as her extreme tolerance, not caring what others do as long as they don't get in her way. Her own journey toward self-acceptance has forged her tolerance.

Another nadir experience has been her worsening health. Although she had long suffered from hypoglycemia, at thirty-five she felt something more mysterious and frightening was happening. She suffered diarrhea, "a small stroke," and mysterious paralysis of her limbs. These symptoms appeared just as she had switched careers, leaving journalism to pursue computer programming. She ignored these symptoms, in order to maintain her computer job, where she did not yet feel indispensable. Despite her stoicism, she was fired for shifting her hours from days to evenings. One day, while jogging, she heard herself say, "The big challenge would be to love the creator as much as the creation." Shortly after this, she felt a jolt in her arm. What she characterizes as "weird physical symptoms" continued for the next three years. At thirty-five and single she saw herself as going nowhere, and questioned whether she would make it. During the next three years she lived in fear that she could not count on parts of her body to work. She went to bed fearing that she would wake up paralyzed, or not wake up at all. She worried that she had become infected with the AIDS virus. Another possible cause she considered was her exposure at the newspaper to chemicals, which she later learned caused symptoms similar to multiple sclerosis. Others at the newspaper also reported an unusually high rate of cancer.

In the midst of her fear, she suffered from an inability to sit down. She switched from bathing to showers and to kneeling or standing at her computer. She wrote an extensive life history filled with significant events that she felt affected her emotionally, but her doctor dismissed it. Unable to find an answer in Western medicine, she turned to Eastern medicine and developed her own special diet, which involved eating specific food at specific times, no spices or sweets, and preparing all her own foods. She also gave up cigarettes and drinking. She did not know why it worked, but it did, so she followed it faithfully. While she improved, she no longer saw herself as the same person she once was, physically.

Probably more importantly, she decided it was time to make some lifestyle changes. She decided to stop her sexual adventuring and seek a serious relationship. Through the help of her church, she was able to resurrect her need for community, protection, and commitment—all of which she had cut off in her search for "independence." Although she says her entry into the Bible study class was the result of a chance encounter, her narrative makes it clear that this was an encounter for which she had been preparing.

A third nadir experience was her father's suicide, which occurred around this same time. She viewed his death not as a loss but a relief, a feeling of being "freed up." Since much of her self-concept for all these years was a reaction against her father, his death freed her to search for more positive models, which she found at church.

Baptism

The turning point in Beatrice's story occurred when she was thirty-nine. After her father's and sister's deaths, her mysterious illness, and her increasingly unhappy relations with men, Beatrice decided to make some critical lifestyle changes. She had left journalism for computer programming. She now followed a rigorous eating program to control her illness and had given up drinking and smoking.

En route to visit her cross-dresser boyfriend at a rehabilitation center, she sat on the plane next to a young woman who "looked like a cherub. " The conversation turned to God and the Bible, and the young woman invited Beatrice to a Bible discussion group. Back home, Beatrice rearranged her schedule to attend this Bible discussion group, composed of six women.

After a time her beliefs changed. She characterizes this change as focusing more outward than inward. Through the reflected appraisals of her new friends, she began to expect something from people, even men. Given a positive and safe source of feedback, she learned to give up some control in her life, to be less self-focused. She cites her reaction to a near collision in her automobile as "the peace that surpasses all understanding," in contrast to her friend's panic. She felt that she was finally permitting God into her life. She now interpreted past events as God's efforts to get her attention. She found she was able to give up some of her independence in order to affect the world in a more positive way.

She credits the church for changing her views on relationships. She used her computer skills to develop a list of older singles at the church, and organized a singles group. There she met her husband. She no longer viewed men as sexual objects, where she had "sex first and dates later." "Now she did the reverse. She began to expect love and caring, where before "she didn't expect anything"—actually a denial of her need for such things. By expecting respect and care, she was able to attract a partner who provided this, just as she learned to respect and care for others. The church, she feels, gave her a sense of purpose, changing her life pattern from Me-centered to God-centered. She finds her life more adventurous now that she has relinquished some control.

Without in any way denying the intervention of God, it is clear that much of the change in Beatrice's life came about through her own efforts. She decided to change, adjusted her schedule to attend the group, used her skills to set up the older singles group, adopted a new attitude toward sex and male relationships, and recognized that her need for control had locked her into a defective lifestyle rather than making her independent. Her lifelong awareness of God was a partly unconscious recognition that her life was not properly based. Since most images of God reflect the image of the earthly father, her father's death may have been an important event in precipitating this change.

Unsurprisingly, Beatrice's husband is the opposite of her. Yet, she is able to integrate his weaknesses and strengths. He is lackadaisical but strong. She can and can't depend on him. She is work; he is play. She is scheduling; he is spontaneity. He is more genuinely caring, she feels, while she is more dutifully caring. She finds marriage difficult—more intense and inclusive than her former sex partners. Her husband comes from a background of foster homes and a broken marriage. Her health is an issue because she does not like to travel on the spur of the moment, as he does. He has trouble with will or discipline. Lacking a sense of moderation, he is driven to excesses. Another problem is his waning interest in sex. Nevertheless, she accepts him and he accepts her because the balance is good. This shows a relaxing sense of rigidity, morality, and control. Her choice also reflects a higher level of self-esteem in choosing someone who can give care and commitment.

The self-disclosure required for intimacy, as Rawlins has pointed out, relies on not only expression or openness but also protection.[7] Refraining from criticism of others' differences is as important as expressing who we are. While Beatrice is well aware of her husband's differences, she accepts them, and in doing so she protects the relationship and him from a sense of rejection. She has learned how to be more resilient. She conveys an empathetic understanding of his subjective world, a good-humored tolerance. This tolerance, along with her love for teaching children and thoughts about adopting a baby, reveals that she has released a maternal side of herself which she could not tolerate before because it reminded her too much of her parents and conflicted with her former reactive identity.

She feels her early years set her values on the wrong course, and she has had to find a new one. Marriage she finds hard but she would not go back to being single by choice. She has found her niche. She describes herself as happy. Beatrice's story is one in which she is able to rework an older identity into one that provides her with a more open and positive one. She has developed a more flexible sense of self, which permits her to have the life she desires.

11

Ian's Story: "Devotion"

Ian's story, also, is a case study in boundary issues. Ian has not yet been able to sustain a long-term relationship due to the thick boundaries he has developed to protect himself against the slavish devotion he felt his mother demanded and by which he now feels threatened when he attempts to enter relationships. He protects himself from what he believes to be both his mother's and the cultural ideal of love—a single-minded devotion that allows no room for other interests—by selecting those who demand this type of devotion. This pattern exacerbates his worst fears of love leading him to end relationships, because they either match or fail to match his model. Ian is struggling with inclusion—the ability to let others in and still feel a safe sense of self without being swallowed up.

The broad theme in Ian's story is a search for love. He is still entangled with earlier conceptions of love based on his relationship with his mother. He remembers this relationship as one demanding total and unwavering devotion, to the exclusion of his own needs and desires. Love, he feels, is a form of merger, which negates his own identity in the service of others, an idea most clearly expressed by his flirtation with being a monk. Even on earth he fears that true love would require complete negation of self, and this has prevented any commitments in his own romantic life. Ian describes himself as inhibited, what he calls "tightly wrapped," a perfectionist with a high need for control and clarity. He thus has difficulty with passion or sexual expression, and ambiguity. Ian has developed a thick boundary system to protect against his fear of intimacy.

He has achieved some degree of occupational success as an independent consultant after a period of "identity confusion" or moratorium.[1] Erikson says that identity confusion is manifested when the individual faces intimacy, occupational choice, task completion, or self-definition yet is unable to engage. Engagement is the test of self-delineation.[2] Beatrice has moved from identity confusion to identity resolution. She has exposed herself and has been able to make the necessary choices and commitments. Ian is still struggling to be intimate in love. The two key themes that he carries over from childhood are love as devotion, and his search for a proper father. Ian divides his life story into the following chapters: "The Gatsby Years," "Sleepwalking," Years of Brainy Discontent," and "Finding a Father."

The Gatsby Years

Like Beatrice, Ian begins his story in the recent present, shortly after college, when he was in his mid-twenties. Just as Beatrice has moved beyond the psychic domination of her childhood, so Ian is moving in this direction. He calls this period his Gatsby Years, a golden period in New York when he "posed as a writer" and had a number of satisfying and exciting friends. (One presumes that he identifies with Nick Carraway and not with Gatsby.) It was for Ian a period of self-discovery, when he had a salaried job for the first time. He had discovered in college that he was "a lot smarter than he realized," and it was exciting to meet people his own age who appeared on the verge of doing something. It was a time of possibilities, and he loved the gritty feeling of New York and the art scene. In contrast to the small town where he grew up, it felt cosmopolitan—an exciting new vista. Many of his friends from the period he met through a church that drew bright and artistic people. He worked for a church magazine.

A part of Ian's problem with love is an uncertainty about his sexual identity. He recalls a relationship from the Gatsby period that was reasonably good sexually, but he could not conceive of it "going on and on," as he puts it. He did not know how to establish a more committed relationship and so reached a dead end. This led him to explore options such as the priesthood and monastic life. Looking back, he says that his path of intimate relationships has been "litter strewn" and has "bent him in ways" that have made it difficult for him to feel connected. A part of that difficulty is that he fears connection because he cannot trust his sense of self to hold. He fears that he might be swallowed up and disappear as a unique individual.

In particular, Ian confesses his love for a close male friend during this Gatsby period, a man who became an important mentor. He believed that this friend would shoot to the top as a film writer, but he works now in corporate communications for a chemical company. Ian admired him because he seemed to know his mind, wrote well, and was very bright. His love for his friend, Ian felt, made it difficult to distinguish between wanting to be like him and wanting to stay with him. He wanted his influence all the time. Although they considered living together, they agreed that doing so would drive them nuts. He was not aware of seeking a physical relationship with the friend and generally rejects the notion that he is homosexual, although he admits to having strong feelings for men more than once.

Ian especially liked the fact that his friend appreciated Ian's better qualities: his brightness and wit, his ability to defend his ideas, and his appreciation for arts and letters. He made Ian feel worth admiring. His friend provided him with a sense of his own uniqueness, something his parents failed to do. Ian compares his sense of deep connection with his friend with going to a foreign country and discovering someone who speaks your language.

The self-imposed limit which he set on this and his female relationship, he considers part of a larger sense of despair which caused him to bring his Gatsby period to a close. He eventually admitted to himself that he wasn't getting anywhere with his writing. What he was writing "disgusted" him and "felt like something that had been in the back of the refrigerator too long." The "thrill and vigor" of the New York art scene left him. He began to look for what to do next. Ian's strong, even harsh, superego is characteristic of thick boundaries. They protect him but keep him from closeness with others.

His quest results in the form of a religious awakening. He explains it as a negative form of mystical theology where the experience of God is not one of comfort or consolation, but of absence. The theme of occupational choice or exploration is an important part of Ian's identity. This search for a career led to an interest in the ministry, an interest that had begun in his youth and which offered him a means of connecting with people emotionally. He began his search by investigating the Episcopal priesthood, visiting two dioceses in New York. He was repelled by the hierarchy he found and sensed "that the bishops were uneasy about considering him," because he was from out of town, not one of their own. Their reaction made him aware that he was seeking to be channeled and directed, rather than opposed. He was seeking to explore possibilities, but resented the notion that the priests would make joining their number some sort of test. A priest advised him that becoming a priest was tough, socially rigorous, and not for the faint of heart. All of this seemed to Ian to make the priesthood a bureaucratic labyrinth rather than a spiritual odyssey.

He recalls how attracted he was to monastic life after reading Thomas Merton's *Seven Story Mountain*. He was attracted by the "clear romance" of it all. As he puts it, "It sounded clear and pure, and the struggles simple and well defined." More importantly, it made it sound "like your battles were picked for you." Another influence he recalls was Annie Dillard's *Pilgrim at Tinker Creek*. Ian is drawn to order. He likes things clear, not murky or gray. This seems to him a good way to be sure that he is not wasting time and effort. The need for clarity, a clear line between order and disorder, is another sign of a thick boundary system.[3]

Exploring his options, he made inquiries into several monasteries. The first one he visited he fell in love with, finding the men fascinating and intelligent. He liked the fact that "they weren't trying to live like they were in the fourteenth century." He became a postulate, and eventually a novice, though he left before he completed the six years necessary to become a monk. Ian later recognized that he had been drawn to a monastic life because he felt the most profound feeling of love for men there, and it offered him a new family. Although he was not aware of it at first, he discovered that most of the monks were gay. This caused him to question his own sexuality, but in doing so he realized that he was not searching for romance but for a father and a home. This eliminated the monastery as an option, and he left with a firmer sense of self.

Ian is the oldest of three siblings and the only son. Sulloway argues that a critical insight into identity begins with birth order, our first means of social comparison. He says firstborns identify with their parents, who tend to favor them in return.[4] As a traditional firstborn without a history of significant parent conflict or rebellion such as Beatrice had, Ian identifies strongly with power and authority. He exhibits many firstborn characteristics such as ambition, conventionality, conformity, and conscientiousness. He seeks a strong father figure to guide him and help him succeed. Unlike laterborns, firstborns tend to take fewer risks and to be more defensive. Sulloway sees them as more closed to experience, compared to laterborns. Their identification with parents leads them to internalize a strong set of rules (or superego), which is reflected in their absence of rebellion and their conventionality. Being oldest and bigger means less identification with peers. The firstborn looks up to the parents rather than down or laterally to peers. Firstborns, as a result, are more closed and harder to get close to—having what we are calling here a thick-boundary system. Laterborns have thinner boundaries, are more sociable, and are more open to experience. They are more creative, and exhibit more empathy and peer orientation. Sulloway also believes that family niches are shaped by gender. He sees status enhancing as a firstborn and male strategy, while cooperation is a laterborn and female strategy.

Sleepwalking

Ian identifies his childhood and youth as a time of sleepwalking. This suggests a narrative tone of gray, or a mixed reaction to his upbringing. His memories of this period are shadows in the dark. Before he left home, he believed he had grown up reasonably normal and well adjusted, but he now realizes that his early experiences created limitations with which he now struggles. He stills feels limited in his ability to get close to people. His parents, he thinks now, were not good at loving one another or loving him. He rarely felt recognized or appreciated as a human being, flaws and all. Rather, he felt either over- or undervalued. His parents did not encourage him to experiment with options because they themselves had a strong need for both clarity and closure. For the same reason, they did not feel comfortable with emotions, which were rarely sharply defined. He felt no sense of his own uniqueness, an important element for forming an identity. He learned to talk about feelings in the past tense, to ensure a happy ending and no uncertainty. Both of his parents had come from expressionless families. Ian believes that the inability to get emotional help from his parents fostered a powerful self-sufficiency in all three children.

Ian has identified with his parents and other models, but suffers from a lack of feeling authentic. He has difficulty with mutuality, is still searching for his niche, and has yet to commit long enough to tend to another. His father was an architect, "silent and busy." He recalls him appearing at five o'clock to read the paper while the children watched TV, but he did not interact with them. He found solace instead by working in the yard, alone. He describes his father as a dispassionate man who rarely got excited or angry. Ian thinks his attraction to men is a need to hear from another man about the right way to do adult things, something his father never provided. He seeks a father figure even in his work to take him under his wing and tell him "Here is how you do business. Here is how you get ahead. Here is how you act like a man."

Ian describes his mother as repressed and uneasy about sex. His most frequent memory of his parents' marriage is a scene in which his mother was working in the kitchen. His father appeared from working in the yard and kissed her, sending her the message that he found her sexually attractive. She then swatted him and scolded him. Ian interprets her behavior as due more to distaste than to playfulness. He thinks she disliked admitting that they had a sexual relationship. This caused Ian to wonder if they were attracted to each other prior to their marriage. Examining premarital photographs, he found pictures where they looked like they were "nuts about each other" yet he did not see much evidence of this now. This lack of affection has led his now-married sisters to conclude that they were they result of Immaculate Conception. Ian also got the message that romance and sex did not go together. Instead, he saw marriage as being like a small business, where you run a tight ship and don't let any of "that" in. His parent's generally considered emotions as untrustworthy and possibly dangerous. Nevertheless, he felt that they loved each other. When he asked his father how he would know who he should marry, his father replied, "You will just know."

Since he and his sisters left the nest, Ian thinks his parents have rediscovered each other in ways that are important. Ian notes that his mother is not as uptight. After the children were grown, his mother returned to nursing, where she found fulfillment. Ian believes his parents were afraid of being close, and were uneasy with themselves. Being the only son, he was closest to his mother. As evidence of their psychic bond, Ian attributes almost telepathic significance to her sending him a check during college because "she had the feeling" he needed it. He finds her capacity to read his mind "unnerving." He sees their mutual ability to influence each other as a significant obstacle to his intimacy development because she was, or is, overinvolved and prying, leaving him feeling unprotected from her intense scrutiny and demands. All of his love relationships have been shadowed by the sense of her watching.

As a child he remembers long conversations with his mother in which his father would not participate. At the end of each conversation his mother would resolve whatever problem was being discussed in a tidy summary that left no loose ends. Everything would now work out and be fine. No ambiguity. Ian has identified with his mother's need for clear resolution. Even now he finds it difficult to tolerate ambiguity or uncertainty, which has become a kind of perfectionism. In business situations he is the one who stands up and resolves the problem with a final summary, like his mother. He calls this his functional neurosis because it is a useful trait in many situations. He has tried to learn to suspend this need in relationships, but knows that he does not fully succeed.

Another quality he associates with his mother is what he calls her capricious, combustible rage, where at any moment she could go up like a trident missile. A ruthless perfectionist, she seems to have passed this trait down to her children. Her children were often uncertain about what triggered her frequent bouts of anger, but Ian assumed that he was the cause. Her anger, he comments, was like a black cloud. He would often get a spanking for no particular reason.

He developed three strategies for coping: he tried to make himself scarce, as his father did; tried to calm her down, using conciliation; or used his magical power to exert mind over matter. If he were good or perfect enough, he thought, he could ward off his mother's eruptions. Later his mother admitted to him that she was mostly angry with herself because she had failed to live up to her own expectations. She finally acknowledged that she hated cooking, which everyone else had known for years. Ian believes she learned to express anger from her own mother, his grandmother, whom he calls a "bitch on wheels." His mother sought perfection for the same reason he did, to avoid her own mother's rage.

Ian's feeling that he was supposed to have some power over his mother's anger required that he be perfectly good, and this need continues in his desire for control. He had temper tantrums, he remembers, into his teenage years, feeling frustrated when he could not finish something or manipulate something successfully. He also learned to disappear like his father, which is a strategy he uses to end relationships.

Ian feels his parents were sleepwalking because they never said anything to him about what he might do with his life and where he might go to college. He remembers a hunting trip where he tried to incite his father into an argument by informing him of his decision to be a conservationist. His intent was to avoid future hunting trips, but his father interpreted his comment as a career decision and told him to do whatever he wanted. Later, he baited his parents at dinner when he told them, tongue in cheek, that he admired them because they never once offered him advice. What he meant to say was "what were you thinking of?" The one time his father did offer his opinion was when Ian informed him that he might be going to a university in the Midwest. His father's response was that it was awfully far away, and he wouldn't get to see him often. Ian remembers this as one of the few times when his father seemed, however obliquely, to express affection, and he changed his plans on the strength of this comment and went to a local college.

An important discovery for Ian occurred as a teenager when he learned that his mother had given birth to a stillborn son prior to his own birth. He was "the replacement" son. This had been a deep family secret, never mentioned by his mother. One of his mother's greatest regrets, however, was that she took her doctor's advice and had the baby buried without seeing it. To this day, she does not know where the child is buried. The doctor also advised her to have a replacement child as soon as possible. In addition to being the replacement son, Ian feels he is a very important child indeed because he was the first child, the first boy, and the first grandchild. He likens this to being the chosen one of God, terribly important, and spoiled.

To the parish priest, a friend of his parents, he credits his interest in the priesthood. Here Ian found a warm and openhearted man who spent time teaching him as an acolyte. Assisting at the service satisfied his need for control and perfection because he knew he would always succeed. He knew the right thing to do at the right time, and the right way to do it. This spoke to his need for clarity and gave him the positive reinforcement of a father figure.

Another peak memory from childhood was his grandparents' annual barbecue. He remembers being wrapped up and cuddled in a blanket, as everyone in a crowd of forty-plus people gathered to listen to an accordion player at twilight.

He felt part of something larger than himself but now feels a little troubled that he has no memory of either parent being a part of that warm scene. This is further evidence of his sense of emotional distance from them.

Two other important characters from this period were his sisters, who he sees as adversarial and competitive. He was especially in conflict with his sister next in age, two years younger than he, who he felt was going to screw up any possibility of his being perfect. As an adult, he has become friends with his youngest sister, but finds Rita still " too tightly wrapped." He characterizes her as a worrier with a paralyzing need for control. Since he is the same, they continue to clash. He thinks that they both want things their own way because of the need to justify their actions to their mother as children.

Years of Brainy Discontent

The next chapter in Ian's story begins with his college years, where he began to explore, intellectually and spiritually, but also romantically. He continues to work backward in time, uncovering his past as a series of layers, and sometimes is surprised to find new insights as he does so.

Ian spent his college years in a fundamentalist Christian College, where he says he spent most of his time drinking coffee and complaining that he was in the wrong place. In particular he resented being treated like a child and, as we saw with Beatrice, he had an adolescent impatience with hypocrisy. His choice of a religious school he traces to a religious experience that he had at age sixteen. At a Pentecostal service he was baptized in the Holy Spirit and spoke "in tongues." This resulted in his coming away feeling changed, a feeling that continued through the next few years. He saw his former faith, the Episcopal Church, as empty by comparison. By college he had realized that Baptist practice could be just as ritualized and codified as the Episcopal had been. This, and the dreary homogeneity of the student body, pushed him away from Christianity, leading him to become a kind of conscientious objector. Not feeling that he belonged anywhere, he questioned his mystical conversion as a teenager.

This period also began a search for romantic love. His longest-term relationship until the age of thirty-seven lasted about one year. Although he had fallen in love in high school, the affair was not consummated, and in the end he felt rejected. When he fell in love in college he was introduced to a new theme— feeling afraid of his sexual desire. He broke up with this college girlfriend because they were too excited by each other. In a fundamentalist college, where sexual activity was number one on the list of no-nos, this was a serious challenge to his values and self-control. Ian sought reason and order, but passion is always more or less out of control. There was no way to channel his sexual feelings at a Christian college. Sexual desire did not fit with the other things he felt. He had learned from his parents that sex and love did not go together, and he worried about losing himself because he saw love and passion as giving the other person the right to impose a power to which he must submit. He feared loss of his own boundaries, and was tormented by his rigorous superego.

He also feared his girlfriend's discovery that he was less than perfect, which provides us with an opportunity to further explore the thickly bound self. Had he and his girlfriend had sex, it would presumably have been by mutual consent. Yet Ian insisted upon taking the whole issue on himself, and his solution was to break off the relationship. It did not occur to him to share the blame (if that is the proper word), because there was no model in his life for that kind of ambiguity. In his world, each person was expected to be perfect on his or her own.

Ian worries that he has never felt toward women the way he has with men. Men offer excitement and tension in their disagreeing, forcing each other to think harder. He likes talking and being intellectually stimulated. He likes feeling there is a solid object to push against. Ian feels more comfortable with men, where he does not feel in danger of being swallowed up. The boundaries of his male friendships are easier to navigate than the murkier ones of his female ones, which threaten his sense of self.

Yet we cannot ignore the terminology of his narrative. He speaks of "solid objects" and being "swallowed up," and says he has been physically attracted to men "more than once." He says that he and his New York friend could not live together because they would "go nuts." He earlier decided that this was not a physical desire but a search for a father figure. As a firstborn he is conventional and may be more likely to see the only acceptable goal to be marriage and family.

He used to like what he calls "high maintenance" women, women with problems who needed help and comfort. At the same time, this need led to problems for him because he came to feel that this was his primary job in the relationship. He also feels attracted to women who are his opposite or complement, who he describes as usually younger, taller, thin, extroverted, and unreflective. However these complements, he allows, have not worked.

His most significant relationship, Abby, was one of these complementary attractions. Abby impressed him but scared him. She came from a world he characterizes as upper class, Harvard, wheeler-dealers. He considered her a prize and felt it was an honor to have gotten her attention. He met and began dating Abby during the summer. Since she was going away to graduate school in the fall, both felt safe dating, and they quickly became close and sexual. Ian felt they challenged each other emotionally and let their guards down because they knew they had a short window of time. Abby rejected his offer to continue the relationship at the end of the summer because "she couldn't see herself marrying him." Ian thinks that she also wanted to keep her options open for graduate school. Although hurt and angry, Ian began a correspondence with Abby by e-mail.

Things heated up again quickly, and they agreed that he would visit her one weekend to sort out the future of the relationship. The weekend turned awkward when both felt odd and ill at ease. At the end of the movie *French Kiss,* Abby informed him that she did not feel toward him the same way that the characters felt about each other in the movie. He replied, "Neither do I." Ian left early, boarding a plane four hours later. Both decided they would not be able to reach the standard of love set out in this movie. Both felt that the cultural reinforcement of love as passion, resulting in incredibly high standards, permitted no negotiation.

Both failed to note the obvious fact that this was a work of fiction, not a recipe for real-life love. Ian felt that love demanded a standard of complete and constant enjoyment and interest in each other, or complete devotion, which he found impossible to sustain. He confused love with devotion. Being devoted would be a full-time job. In looking back, he concluded that devotion is what had made them fit in the first place. He had been doting and devoted that summer, but only because the relationship seemed to have a clear terminus. He could not continue to live up to this standard. What he failed to recognize was that this was the wrong standard.

This left him disappointed. He felt Abby was infatuated by what she remembered rather than by the real Ian. The difference between what he had expected to happen and what indeed happened was significant. As he puts it, the "me" that she remembered was, in reality, "no good." He had failed. He now feels that they were both too guarded this time, because their expectations were higher. He suspects that he did not seem as warm and compliant as she had remembered. This change was obviously brought about by the prospect of a more lasting relationship, as contrasted with the torrid summer affair.

Another problem in the relationship was that Ian saw Abby's family as the polar opposite of his own. They were affectionate and demonstrative, so much so that it "gave him the creeps." He felt ill at ease with her family, feeling he was being "tested for the real thing." He responded by holding them at arm's length. Since Abby was so close to her family, he knew that it was extremely important that he be liked, but he did not feel he fit in well. He found her family too much involved with each other's personal lives. He was unable to match their outgoingness or demonstrativeness.

Ian makes a strong distinction between his own family and himself. Whereas he saw Abby's family as overinvolved or enmeshed, he feels disengaged from his own family. He remarks that he often feels he is so different from his own family that he might have been found under a tree or mistakenly placed in the hospital. This is a notion that we have encountered before, and we have already noted that it is an almost stereotypical idea for those disaffected by their family. As an example, remember Adam's sense that an alien ship had dropped him and his brothers.

Ian recalls a telephone conversation with Abby in which he tried to be honest about his feelings and doubts about the relationship prior to his visit. She responded by suggesting that maybe he should not come if he felt like that. Although he felt his doubts were no different from hers, he felt she expected him to anchor the relationship. He saw this as a significant warning that something was wrong or missing. In part this showed only a difference in their family backgrounds, but it again raised Ian's fear of commitment.

When he sent a note explaining how bad the conversation had made him feel and how much he had thought about their relationship, she responded by saying that she had hardly thought of it at all. Ian was hurt that his self-disclosure had not been reciprocated. Since revealing who we are makes us susceptible to hurt, we must decide if the risk is tolerable. Ian decided courageously to act with openness rather than restraint and discretion, but since trust is built on the interplay between protection and expression, Ian ended up feeling hurt. This might have been the kind of issue that needed to be discussed face to face. Still, Abby might not have developed an appropriate strategy for intimacy and managing relationships either. Since we have no objective report we cannot decide.

This relationship is ongoing. Abby has returned to Boston, and they remain friends. They are planning to work together to develop a training program.

Finding a Father

A theme that reverberates in Ian's story is his attempt to find a father who would offer advice and direction. Particularly we see this theme in the world of work. In his thirties Ian joined a business firm, a small company where he became a close friend of one of the male principals, a man ten years his senior. Ian felt their friendship offered him an opportunity to grow with the company and to become someone of great importance. Six years later he was disappointed at his lack of advancement. He began to feel he had reached a dead end. After a period of disgruntlement, he decided to leave and become a consultant, a position he still holds. He feels this chapter of his life has been a lesson in the benefits and detriments of independence. In particular, he has discovered that communication is his strength. In fact, this new position makes use of several of Ian's strengths. He is organized and able to plan ahead; he has some writing skills, even if he is not F. Scott Fitzgerald; and he has other verbal skills appropriate to salesmanship. In his own terms, this new job makes use of his "functional neurosis."

Ian feels that his former employers betrayed him, in that they were not willing to provide the time and effort to train him but instead hired someone from the outside, for more money. While at first he found their support exhilarating, he soon began to feel discouraged and unappreciated. He became angry and his feelings created misbehavior in meetings. He now thinks that the job was a continuation of his theme of finding a father. He loved his boss and thought he had found someone who would show him how it felt to grow up. His boss had what Ian wanted, and Ian was furious when his boss let him down. Ian has salvaged the relationship with his former boss, however, and it has come full circle. The former boss now admits that letting Ian go was probably a mistake. They continue to work together, with Ian hired as a consultant (at a higher rate of pay), so it was a good move. He has turned a negative into a positive. Where he had sought a father figure to compensate for his own dispassionate, uninvolved father, he now seems to be more realistic.

Ian's current romantic relationship, with Martha, has lasted for six months. He sees her as different from the other women he has dated. She is not high maintenance. She does not expect him to place her on a pedestal. She accepts him as ordinary and flawed, which is a great relief for him. Martha is a photographer. She is visual and he is verbal, and this provides him with an opportunity for the kind of give and take that he enjoyed in the Gatsby Years. She has some of the qualities of his New York friend in her desire to make a living without sacrificing her integrity. Ian feels that he is doing the same thing in his consulting business, so they offer each other support.

Yet Ian is having a hard time saying he is in love, since he is not using his standard of complete devotion. He was drawn to Abby because she demanded his attention. Martha is not pushy about demanding affection or attention. She is more realistic and distracted; she has her own life. Attending to Abby was taxing but thrilling. He does not have the same thrill with Martha, yet he is less afraid of making a life with her. He is comfortable with Martha and not concerned about whether she impresses his friends in the way Abby did (Abby was apparently a striking woman). His friends' opinion of her is no longer a reflection on him. This shows growth, in that Ian can choose a partner who permits him to maintain his sense of self. In some respects Martha seems to have the qualities he seeks in a father. She is that "solid object" he can push against.

Ian is still worried about getting too close, because his idea of love is so strict that it will be difficult to live up to. He has learned from his mother that there should be no shadow of turning from devotion. If he lets down his guard and is less than perfect, his mother (or partner) might become unhappy, or perhaps even angry. Ian recalls another woman, a painter, whom he dated and was infatuated with for a while. Yet the problem was that she made the ordinary so extraordinary. She made each occasion special, whether cooking dinner, or going out. He could not see any way to have an ordinary life with her. Her artistic talent had attracted him in the first place, but she soon gave up painting to focus on him. She stopped all of her outside interests, and he began to feel he was her only interest. This imposed too heavy an obligation—he began to feel he needed permission not to think about her. Disliking this, he began to distance himsef from the relationship, and soon broke it off.

The Future

Ian would like to form a relationship with someone and make a home, but he still needs the certainty of knowing that he has found the right person and situation. Like his parents, he demands a level of certainty that is unrealistic—no relationship is ever guaranteed. He would also like to spend more time writing and traveling and is concerned that marriage, and especially children, would demand too much of him. It is clear that Ian is not going to be able to have everything he wants, as no one can, and the question is whether he can relax his standards and goals enough to form a longer-term relationship.

He has found that his neurotic need for clarity and perfection is an asset in his work activities, but personal relationships never have the same clarity of structure and goals of a business. Ian is still in moratorium, in many respects, as he actively searches for an achieved identity. He tends to have intense and brief relationships, and has tried relationships with a wide range of different types of women—those like him, those different from him, artistic women, businesswomen, and so forth—but he is still struggling to find a stable commitment. Ian thinks he has made significant strides in this regard, and he is now engaged in a new kind of relationship with Martha. He describes it as permitting him new categories of commitment, which protect him from earlier fears of merger. He does seem to have made some progress. Yet his history is not such as to permit us great optimism—each of his previous enterprises—relationships, the priesthood, the monastery, business—begun with a great burst of enthusiasm and conviction that "this was it," but none worked out that way. We must therefore be only guardedly hopeful.

Completing the Self: Identity Resolution and Consolidation of the Authentic Self

"When we wound our bodies the nearby muscles cramp around it to keep it from any more violation and from infection. We have to learn to use these muscles to get them to relax. Something similar happens with our psychic muscles. They cramp around our wounds—pain from our childhood, the losses and disappointments of adulthood—to keep us from getting hurt in the same place again and to keep foreign substances out. So these wounds never have a chance to heal."

—Annie LeMont, *Bird By Bird*

Just as a secure base underlies our affectional skills and the Oedipal process underlies conflict skills, boundary issues determine our inclusion/exclusion system. When offered feedback, our sense of self is protected by what psychologists call our ego boundaries. Our ego boundaries determine the degree to which we let others close, determining whether we become overinvolved or underinvolved. Human relationships turn upon closeness or distance from others. It is the flexibility—the ability to be situationally appropriate—with which we employ these boundaries that indicates a resolved or matured sense of identity. Those with healthy boundaries have a realistic ability to separate feelings from actions and thoughts, and to judge what is inside and what is outside. Those with poorly formed ego boundaries have difficulty making these distinctions. Having what psychologist Ernest Hartmann calls thin boundaries results in an urge to merge, while having thick boundaries defends an incomplete self through separation. Interestingly, Hartmann believes that narcissists tend to have thick or solid ego boundaries while masochists have thin ones.[1] Although nearly all of us fall somewhere between these extremes, the two extremes help us understand the explanatory power of the boundary concept. Boundaries determine our receptiveness to internal and external stress and feedback by the way they organize and filter our experience. Ideally, boundaries protect the self but also allow it to grow. For this reason, I believe boundaries represent a neglected dimension of personality that helps explain aspects of communication that no other measure does.

Building on the insights of Freud, Federn, Hartmann, and Erikson, I extend the notion of boundaries to the communication process. The larger issue is the development of our sense of identity, or our degree of separateness and relatedness. The boundary system determines the breadth and depth of our self-disclosure and is an important factor in our ability or inability to be intimate, since it determines how much information we give about the self and how much feedback we take in.

As I have argued earlier, self-disclosure, or revealing who we are to others, is critical to intimacy. Since the word *intimacy* is derived from a Latin word meaning to make known, this could be considered a definition. Self-disclosure is a necessary condition for intimacy but not a sufficient one. It must also be modulated by the ego boundaries, in such a way that we strike a happy balance between self and others.

Boundaries shape our identity—what is us and what is not us—revealing or concealing who we are. They control the persona or face, our presentation of private self as public image. A healthy persona allows us to accept ourselves and let others in because the boundary system is sufficiently selective and flexible to control this interchange. We can consider negative information and possible change without being overwhelmed. Fragile, porous boundaries threaten our self-definition by bombarding us with experience. Thicker, solid ones protect our sense of identity against fear of merger, attack, abandonment, and exposure, but also cut us off from new experiences that might be valuable. Either boundary extreme creates problems for intimacy.

Erikson believes that boundaries develop to confine and protect our sense of identity from internal and external stress. He views adolescence as just such a time of crisis, as we separate from parents and so find it necessary to synthesize a new boundary system outside our family in order to develop our first sense of adult self. A sense of committed identity is not possible prior to adolescence, he believes, because it is not until this stage that all of the necessary constituents are available to be integrated—our full physical, sexual, and cognitive components.

For Erikson, the synthesis of a fully integrated adult self requires the completion of a number of emotional tasks. First, it requires achieving and maintaining mature ego defenses against the control of our immature defenses and their intensity, a process that ideally resolves many of the key emotional tasks first begun in the Oedipal stage. Adolescence also means choosing an occupational identity, a task that necessitates such "virtues" as a sense of competence, responsibility, and commitment. Adolescence transfers our experience of being cared for as children into adult affiliations where we both care and are cared for. For Erikson, a good test for a completed sense of identity is both the ability to engage in emotional intimacy and the ability to commit to occupational choices. Failure in either area indicates identity failure, or what he calls identity confusion, a problem that trails many of our case studies into adulthood.

The end of adolescence ideally results in an ability to resynthesize our childhood experiences in a first attempt at mature identity. During this phase we develop our first version of our life stories. We do this by selective repudiation and assimilation of all our childhood identifications, in much the same way that we might try on clothes in a store until we find a wardrobe that fits our idea of who we are. This complicated process often requires a period of time, or passage, through which we enter as adolescence and from which we exit as adults. This period Erikson calls a moratorium.

Moratorium: Seeking an Adult Identity

Erikson believes that every society sanctions a period of psychosocial delay between childhood and adulthood, which, as I have noted, he called moratorium.[2] This time allows the adolescent to experiment with different identities. In simpler societies, it is often formalized into a period of withdrawal, instruction, and testing, ending with an initiation which declares the person officially an adult. In our more complicated society, moratorium takes various forms—college, apprenticeships, travel, or delinquency—and some individuals create their own periods of moratorium based on patienthood (chronic fatigue syndrome, psychoses), delayed choice, or in completion of career (graduate school).

Adam, in his forties, is still in graduate in school. A part-time writer and editor, he puts off full commitment. Jonathan continues his minimum-wage security jobs, for which he is overqualified, and fails to complete any attempts at graduate school, which would provide him with a more committed career. Laura, in her late thirties, is also in graduate school, and Beatrice, though more committed to a career than the others, went through a series of sexual adventures before settling into her marriage.

During this time of moratorium we engage in transitory and often multiple commitments as we try on different identities, and we may have other moratorium periods throughout our lives. A divorce, for example, often requires both partners to reconsider occupational and personal goals and plans. The midlife crisis is also such a time.

Erikson believes these periods of exploration go hand in hand with periods of identity confusion, and are crucial to an authentic adult identity. Arriving at an identity too soon, without a period of exploration, produces a failed or false identity. Since identity is not fixed, these periods of exploration are crucial in updating and creating new identities as we progress through life.

Conversely, he believes that prolonged or extended periods of psychosocial delay signal identity confusion, and this confusion is manifest less through biological or sociological indicators than through emotional ones. Superficial qualities such as looks, charisma, wealth, or intelligence, do not accurately gauge emotional health. Better indicators are the length and endurance of current and past intimate relationships.

Similarly, an individual may not have integrated the emotional and social skills that allow career selection or success. Our stability of employment and the amount of negative conflict experienced in the workplace are also indicators of emotional health. These periods of delay, which are formalized by culture (during adolescence) or determined by individuals (to meet their unique time schedule), mean that individuals experiencing them are, at least for the moment, not ready to meet adult obligations and commitments.

Ian's twenties were a period of work delay during which he experimented with different professions, including writing, the priesthood, the monastery, and business, until he finally settled on the last. Although his range of experimentation was rather wider and longer than most, the process itself was normal. Beatrice experimented both in love and in work before settling into an achieved identity in her forties, later than usual.

In extreme periods of delay Erikson postulates that a disturbance of time appears. There is a great urgency to settle the issues, and yet also a loss of a sense of time as a dimension. There is a fear of missed opportunities and hope that time will bring change, and yet fear of change leads to paralysis. Erikson cites other indicators: an inability to concentrate on any one occupation; a self-destructive preoccupation with a one-sided or nonproductive activity (such as Jonathan's obsession with the writing which he fails to market); or an excessive fear and abhorrence of competitiveness.[3]

The roots of work moratoria may be traced to elementary school, where Erikson believes the prerequisites for participation in a particular culture and its technology are established. Here we are given the life task of developing a sense of workmanship, to concentrate, to focus attention, to identify with a group, to develop friends and enemies. He calls this stage the age of industry,[4] a time between five and ten years of age typified by the thickening of boundaries. The school-age child identifies with parents as workers as well as family, which causes the child to considers his or her own place in the world of work. Work goals enhance the ego through constructive activity and pride in accomplishment. Adults who fail to develop their capacity for work, Erikson believes, allow their infantile fantasies to continue, turning their focus toward early significant others in order to attempt to rebuild shaky identification. Such a person attempts to be reborn, to learn again those emotional skills and beliefs that have prevented growth. Certainly we see this as true with Jonathan, Adam, and Laura. Beatrice literally had to be reborn in the church in order to achieve identity, because her early life had not offered the security and protection she needed.

Erikson sees our adult identity as the result of weaving our childhood identifications and interactions into a coherent whole. This frees us to affiliate with others beyond the family. Those who have failed to develop a sense of committed ego identity, complain of not feeling alive or vital. When the identification process failed, identity confusion results.[5] Those who lack a firm sense of identity avoid intimacy within others, because engagement threatened their fragile and precarious identity, as we have seen with Ian and Beatrice. To quote Erikson, "True engagement is a test of firm self-delineation."[6] Intimacy becomes virtually the definition of adulthood.

Boundaries and Relationships: Overcoming the Narcissism of Childhood

In the frontier society of 150 years ago, men and women were often sufficiently happy to have a partner that they were willing to overlook details of appearance, intelligence, and background, or personal faults. The desire to be married, to produce children, and to be socially "normal" was sufficient reason to tolerate a partner's less desirable qualities. As society has become more mobile, more complex, and more self-concerned, however, we are less and less willing to accept "less than the best," or even less than perfect. We have inherited a romantic ideal that is difficult to meet in the context of a society without clear norms. To some extent our high divorce rate may reflect this higher level of expectation and wider range of choices.

An intimate relationship can be a healing or maturing experience for both partners, permitting differentiation and growth, but Karen Horney warns that closeness also has the potential to constrict and inhibit growth.[7] If we choose partners who mirror our childhood psychic world, the need to comply with each other's projections, and our continuing attempts to gain approval, can set back our development.

Those who lack a solid sense of self raise the level of anxiety in their relationships. Whether they have thick or thin boundaries as a defense, their experience anxiety over closeness. An intimate partner expects boundaries to be lowered, and this is one of the reasons we enter a relationship in the first place. Those with only thin boundaries lack the ability to make appropriate and judicious decisions to protect themselves from hurt. These are the people who rush into closeness and then flee. Those who have thick boundaries protect themselves with a strong emotional hide that makes others feel excluded. However, it is not the absence of boundaries that characterizes healthy relationships but the flexibility with which they are employed. Flexibility requires confidence in one's sense of self, much as athletic achievement requires confidence that one's body will perform as expected.

Disturbed relationships often mirror early parent-child relations. We may respond to our partner as an extension of earlier relations with our mother or father rather than as a unique and real self. Karen Horney thought that the degree of resolution in these primal relationships determine our ability to love, and account for many of the problems in marriages. Whatever we do not get from our parents, we may try to find in our adult partners. Horney called these type of marriages "narcissistic" and considers them to be destructive.[8] The reasons people cite for the failure of such marriages are often the failure of the partner to fulfill their hopes. A man may expect his wife to provide the warm and cozy home that his mother did not; a woman may expect her husband to provide the protection and security that her father did not. These are issues that ought to be negotiated, with each partner discovering what the other wants, needs, and expects. Unresolved childhood longings, Horney believes, lead to rage at the depriving partner—the same rage once directed at the parent. We may hold against our partner his or her inability to give us that which we were deprived of by our parents, while taking for granted or devaluing real gifts. This is because we are not seeing the partner as a person, but only as a representative of the failed parent. Having any relationship at all may increase our security, because it is a socially approved condition, but that does not necessarily lead to personal growth.

What of those whose failure was not in maintaining intimate relationships but rather in failing to form them in the first place. Erikson identifies what he sees as critical signs of a lack of readiness to form intimate relationships, which he connects to those who have not achieved completed identities. One such sign

of inner reservations is when someone seeks intimacy with an improbable partner. Beatrice's seeking out of unlikely partners confirmed her reservations
about intimacy. She had affairs with a married man and an alcoholic transves-
tite, both obviously poor candidates for a lasting relationship. It was only when
she decided to turn her life around and develop a positive identity that she was
able to commit to a more realistic relationship. None of Adam's marriages has
proved satisfying, in part because he has chosen women with physical and psychological problems. These allow him to continue the caretaker role of his
childhood, the only caring role he can imagine. Until he is able to free himself
of childhood projections, he will be unable to form an adult relationship.

Another manifestation of identity confusion Erikson sees as the inability to
enter more committed relationships. Instead, individuals stop with formalized
relationships where the boundaries are clearer, such as dating and friendships.
If threatened by closeness, they react in bewilderment and rage, pulling away
from the threat of intimacy to start all over again.

For Erikson, the capacity for intimacy is the defining quality of healthy
adults. Identity, he believes, is the healthy outcome of adolescence. Using our
powers of reasoning and trying on a series of identities by observing those
around us, we should be able to reach some notion of who we are and what we
want. We may also make realistic judgments about what is possible. Unresolved
identities can reach into old age, and may lead to such despair that we question
the worthwhileness of life.

Both Ian and Beatrice are struggling to develop and integrate an active
identity. Although Ian thought he had a normal adolescence he realizes in retrospect that his parents provided no guidance and refused to allow him the
normal period of adolescent groping. Beatrice has spent most of her life in adolescent rebellion and is only now finding a positive position. We reformulate
out identities throughout our lives. Therefore, the search for identity is not a
closed system but a psychosocial process, which preserves some essential features while adapting to change.

Since revealing who we are makes us susceptible to hurt, we must decide in
each case whether the risk is tolerable. Those who have not yet formed a strong
ego boundary that permits them to be resilient often unconsciously defend
against risk by developing a boundary system that keeps them alone. When
trust is uncertain, it seems safer to act with restraint and discretion than with
openness and revelation. As the saying goes, fools rush in where angels fear to
tread. If we fear a negative response we will be cautious about disclosing. Since
intimacy is an interaction rather than an individual quality, assessing the effect
of these interactions becomes a critical skill. When we are too quick to criticize

or judge others, they may withdraw from the relationship. Similarly, if we are too thin-skinned, we may withdraw too quickly, without developing the ability to negotiate.

All relationships are a process of negotiation, as we test, adjust, and test again, until we build trust in the self-disclosure process. If trust does not grow, the relationship stalls or deteriorates. One woman found her relationship increasingly superficial when fewer and fewer friends disclosed the details of their lives. She had made unrestrained remarks that hurt her friends, so they stopped revealing vulnerable information. While she may have considered herself "candid," her friends found her reactions abrasive and insensitive. When one friend tried to provide the feedback she needed, she terminated the relationship.

Those who see themselves as weak in one area are frequently hypercritical of that same weakness in others. People often act exactly the opposite of the way they feel, especially when they are unhealthy. The woman cited above, because of her own vulnerability, demanded that others be invulnerable to her caustic remarks—a sort of "first-strike" defense. When she received candidness in return, she eliminated the feedback system that might have helped her to correct the problem.

The ability to self-censor and to evaluate the impact of information on others is crucial to intimacy. When we experience problems in these areas, we must consider the role of our ego boundaries and determine whether they are providing us with accurate feedback. In the earlier example, the woman had developed a boundary system that walled-off the feedback she needed to maintain her friendships. Unguarded self-disclosure is not intimate communication but self-indulgence. When we say whatever pops into our mind, we put trust at risk, and may cause significant others to withdraw in order to protect themselves. Selective protectiveness and selective expressiveness must be balanced for trust to occur. This requires developing a healthy boundary system, and we turn next to an explanation of how the ego boundary develops.

The Development of Ego Psychology

It was Freud who first proposed the concept of the body ego, a boundary around the ego to defend it from identification with the outside world.[9] The way we hold the world together is determined by this boundary, which filters and controls our apprehension of events. An analogy is the semi-permeable membrane that controls the flux of chemical substances in and out of the cell. The purpose of this boundary, Freud believed, was to delay gratification (which he called the reality principle), as opposed to insisting on immediate satisfaction (what he called the pleasure principle), so that we might achieve gradually or indirectly what would be unacceptable if we attempted to gain it directly. Where the pleasure principle demands a temper tantrum, the ego recommends talking it through. We may feel like slamming down the phone receiver, but we hopefully decide to maintain the connection.

Freud's followers extended the concept of ego to refer to boundaries or divisions between the ego and the external world.[10] The basic difference between a healthy individual and a psychotic one is the ability to distinguish what is inside from what is outside, to distinguish between fantasy and reality. Both Freudians and neo-Freudians call these filters the ego, as discussed earlier, the central feature of personality. The ego organizes, and guards against, a too-direct expression of physical drives for food, warmth, and sex, and keeps too-painful memories in the unconscious. We differentiate our self from instincts or drives by gaining more control over the sense organs as we develop. A strong ego actively defends against our internal impulses or external stimuli and integrates our internal impulses and the external world optimally to meet our needs.

The term *ego boundary* is neo-Freudian. This school emphasizes the ego's role in adapting to the world, and in acting as a defensive barrier between the conscious and the unconscious. Federn imagined two ego boundaries—an inner boundary protecting the ego from disturbing memories and drives in the unconscious,[11] and an outer boundary dividing inner from outer reality, like a peach pit, which separates the inner seed from the flesh. If the inner boundary is weak, we have trouble differentiating between fantasy and reality, resulting in delusions, hallucinations, and paranoia. If the inner boundary is strong, we are walled-off from our feelings. If outer boundaries are strong, we are unavailable to others; if weak, we may be overwhelmed by outside events. Boundaries determine whether something belongs to the self or to the nonself.

Although we typically think of outer boundaries as conforming to our bodily boundaries, they need not. Our boundaries are capable of being expanded or restricted. In some cases, our sense of self may exceed our bodies. Some motorists, for example, take personally such everyday driving experiences as having someone cut ahead of them in traffic. They have extended the sense of ego to include their cars. In a recent incident in Boston, one driver cut off another one who he believed had cut him off, and then killed the offending driver with a bow and arrow. In Los Angeles, freeway shootings are endemic. In other cases, our sense of self may differ from or be less than our bodies. Some grow up uncomfortable with their body size or weight, or even gender, not seeing it as belonging to them. Consider the "absent-minded professor" whose focus on his inner reality reduces or contracts his sense of outer reality. This has the virtue of increasing his concentration, but puts him at risk of stumbling over some obstacle.

Ego psychology, first developed in the 1930s, stresses the meaning-making and social dimensions of personality, as opposed to the Freudian notion of unconscious childhood events. The ego, the perceptual, evaluative, and integrative component of our thinking, includes memory, language, and motor skills, and its healthy integration leads us to the ability to distinguish self from non-self. A central conviction of ego psychology is that development depends upon interactions between the organism and the environment, rather than the Freudian over emphasis on an internal process alone. The very essence of ego activity is that object relations, influences from outside the self, begin at birth.[12]

The goal of a healthy ego boundary is what Carl Rogers calls the "actualizing principle." As we are actualized our ego grows and expands toward autonomy, while control by the external environment and by our internal fears is reduced.[13] As we take charge of our lives and strengthen our sense of self, we become less vulnerable to external and internal stresses because we are better able to select and integrate them. The tension between defenses and growth Rogers sees as integrated into a single system by ego whose function is maintenance, balance, and change. This process gives rise to the self or identity, the meaning-making system, which defines who and what we are. Defenses, he believes, are attempts to maintain the self in the face of external and internal threats—even though, in some instances, the self would be better off to accept these influences and change. Psychotherapy, according to Rogers, is an attempt to assist the self-system in this natural function so that healthy growth can occur.[14]

The Primitive Ego

The ego's boundaries or filters are virtually nonexistent at birth, but emerge through gradual differentiation between self and world. Objects (including other people) are experienced by infants as an extension or part of the self. Freud thought the primitive ego developed from the id, responding to the external world as emotional symbols, and is unable to separate internal from external stimuli. Using images rather than concepts, the primitive ego relies on wishes or magical thinking, which continue later in life, as dreaming in normal people or as hallucinations in the psychotic. The primitive ego follows the pleasure principle, seeking immediate gratification as much as possible. Left to itself, the ego selects defenses that are compulsive and repetitive, and represses or distorts unpleasant information that is not pleasant.

The Abstract Ego

As we mature, our thinking processes become less influenced by these early instinctual or imagistic material, or what Freud called our primary process. Imagistic thinking clouded by emotion is reduced and rational thinking increases. For this to occur, however, feedback from the environment is necessary. Deprivation leaves us with only primordial, infantile, imagistic thinking, a blurring of the boundaries between inside and out.

The primitive ego gradually becomes more realistic as it grows into a relatively autonomous, rational system of abstract concepts and ethical restraints; what psychologists call the abstract ego and Freud called the secondary process. In order to channel our basic needs into socially acceptable behavior, the ego must have a repertoire of defensive functions and strategies, which I have detailed in chapter 8 as part of the control system. The master control is adaptability, changing strategies to fit the situation, and, as we mature, we use the higher-level defenses rather than the lower-level ones such as simple repression or denial. As the ego matures it defines and redefines boundaries between self and nonself, allowing us to make important distinctions between internal and external influences.

A key prerequisite for the abstract ego is language. As a child learns to symbolize, he or she separates thinking from actions and learns that his or her projections are part of imagination. We learn this by trial and error, based on environmental feedback. We learn that reality is flexible and not static, that our parents' values are not universal, that facts are different from inferences, and that love and hate may be evoked by the same person.[15] The abstract ego continues to mature over the lifespan and changes as a function of new experiences.

Language and symbols also permit us to develop conceptions of things that do not exist, including not only a past but a future, what we might become. We have earlier called this the ego ideal. It is not the same as the superego, or conscience, because the distinction is not a moral or ethical one. It is simply the recognition that there is a difference between the actual and the possible, a reference point for the ego's evaluation of achievement. By comparison, as we have noted, the superego develops as a result of criticism by parents and significant others, and becomes internalized as a self-observing function, or watching agency, concerned mainly with moral and ethical issues. We submit to the superego out of fear but to the ego ideal out of love—the stick and the carrot.

The superego and ego ideal are the last components of personality to develop and represent an internalization of parental and other formative images, as well as our capacity to visualize our own potential. Maturation is a process of learning to moderate anxiety, to control impulses, to separate thoughts from feelings, and to develop flexible boundaries. When overwhelmed by new or threatening experiences, we may regress to our primitive selves as a kind of last bunker against annihilation. It is the ultimate defensive strategy, but it is an abandonment of growth.

The abstract ego provides a sense of mastery, wholeness, centrality in time, and freedom of choice. Through it we come to believe in our competence and effectiveness in influencing our environment. As we gain competency we have a positive sense that we will be able to manage experiences as they occur, and are therefore free to seek out new ones and continue our growth. Conversely, when we are unable to manage new experiences without anxiety or the need to defend, we must retreat to some earlier position, ceasing to grow.

Boundaries: Permeability versus Impermeability

The extent to which the ego boundary is accessible to outside stimuli is called its permeability. Other psychologists have described permeable boundaries through such terms as solid or fluid, or resilient or unrebounding, but all of these metaphors are a way of describing the ego's degree of receptiveness to feedback. As we shall see, Hartmann uses the terms thick versus thin; Erikson, wholeness versus totalism; and Sullivan, open versus closed. Optimally, ego boundaries should be open, fluid, and variable, yet with some inner core of permanence, a stable sense of who we are, where we are going and what we stand for. Weak or fragile egos may be readily permeable. They tend to overidentify and fuse with others. Conversely, another form of ego weakness is to be closed off and impermeable, with rigid boundaries. The rigid ego is well defended, but unable to accept new experiences and thus grow. All egos expand and contract as circumstances demand, but it is the flexibility of boundaries that is important. Openness leads to closer relationships, but too much openness suggests a lack of firm identity. The result is diffuse and clinging relationships, where partners have difficulty distinguishing between self and other. At the other end of the spectrum, some distance shows appropriate respect, but too much may be interpreted as coldness and isolation. Finding the right balance between an open and closed ego is called ego integration.

Hartmann: Thin versus Thick

A psychologist seminal for his work on ego boundaries is Ernest Hartmann.[16] Hartmann distinguished between what he called the thick and thin boundaried.

He, like Federn, envisioned two boundaries, one between the id and the ego, and one between the ego and the outside world—the peach pit. His study of boundaries began with sleep research. Because sleep puts the ego off guard, he used this state to study the fluidity and extendibility of the ego boundaries. He concluded that those who have thick boundaries saw sleeping and waking states as distinct. They have fewer fantasies or daydreams and wake up instantly, with little dream recall, as compared with the thin boundaried, who see dreaming and waking as more continuous and take longer in waking. As children, the thick boundaried engage in structured games, while the thin boundaried engage in fantasy.

He also noticed differences in how the two types of people structure time. Thick-boundaried persons see a solid line between their early years and adulthood. Their memories are organized and kept in a tight compartment, brought out only when useful to a specific problem. They store memories as though in filing cabinets and their perceptual focus is like a spotlight, one thing at a time. Similarly, they impose this precision and organization on their personal space.[17] They have more difficulty with free association, since they see things as complete and separate, and organize the world as black and white to protect from pain. Those with thick boundaries get along and live at peace by avoiding closeness or conflict. They do not get involved. While they might lead normal lives, they surround themselves with walls and made others feel excluded. In conversation, he noticed, they tend to speak in clichés and give brief answers, avoiding self-disclosure. Despite these defensive tactics, Hartmann saw them as having conventional, well-organized lives, following societal expectations, and staying in long-term marriages, even if those marriages were less than ideal. He also observed that they identify more with social or class groups and tend to see these divisions as given. As a result, they make excellent team players and live by group standards, finding anyone different from them to be sick or even evil. Those with thick boundaries see themselves as solid, reliable, autonomous, and independent, while they see thin-boundaried people as flaky. Hartmann concluded that the thick boundaried store a great deal of material in the unconscious by using repression and other primitive defenses. Such defenses are highly effective in protecting them from pain and hurt, but prevent closeness and make learning difficult, since they cut off feedback.

Thin-boundaried people, by contrast, remember infancy in vivid detail and have difficulty separating memories, fantasies, and reality. They have no filing cabinets, or at best, cluttered ones. They focus on a number of things at the same time, so their focus is more diffuse. They have an easier time with free association since they see things as connected, but they have a harder time defending against anxiety. Their defenses are more porous and are more easily taken advantage of and more easily hurt. In failing to repress dangerous thoughts and feelings, they are more sensitive, open, fluid, and vulnerable. Forming relationships easily, they typically champion love at first sight and offer an immediate sense of closeness and trust, following their impulses despite social pressure. Although they fall in love intensely, their relationships are more emotional, changeable, and shorter term, often ending in traumatic breakup. Their feelings of betrayal and pain outlast their relationships and they end by nursing a grudge.

Hartmann believed that boundary development is influenced by timing and intensity. Those with thick boundaries, Hartmann hypothesized, grew up rapidly and more intensely, as compared to those with thin boundaries, who are more childlike in their vulnerability.[18] Firstborns, who have less interaction with siblings and more identification with parents, tend toward thicker boundaries, they have less spontaneity, less inclination to form new relationships, less vulnerability, and less openness to experience. While thick boundaries may be a necessary adaptation at the time, too rigid an orientation makes them less adaptable as adults. By comparison, those with thinner boundaries may have had a less intense need to grow up quickly, retaining the thinner boundaries of childhood.

According to Hartmann, the rate and extent of boundary thickening in childhood strongly influences our boundary structure as adults. Our thinking processes, whether still primitive or abstract, reflect this early period and how much we are able to separate and integrate the self and others.

Identification is another factor important in the development of our boundaries. Those who have a strong identification with the same-sex parent tend to have thicker boundaries. As part of the identification process, a strong superego is internalized, and this is reflected in a need to follow values and rules in order to fit a definite role. For example, Ian has thick boundaries, having identified with his father's emotionless demeanor, even though a key part of his adult journey has been a search for a more emotionally rewarding and satisfying father. By comparison, Adam, more alone and neglected in his childhood, has thinner boundaries, having failed to identify with what he sees as his father's obsessive, pathological, and destructive need to control. Another factor in boundary development is gender. Men culturally are expected to develop thicker boundaries and women thinner ones—the hard and the soft, the aggressive and the nurturing.

Either childhood or adult trauma may contribute to thinner boundaries. The ego is, in effect, bruised by the loss of a parent, by serious illness, by mistreatment, or other painful conditions. There may even be some innate personality factors that affect boundary development. For example, some children seem genetically disposed to experience the traumas of childhood as unnaturally hard. The intelligent, sensitive child may see even normal punishment as harsh and rejecting, thus never developing a firm ego and retaining the thin boundaries of childhood.

Erikson: Wholeness versus Totalism

Erikson's theory of ego development encompasses the lifespan, focusing on qualities, what he called virtues, that emerge at unfolding stages and form the ground plan of identity. Each stage has a period of optimal domination, leading to a "fully functioning person."[19] Virtues are qualities of human strength and are related to the process of ego strengthening as it grows from stage to stage. He envisioned two ends of the spectrum for what he saw as the constituents that made up each virtue. Ego development derived not from the external world but from the interhuman one.

His first constituent he called trust versus mistrust. The impairment of trust characterizes individuals at odds with themselves and others. Proper development leads to the virtue of hope over despair. I have earlier identified consistency in emotional communication as the crucial task of the caregiver, leading to what I have called affectional communication.

The central goal of the second stage of ego development, according to Erikson, leads to either autonomy or shame. This stage is tied to our ability to use action, language, and imagination to control our unconscious influences. This leads toward the virtues of will or self-control versus their absence. Initiative versus guilt, the third constituent, determines whether we choose the freedom to act or continue under control of the unconscious influences. It leads to the virtue of purpose. The fourth constituent, our degree of industry versus inferiority indicates our sense of confidence and ability to complete tasks versus a sense of infantile inadequacy. This leads to the virtue of competence. These key stages I have associated with the task of ethical communication and our ability to turn passive into active as we learn to handle conflict by using mature defenses.

Finally, the developmental task of adolescence is identity versus identity diffusion. This leads to the virtue of fidelity. The childhood virtues—hope, will, purpose, competence, and fidelity—provide the foundation for what Erikson calls the "inner capital accrued from the sum of childhood," or our sense of ego identity or integration. This integration determines our ability to maintain inner sameness and continuity of meaning for others. It consists of an ability to actively master the environment, to have unity of personality, to perceive self and world correctly, and to connect to others, leading to authentic communication. When identification fails, confusion results. As we have seen, a good test of the integrated adult is the capacity for intimacy and the capacity for work. Erikson believed that those who were not sure of identity shunned intimacy and career choices and that the surer one was of identity the more that person was capable of both friendship and love and commitment in work.

According to Erikson, the opposite of intimacy is readiness to repudiate, isolate, and destroy those whose closeness seems dangerous to our independent self. This lack of ability to be intimate often indicates a fear of being absorbed by another. Erickson associated the ability to be intimate with having reached a wholeness in identity, which made intimacy possible.

Erikson identified four levels of identity status: the identity achieved, the moratorium, the foreclosed, and the diffuse.[20] Each state reflects the absence or presence of exploration and commitment, but only the identity achieved has both. Those in a state of moratorium are exploring but not yet committed keeping their options open. Those, by comparison, who are foreclosed have committed early and have not been characterized by significant periods of exploration. The diffuse have not explored or made commitments in work and love.[21]

Negative Identity

Some individuals express their identity perversely or in opposition by rejecting the identifying roles presented to them by family or community. Membership in groups—male or female, national or ethnic groups, class or occupation— becomes a source of disdain because these roles, connected with parental power, seem dangerous and undesirable while their opposites appear to offer life and strength.[22]

A vindictive choice of identity represents an attempt to gain mastery in a situation in which the choice of positive identities will cancel a child's sense of self. The child prefers to assume a negative role and feel real, rather than assume a role defined by others. Erikson believes our boundaries rigidified, or what he called a totalistic orientation, at critical stages when wholeness seemed impossible. A psychotic break, a complete reversal of parental values, a refusal of expected career, all indicate a means of treading water until the necessary healing can occur. Beatrice's "Reversal" illustrates such a negative identity, one she is able to exchange for a more positive one at midlife. We see other instances of negative identity in Adam's attempt to break from his family by joining the Moonies.

Erikson thinks that a negative identity is not sufficient to mark the end of adolescence. Only a positive identity signals the readiness for adult activities. An adult readiness for intimacy requires the weakening of a harsh or overstrict superego so that the individual accepts the imperfect self and imperfect others. He or she no longer needs to repudiate, ignore, or destroy that which seemed dangerous.

Erikson calls the boundary-building task ego synthesis and, like Hartmann, see the ideal as boundaries that are open and fluid, which he calls wholeness. Rigidified boundaries are based on a need for a clear delineation. Nothing that belongs outside could be in, and nothing that belongs inside could be out. Wholeness, by comparison, means having open and fluid boundaries. For Erikson, being alive means being vital or whole and requires an achieved identity. The vital personality enabled us to weather and to emerge from every crisis with an increasing sense of inner unity, while helping us to develop good judgment and take pride in doing well.

Sulloway: Openness versus Closedness

Frank Sulloway's *Born To Rebel* offers further insight into the development of our boundary system by examining the role of birth order in identification. Sulloway says siblings compete for family resources, They develop different strategies to gain their parent's attention. Childhood, in Sulloway's view, is about our search for a family niche. Identity is based, Sulloway believes, on comparison with other siblings, and can be traced to systematic differences in niches, rather than idiosyncratic experiences. Birth order establishes these niches. He uses the term *contrast effects* to describe the tendency of younger siblings to be drawn to interests and activities that older siblings have not staked out.[23] Sulloway argues that it is the siblings' partitioning in the family that determines whether they are open to experience or closed (thin or thick boundaried). In this regard, sibling conflict and parent-offspring conflict are flip sides of the same coin, in Sulloway's view, since in both cases the conflict springs from birth order differentiation.

Sulloway cites a study by Schachter, who proposed the term *deidentification* to discuss sibling differences.[24] Deidentification is a defense against a disruptive rival where we stress our differences rather than similarities. In her study, Schactner found that siblings closer in age manifested the greatest dissimilarity. Differences among siblings further apart in age were smaller. Same-sex siblings also chose to adapt by emphasizing greater dissimilarities. Schactner explained these results by saying that siblings next to each other in age chose a different one of their parents with whom to identify and were more inclined not to identify with siblings close in age or of the same gender, seeing them as rivals for the parents' attention.[25]

According to Darwinians, the primary reason siblings seek to be differentiated, Sulloway notes, is offensive rather than defensive. Siblings are motivated to exploit unoccupied niches because they gain greater emotional investment from parents and reduce conflict between siblings. They pick different abilities in order to avoid adverse comparisons.

Conflict with parents, Sulloway suggests, causes firstborns to act like laterborns. In other words, the more conflict between parents and child, the more open to experience is the child. This is borne out by the life stories of Adam, Laura, and Beatrice, all of whom rebelled against their parents openly. Of the three, Adam and Laura are laterborns while Beatrice, like Ian, is a firstborn. Conversely, firstborns minimize parent-offspring conflict by adopting a closed or conforming style, like that of Ian.

Firstborns, like Ian, identify with the parents, and with power and authority in general. They are more achievement-oriented and ambitious, more conventional, conforming, and defensive, all attributes that are likely to be opposed to openness of experience. Thus, using Hartmann's term, firstborns form thicker boundaries due to stronger identification with parents and the resulting need to grow up fast. They internalize strong sets of rules, reflected in their absence of rebellion. In defending their special status, they become more assertive, socially dominant, ambitious, jealous, and defensive, more amenable to parental wishes and standards, and more conventional in morality. They take fewer risks and so are less open to experience.

By comparison to their older brothers and sisters, younger siblings are more inclined to question the status quo and challenge authority, since change favors the underdog. They have more permeable boundaries and tend toward higher degrees of fusion and empathy. As a result, they tend to be more socially successful. Laterborns are more sociable, altruistic, and peer-oriented, less conscientious in following parental values, less neurotic, and less conventional. Thus they are adventurous, rebellious, and more open to experience. It is their sympathy for the downtrodden or underdog that led Sulloway to conclude that laterborns are "born to rebel."[26]

Sulloway argues that openness and versatility (thin boundaries) are tactical responses to birth order, leading younger siblings to what he calls divergent thinking, which generates a number of potential solutions to a problem, as opposed to convergent thinking, which aims to find a single answer to a fixed question (more common with thick boundaries). Divergence he sees as an adaptive strategy response wherever there is competition for scarce resources. It minimizes direct competition and increases parental investment, but makes offspring more independent of the parents. This is very similar to Hartmann's idea that the perceptual focus of the thick boundaried is like a spotlight, seeing one thing at a time and with a need to store feelings and ideas into completely separate compartments, as opposed to the thin boundaried who see things as more diffuse and connected.

Sulloway also believes that family niches and roles are shaped by such factors as gender. Birth order and gender interact in two ways. While he sees competition as a firstborn and male strategy, he sees cooperation as a laterborn and female strategy. In the absence of brothers, female sibling dyads assign themselves masculine and feminine niches, according to Sulloway. As the mother shifts her attention to the younger child, the firstborn shifts in identification to the father, a process that encourages instrumental orientation. We have seen this shift occur in Beatrice's life story. Sullaway believes that the presence of brothers increases the likelihood that sisters will adopt traditional sex roles. For most personality traits, Sulloway concludes, sibling differences are more important than gender differences.

Boundaries and Identity Resolution:
Relatedness versus Separateness

A key issue for contemporary developmental psychologists is whether men and women develop differently. Some researchers think women develop intimacy before identity, while men develop identity before intimacy. As a result, male identity is threatened by intimacy while female identity is threatened by separation.[27] Traditional research on identity has focused on becoming our own self by separation and individuation. For example, Erikson's model of psychic development, in seeing identity resolution as a prerequisite for intimacy, errs on the side of differentiation and individuation. Recent research, initiated by Carol Gilligan and others, has placed more emphasis on connection with others. This shift suggests a greater recognition that we are social animals and that our "self" includes a network of other people. In this view, intimacy is not only a desirable condition, but perhaps the only condition in which we develop as fully as we might, since it is through our web of connections that we become fully ourselves.

We might argue that both Laura and Beatrice have achieved greater identity resolution through intimate partners and commitments than their male counterparts in the book. Laura is less resolved in her occupational identity and has yet to enter a profession full time, but is moving to complete a Ph.D. in counseling psychology. Beatrice, disillusioned with journalism, has made a career switch to computer programming and has married. Jonathan is the least identity resolved, what Erikson calls identity diffused, of the males in the book, having failed as yet to commit to a career appropriate for his ability, and has yet to form any meaningful relationship. Adam and Ian are opposites to each other in their identity resolution. Adam has committed to three marriages but has yet to enter the world of work full time. He has written and published a successful book but has not built on that early success. His relationships are what Erikson calls foreclosed, in shutting off the necessary periods of identity exploration he needs to flesh out a fuller sense of self. Ian, conversely, is more identity achieved in his work as a management consultant, but his longest relationship has lasted only a year. Yet he is attempting to find a new self-definition, which will allow him the intimacy he seeks.

Josselson and Identity

Certainly the case studies in the book offer evidence for this increased emphasis on relatedness as well as separateness as critical to identity development. In fact, one could say that that a focus on the importance of connection or intimacy is the theme of this book. As we have seen, there are two poles to the self: isolation and relatedness; aloneness and connection. Freud and Erikson have emphasized aloneness, the existential process of creating the self, framing development within a context of self-sufficiency and agency. Winnicott, Bowlby, and Ainsworth emphasize relatedness and making meaningful connections with others, insisting that no one creates a self without reference to others. As we recall, David Balkan earlier identified these same two fundamental needs, which he called love (communion) and power (agency). Whereas agency is the striving to be separate from others, to become a force that masters and controls our environment, communion is the striving to lose individuality by merging or relating intimately. While Erikson has provided a language by which to discuss the process of differentiation, psychologist Ruthellen Josselson suggests a language by which to discuss the process of relatedness.[28] She proposes eight relationship dimensions. Just as Erikson's virtues suggest tasks critical to separation, Josselson's suggest tasks critical to connection.

The first four dimensions develop in infancy, but the last four develop later because they require cognition. The first dimension she calls holding. Holding has a powerful consequence for the formation of identity. Without safety and trust, we not able to risk separation or individuation. The inability to find a meaningful place in an unreliable world is at the heart of identity diffusion. A second critical dimension she calls attachment. Attachment requires an external object, the first of which is the parents. Attachment to parents may be revised during our lives but it is never obliterated. Holding and attachment I have associated with affectional communication. It is our experience of holding and attachment associated with our early caretakers that establishes the narrative tone for the life stories presented, whether we are predisposed for optimism or pessimism, for hope or failure, for feeling we are lovable or not. Jonathan's insecure attachment continues to prevent growth, keeping him stuck in his "torn net."

Third is passionate experience. Unlike holding, which is solid and secure, Josselson sees passion as noisy and affective. We seek intense connection but, since we cannot have this all the time, it becomes ambivalent and must be directed and channeled. Fourth is eye-to-eye validation. Josselson calls this the need to be known for the true self, to feel affirmed and real. Feeling real builds confidence in our experience and leads to empathy and validation. Whatever is not responded to in our selves, she believes, may be lost, extinguished through lack of being rewarded. Fifth is identification and idealization, which are based on models. Identifications are the building blocks of identity. Through them we develop careers, interests, and values that form the narrative of identity. Models and heroes are internalized to give life guidance, goals, and meaning. Sixth is mutuality and resonance, which allow us to develop bonds and companionship. They provide a sense of vitality.

The integration of identity occurs as we construct the emotionally charged symbols that power our personal myths. We begin to think logically and to create stories with themes, plots, and motivation. Jonathan's attachment to uniforms, Adam's captivity in the garden maze of his father's prison, Laura's gravitational pull to her "castle on the hill," which is silent like a morgue, Ian's search for devotion, Beatrice's conversion into adulthood all were themes and plots begun during childhood. Each story is shaped by formative relations with parents, who color the adult lives of their children. In particular, the motives driving the plots of each life story are not only the need for love but also the need for agency, for power. Our choice of mature versus immature defenses indicates our capacity for ethical communication and our ability to delay gratification and resists aggression. They signal an integrated ego, which can turn passive into active, the imaginistic unconsciousness into the linguistic consciousness. Adam and Laura, caught in the prisons and the orbits of their families, are struggling to lead vital lives.

The seventh dimension is emboldening or courage . Even the ugly duckling can find a place among the swans if it has the stamina to persist. The eighth dimension is tending, the ability to look after and care for others.[29] Adolescence is marked by preoccupation with how we are seen. Feeling criticized, or rejected, not being chosen, or treated as important, create negative self-images. We are most at home when we are sure what we mean to our selves and what we mean to others. Courage and tending reflect our ability to self disclose and manifest our degree of boundary resolution that has been identified with authentic communication. The end of adolescence marks our first attempt to formulate an adult identity.

Our capacity for the kind of self-disclosure demanded by intimate relationships is ultimately rooted in identity resolution. However, identity resolution is rooted in not only differentiation, but connectedness. The type of boundary system we employ indicates the type and the degree of our individual resolution. Those with thin or thick boundaries or other extremes signify unresolved identity issues. They are like broken-winged birds that cannot fly.

PART V
*Your Life,
Your Masterpiece*

13

Conclusions

Development is not an object to be desired.

—W. R. Bion

Men die because they cannot join the end to the beginning.

—Alcmeon of Groton

Old age is like a rock on which many founder and some find shelter.

—Anon.

For the unlearned, old age is winter. For the learned, it is the season of the harvest.

—Hasidic saying

Second Acts of Love

Throughout the book, I have synthesized life history analysis with theories and individual cases of emotional communication in midlife in order to illustrate the paradigms of affectional, ethical, and authentic communication. In building theoretical paradigms in order to analyze these case studies, I hope to offer a fruitful way to approach the social pathologies of loneliness.

I hope that I have, at the very least, dispelled the notion that intimacy is a process that simply happens to everyone. As we have seen from the different case studies in the book, intimacy development is a set of complex, multifaceted processes consisting of affectional, ethical, and authentic communication, which are nurtured through a set of developmental processes. Certainly I do not mean to imply that these paradigms tell the whole story.

A sociological analysis would no doubt point to larger charges in our social structures and to fundamental changes in modern society. The social conditions that have led to partnerships (and hopefully intimacy) in the past function less frequently in our modern era, leaving more adults bereft upon the rock of solitude and loneliness as we confront our middle passage. While these changes are larger than the scope of this analysis, certainly the creation of a modern society of isolated individuals where both the need to connect and the social support for doing so are drastically reduced is undeniable. The older notions of marriage were based primarily on prevailing economic and social conditions. The first industrial revolution drew men off the farms to create an industrial workforce of male wage earners. Women were left at home as a vestige of continuity to the older, preindustrial lifestyle. A woman's role was to support her husband and raise the children while he assumed the role of wage earner for the family.

In the past twenty years, we have witnessed a second industrial revolution. Now it is women's turn to be drawn into the industrial workforce, leaving in their wake what Arlie Hotchschild, in her book *The Second Shift*, calls a "stalled revolution."[1] In this stalled revolution, industry has failed to keep pace with the social changes it has mandated, having yet to develop a nurturing system for the entire family, as it did previously for the husband. Unlike men, working women are not provided a support system of "wives," and no child care is provided for the now empty working family household. Women have therefore had to pick up the slack of this stalled revolution by doing two shifts—one at home and one at work.

Hand in hand with this shift we have seen the ideology of romantic love grow, replacing the older notion of marriage as an economic arrangement. We have witnessed the breakdown of stable communities where men and women chose lifemates based on familiarity with the partner's family's standing and good name in the community as well as economic and practical need. During this older era, it became normalized to marry young, during the late teens or early twenties, to a man or women of good community standing. Since women were not a significant part of the workforce, the woman's role, for the most part, was as a homemaker and mother. Intimacy development was not crucial to those entering marriage in this generation, since marriage was based on other personal and social considerations. For those underdeveloped in their capacity for intimacy, marriage offered a longer-term relational context through which intimacy could be developed.

Today, thanks to the media, popular literature, and changes in the economic conditions that govern our life, we have seen increasingly institutionalized the myth of romantic love, which combines passion and intimacy without commitment. The modern notion of love as obsessive longing creates much confusion. The assumption is that falling in love leads to union and to intimacy.

This perhaps accounts for the many contradictory and bizarre manifestations of love, such as killing or battering the partner we claim to love. While many of us pass through youth and adulthood seeking "the one" to whom we will feel intensely attracted, we may never find this person, or even if we do, this type of love often produces very unhealthy relationships.

Today the myth of Romantic Love holds an ever more powerful grip on individual and popular imagination. Many adults continue to wait for that one magical person to come along and transform their lives, not realizing that the power of transformation is not without but within themselves. Many who are still unhappily alone at middle passage are so because they continue to uncritically invest in what I call the myth of Romantic Love. (This is not to say that there are not pleasures in being alone. Yet typically to enjoy the many advantages to being alone we must feel our lives are on track and not feel, as one never-married fifty-year-old so poignantly stated in a recent letter to Ann Landers, that life is passing us by.) The myth of Romantic Love assumes that falling in love leads to union and intimacy. In the popular media, this is the type of love that creates butterflies in our stomachs, causes loss of appetite, leads to intrusive thoughts ("I can't get you out of my mind"), results in feelings of elation and euphoria, and leads to intense anxiety when separate. It is the essence of popular songs and movies. Triggered by physiological arousal, it is lust clothed in a more romantic form. Much in our culture heavily endorses the notion of love as inseparable from longing. We grow up inundated with fairy tales, movies, books, and songs that celebrate almost exclusively this model of love. If Romantic Love is longing, then at its weakest extreme it creates an obsessive emotional state that leads to pain and jealousy. At its more powerful extreme it results in abuse or death of those we claim to love, when we cannot possess them. At its best, it is the stuff of our cultural notions of passion where we are swept off our feet, marry, and live happily ever after. Like the lottery or the American Dream, it may happen to enough individuals to convince us that we too can be winners. Though many never find Romantic Love, they continue to seek some sort of Grand Passion. If and when they do find it, the result is often very unstable and unhealthy relationships.

Finding intimacy is a horse of another color altogether. Finding intimacy requires moving away from our mistaken ideas of love, much like Ian's devotion, toward a reevaluation, or what I call Adult Love. Based on what I earlier called Adult Communication, Adult Love begins with a necessary condition or a state of readiness, but it is not physiological arousal, as in Romantic Love, that creates this condition. Rather it is when we can give back rather than receive, when we can take responsibility for getting our needs met rather than remaining in a state of childlike passivity, and when we can let others know us appropriately rather than shutting them out. The goal at midlife must be to move beyond this romantic mythology, culturally indoctrinated, and understand intimacy as growing in love, not falling in love.

The Two Poles of Maturation: Differentiation versus Intimacy

As we have seen, the axis of maturity involves two dimensions—autonomy and intimacy. Our ability to differentiate a self is fundamental not just to human identity but also to our capacity for intimacy. As we have also seen, in assessing the viability of relationships, the question of matching—finding others at the same level of differentiation or emotional maturity—is essential. Even when we choose partners who seem for all apparent purposes unequal, we typically choose partners who match us in their degree of differentiation.

Psychologist Murray Bowen has devised an interesting measure of what he calls differentiation of self to ascertain where a person ranks on the scale of human maturation.[2] He notes that a good test of self-differentiation is how long we can remain ourselves when we visit our families, join groups, and enter relationships, without reverting to the childhood self or shutting out others emotionally. People at the low end of the scale lose self—which includes a firm identity, the courage of our convictions, and the strength of our perceptions—under the pressures of groups and relationships. Jonathan needs his mother in order to create a high-functioning self. He is still poorly differentiated, a pseudoadult. Adam's self is similarly poorly differentiated. He uses his marriages to differentiate a sense of self and escape the glass prison of his enmeshed family, where he feels diffuse and unclear. Yet so far his marriages replicate his earlier relationships rather than offer growth. He has problems with identity in groups, merging his sense of self with cults and father figures. Laura's struggle has been to escape the magnetic field of her family of origin and to differentiate a firmer sense of self, while Beatrice's has been to convert an earlier self defined in negative opposition to one more fully developed and positive.

Families of origin tend to stifle attempts to change and implicitly demand that each family member remain a vague or limited self. The temptation to avoid change is great either by running away from relationships or finding ones that allow us to match our own family's emotional level of selfhood. In relationships, those who are poorly differentiated, or pseudo-adults, merge together, often confusing and mixing their strengths and weaknesses. They undergo fusion, the submerging of autonomy, where both their own individuality and their partner's individuality are denied. When they are pressed to change—to differentiate—they experience anxiety or fear. Many attempt to avoid change, either by running away or by attempting to change others.

Yet, differentiation of self is not the only factor critical to development, for change in the self—creating a more autonomous self—takes place only in the context of real relationships. As we have seen, relatedness in the context of real relationships is as important as differentiation. Therefore, psychiatrist Peter Kramer advises his patients when they ask the critical question of whether they should leave their partners to consider whether they are at the same level of emotional maturity as their partners. If so, then they should pause before moving on.[3] For what holds them in the relationship, he believes, may be their concern that changing partners would simply mean working out the same problems with someone else. If they are tempted to run away from relationships (the cut bait and run strategy), or to try to change others (you change first strategy), they may be avoiding their own fears and anxiety about growth. They may be avoiding their own maturity.

The solution implicit in finding someone at the same level of differentiation, in this case, is not to leave or to change the other but to grow themselves. As they grow in differentiation, they retain their identity and autonomy while remaining in emotional contact with their partners. As this happens, they allow their partners to grow, or, as psychologist Carl Rogers puts it, to become self-actualized. In each of our narratives, we witness individuals struggling to bring conceptual order and meaning to their personal story and in doing so to develop a larger sense of identity—a sense of both their uniqueness and separateness, but also of their connectedness. It is the problems of connectedness—or intimacy—that I have focused on in attempting to link the sources of communication difficulties to unresolved developmental issues.

Critical to our ability to become differentiated is staying connected with those around us. Intimacy is difficult to develop outside the context of relationships. Maturation involves a dialectic tension between intimacy and autonomy; it involves growing toward as well as growing away from. It is concerned not just with the impediments to individuality but also with the impediments to connection. While the traditional culturally endorsed recipe for self-improvement—growth in autonomy—is vital, it overvalues self-enhancement at the expense of affiliation.

In particular, I have focused on problems of connectedness, and I believe that the three theoretical paradigms of affectional, ethical, and authentic communication which integrate the case studies do not simply assume but provide strong evidence that the constituents necessary for intimacy first are available during adulthood. They are the ability to move from narcissism (self) to other (adult) focusing, to move from passive (immature) to active (mature) defenses, and to move from too closed or too open to healthy boundaries. If we fail to integrate these constituents successfully, our lives will be ones where we fail to commit, to explore, or both.

The Pathology of Loneliness

As opposed to the passive view that relationships are based on attraction, I take the view that active social processes based on talking and acting are key to intimacy. Many studies on interpersonal relationships arrive at the same conclusion: the more adult the two partners are, the better the relationship. The chronological concept of adulthood is useful in limited contexts, but it tells us almost nothing about the affective lives of individuals and the ways that men and women relate in relationships. The biological clocks that indicate maturity, such as the physiological changes in the aging process, reveal little about an individual's capacity to cope with the social demands of adulthood in contemporary society.

A successful relationship—a true marriage—requires as a precondition the achievement of some hidden potential—what I have called adult communication—which emerges in the course of negotiating a relationship. Throughout each of the three sections of the book, I have identified and traced the cognitive shifts necessary for what I have called an adult perspective. It is these shifts that signal and determine our adult communication and suggests a capacity for Adult Love, a developmental process in its own right, though not tied to changes in the body.

As we have seen, some of those who are disconnected in adulthood are not in perfect control of their communication, since much occurs beyond self-awareness. (Of course, I do not mean to suggest that all disconnected adults have disabled communication skills, as there are, no doubt, a multitude of other reasons for disconnection.) The roots of loneliness may stem from sources in the personality that lie deeper than communication, although, as we have seen, there are communication markers concerning affection, control, and inclusion that predict underlying developmental processes which have yet to be resolved. Intimacy is conveyed through such features as context, mode of presentation, and manner of communication—in other words stylistically as well as through content—but the larger cognitive markers of turning inward into outward, turning passive into active, and turning closed into open are important indicators of having made the passage to adult communication and having developed the capacity for intimacy.

The adult developmental task may be accomplished through adaptive insights into the self and others and psychological turning points. These tasks involve recognition of limits, redirection of goals, and recognition of strength. As we have also seen, maturity requires both differentiation and connection. If the tasks of emotional development are successfully achieved, middle age may be the best time of life.

Integrating a Coherent Self

Each story that we have examined operates as a personal myth, supplying the symbols that carry the human spirit forward, in contrast to the momentary and transitory daily events that tie it back. From adolescence onward, we impose a mythic plan on our lives in order to make sense of it. While identity is constantly revised as we go through alternating phases of exploration and commitment, young adulthood first provides us with the emotional tools necessary to construct a coherent sense of self.

Whether we have been able to overcome the psychic and emotional realms of childhood determines at midlife what we have called, following Agnes Hankiss, the ontology of the self. Imagoes, such as Jonathan's loner, Laura's sexual magnet, Adam's caregiver, Ian's spiritual devotee, and Beatrice's rebel, reveal motivations and provide a sense of theme and ending. They provide a sense of turning points, where significant changes occur in the understanding of the self. To the extent that each has undergone transformation of the childhood self, we are able to grasp the degree of integration of each self, and identity. We are able to see how they make sense of their lives. Jonathan is still the loner, clinging to his insecure base. Laura has taken a rocketship from the magnetic field of her family, turning from being controlled to taking active control. Adam is still seeking to be the caregiver, recreating an earlier relationship where love and sex have yet to come together. Ian is beginning to rethink his idea of love as devotion and is now engaging in a different type of relationship. Beatrice has turned from rebel, reacting against, to marriage and religion, as she attempts to restore a sense of self that she had shut out.

As heroes or heroines of our own tales, we frequently like to portray ourselves as innocents struggling against impossible odds to win a battle against external forces. We may admit to some minor errors in judgment but fail to acknowledge that our external forces are often internal ones. This personal innocence requires a high price. In our unwillingness to take the necessary steps to transform our lives, we may remain vaguely unhappy, often fearful of examining our own complicity in not having the lives we seek. We fear acknowledging our own desires and hopes and resign ourselves to our lots. As we have seen, critical to this adult passage is the ability to define a solid self within a committed relationship and the need to triangulate self from toxic family of origin issues and relationships as well as to find connection and affiliation at midlife through a web of intimate relationships.

Midlife Adventures

Each individual faces a midlife summons or opportunity for affirmative action. Yet affirmation requires autonomy. It requires affiliation and commitment. It requires clear communication. It requires not making a mystery of our lives. Refusal of the summons converts adventure into a negative. When we refuse, the future is regarded not in terms of death and rebirth, but as though the present system of ideals and virtues were fixed. The literature of psychoanalysis is littered with these desperate fixations. Joseph Campbell refers to these continuing fixations as showing the impotence of the infantile ego and its refusal to move beyond its sphere of emotional relations. Campbell sees these adults as continuing to be bound by the walls of childhood, father and mother still standing at the threshold. The fearful soul fails to make the passage through the door and to come to birth in the world without.[4] However, when we face our Ur-moments and the crisis they entail affirmatively, we learn new processes and cloak our communication in more soulful clothing. By the term *soulful* I suggest the degree to which we choose to consciously participate in order to make our lives more meaningful and the quality of our relationships richer.

A good ending seeks a beginning, middle, and end. It includes a sense of inner completion and outer connection. A good story seeks reconciliation and harmony among a number of possible stories. It raises issues and contradiction but also seeks what Erikson has called generative integration. Since our lives exist in a social and ethical context, maturity means the ability to function in a productive and useful way in the spheres of family, work, and larger society. Living a myth provides not so much a sense of happiness but of purpose, of unity and meaning.

Earlier I quoted Erikson's definition of intimacy. Erikson defined intimacy as the capacity to commit oneself to concrete affiliations and partnerships and the ethical strengths to abide by such commitments even though they call for significant sacrifice and compromise. Failing to explore is a critical blow to intimacy, but just as critical is the failure to commit. What we can conclude, following Erikson, is that intimacy is inextricably, but no longer inexplicably, tied to adulthood and to fundamental cognitive shifts that make adult communication possible.

My goal has been to develop the communication processes as a tool for finding meaning, helping us to understand and expand our capacities for intimacy. While certainly early environments provide opportunities for nurturing the development of processes that I believe are critical for intimacy, as adults we have the opportunity to make different decisions about our communication. These Ur-moments provide an occasion for redefinition of self as they disrupt the equilibrium of identity.

Good communication is critical to relationships. Yet, as I have suggested, effective communication is a set of learned skills, not a natural one. I believe that a particular set of markers, both verbal and nonverbal, in the communication process may be better understood as symptoms of deeper unresolved developmental processes. In detailing three crises of wholeness, mother-child separation, the development of the superego, and the end of childhood, I have attempted to examine the assembly of various parts that enter into fruitful association with wholeheartedness as well as those which do not. An organic mutuality between these parts creates open and fluid boundaries. When individuals, because of developmental shifts, lose an essential wholeness, they restructure themselves and their worlds accordingly. Failures in alignment invoke primitivization of affect and absolute boundaries in order to provide some sense of identity. Such adjustments are made on a primitive level, by increased anxieties of infantile origin called forth by acute life crises.

Affectional communication is linked to what researchers have called the quality of our base, or mother-child communication. The crises of mother-child separation determines our attachment system and our style of attachment and patterns of response, whether stable or not. Our affectional communication, whether we are narcissistic or develop an outward focus, I have tied to what John Bowlby has called our stable base issues.

Ethical communication, our degree of responsibility versus victimization, is evidenced by our choice of mature versus immature self-defense mechanisms. I have tied ethical communication to resolution of emotional problems that occur during the Oedipal stage of development. The Oedipal stage is the second crisis of wholeness and reflects not only the sternness and limitations of parents but also the crudeness of infantile states during which our conscience is imposed. A combination of firmness and tolerance ideally guides the process but an overly strict identification process can turn against the self and others, attempting to overcome all moral vagueness by replacing ambivalence with total goodness and badness. A key task of conscience, at the same time, is to maintain healthy ego defenses, and delay gratification, against the intensity of impulses.

Finally, authentic communication represents our third crisis of wholeness and is linked to our degree of identity resolution, or the boundary system that we develop which uniquely frames self-determining inclusive and exclusive communication. Authentic communication determines our ability to let others in appropriately. Problems in self-disclosure I have tied to boundary issues that are related to our degree of and means of identity resolution. In adolescence, at the end of childhood, we attempt for the first time to resynthesize childhood in a unique way. Here we feel the need for the first time to see progressive continuity between how we see ourselves and what others see and expect from us. Identity is now placed in the hands of peers and figures outside the family as we search to align the scattered pieces of childhood into a unifying picture.

Together these crises and their resolution determine our levels of closeness and distance in relationships, and offer an emotional geography of intimacy. Our capacity for adult communication is forged on the interaction of our internal organization with external social systems, such as families and significant others. Deficiencies in these processes may lay dormant until adulthood, when we first attempt to form intimate relationships. It is in adulthood that we attempt to reintegrate the missing pieces by examining our strengths and weaknesses. These processes are markers of intimate expression. Each communication/developmental process provides emotional and linguistic tools essential for intimacy.

It is important to note that the skills we value in building relationships have their roots in earlier developmental processes, processes that often privilege the nonverbal more than the verbal. Naturally, this makes the task of deciphering relational problems more difficult and rife for misunderstanding. We may simply not be able to translate the nonverbal behaviors of others correctly, a source of many difficulties. Alternatively, we may find certain behaviors missing from our own repertoire. In both instances I believe we have the opportunity to consciously learn about our own deficiencies and to remedy them as adults as we attempt to build healthy and more satisfying relationships. For some, who have had little opportunity to learn them at an earlier time, these skills will be essential to being in a relationship at all.

Learning about the self is not an easy process and can be fraught with defensive behaviors and self-deception. Intelligence is not necessarily a guarantee of success. Even when we learn new behaviors it's tempting to allow our earlier learned patterns to control us, no matter how destructive they may be to our lives. However, as with many choices in adulthood, we must face our Ur-moments and learn to accept that which we cannot change and change what we cannot accept. By examining common problems in communication, and rooting them in developmental stages, I have hoped to offer insight that can improve the quality of our lives by improving the quality of our relationships.

Endnotes

Introduction

1. U.S. Census, 1997, as stated by CNN online services 1998 with assistance by Associated Press and Reuters; and Cowles Business Media in "Aging Boomer Bachelor Pads" 1997 (online). Women comprise 58 percent of all people who live alone, and half of all women who live alone are aged 65 and older, 29 percent are 75 and older. Men who live alone are far younger—nearly half are aged 25–44 (47 percent). Only one in ten males who live alone are 75 and older. Older men and younger men who live alone will slowly loose ground to a wave of middle-age singles in the next fifteen years. The number of women age 45-64 will increase 65 percent by 2010, men in the same age group will increase 83 percent. All these figures suggest a growing population of single lifestyles. "Single Persons Households on Rise," *Reality Times*, 19 January 1998.

2. Ibid. The number of single-parent families doubled between 1970 and 1990, from 6 to 12 percent. The number of single, never-married women giving birth increased from 33 percent in 1990 to 41 percent in 1997. The number of single fathers increased to 17 percent during the same period. A surprising trend was the growing number of adult sons and daughters who continued to live with their parents (from fifteen million in 1970 to twenty-two million in 1997). With the age at which most adults enter their first marriage increasing, fewer in the 1990s are setting up their own households.

3. W. C. Schultz, *FIRO: A Three Dimensional Theory of Interpersonal Behavior* (New York: Holt, Rinehart, Winston, 1958). Inclusion, control, and affection are reflected in the way we assign meaning to verbal and nonverbal behavior. Osgood labeled these dimensions dynamism, potency, and evaluation. Mehrabian called them responsibility, power, and immediacy. See C. E. Osgood, G. J. Suci, and P. H. Tannenbaum, *The Measurement of Meaning* (Urbana: University of Illinois Press, 1957) and A. Mehrabian, *Nonverbal Communication* (Chicago: Aldine Publishing Company, 1972).

4. Alfred Adler, *The Pattern of Life* (New York: Holt, Rinehart, and Winston, 1930). See also idem, *What Life Should Mean To You* (Boston: Little Brown, 1931); idem, *Understanding Human Nature* (Garden City, N.Y.: Garden City Publishing Company, 1927); idem, *Social Interest: A Challenge to Mankind* (New York: Putnam, 1939); and H. L. and R. R. Ansbacher, eds., *The Individual Psychology of Afred Adler: A Systematic Presentation of Selections from His Writings* (New York: Basic Books, 1956). On Freud, see Sigmund

189

Freud, *Three Essays on a Theory of Sexuality* (New York: Basic Books, 1962); idem, *Inhibition, Symptom, and Anxiety* (New York: W.W. Norton, 1977); idem, *Introductory Lectures on Psycho-analysis* (New York: W.W. Norton, 1966); idem, *On Narcissism: An Introduction to the Essential Papers on Narcissism* (New York: New York University Press, 1983); and idem, *Character and Culture* (New York: Macmillan Publishing Company, 1963). On Horney, see Karen Horney, *Our Inner Conflicts: A Constructive Theory of Neurosis* (New York: W.W. Norton, 1945); idem, *The Neurotic Personality of Our Times* (New York: W.W. Norton, 1937); idem, *Neurosis and Human Growth* (New York: W.W. Norton, 1970); idem, *Female Psychology* (New York: W.W. Norton, 1967); and *Collected Work of Karen Horney* (New York: W.W. Norton, 1964). On Bowlby, see John Bowlby, *A Stable Base* (New York: Basic Books, 1988). On Winnicott, see Donald Winnicott, *The Maturation Processes and the Facilitating Environment: Studies in Emotional Development* (London: Hogart Press, 1965); idem, Home Is Where We Start From: Essays by a Psychoanalyst (London: Pelican Books, 1987); and Adam Phillips, *Winnicott* (Cambridge, Mass.: Harvard University Press, 1988). On Gilligan, see Carol Gilligan, *A Different Voice: Psychological Theory and Women's Development* (Cambridge, Mass.: Harvard University Press, 1982). On Erikson, see Erik Erikson, *Identity and the Life Cycle* (New York: W.W. Norton, 1959); idem, *Identity: Youth and Crisis* (New York: W.W. Norton, 1968); idem, *The Life Cycle Completed* (New York: W.W. Norton, 1982); idem, *Childhood and Society* (New York: W.W. Norton, 1963); idem, *Vital Involvement in Old Age* (New York: W.W. Norton, 1986); and idem, Insight and Responsibility (New York: W.W. Norton, 1964); Melanie Klein, *Contributions to Psycho-Analysis* (London: Hogarth Press, 1948).

5. George Valliant, *Wisdom of Ego* (Cambridge, Mass.: Harvard University Press, 1993); idem, *Adaptation to Life* (Cambridge, Mass.: Harvard University Press, 1977); and Robert Kegan, *The Evolving Self: Problems in the Process of Human Development* (Cambridge, Mass.: Harvard University Press, 1982).

6. On Erikson, see note 4. See also Thomas Cole, *The Journey of Life: A Cultural History of Aging* (Cambridge: Cambridge University Press, 1992).

7. Ernest Hartmann, *Boundaries of the Mind* (New York: Basic Books, 1991).

8. Dan McAdams, *Stories We Live By: Personal Myths and the Making of the Self* (New York: Morrow and Co., 1993); and idem, *Intimacy* (New York: Doubleday Publishing, 1989).

9. McAdams, *Stories We Live By*, i–xx.

10. Ibid.

11. Ibid.

12. McAdams, *Intimacy,* 46

13. Gilligan, *A Different Voice,* 5–23.

14. McAdams, *Stories We Live By.*

15. The term *moritorium* was first used by Erikson.

16. Paul Watzlawick, Janet Beavin, and Don Jackson, *The Pragmatics of Human Communication: A Study of Interactional Patterns, Pathologies, and Paradoxes* (New York: W.W. Norton, 1967, 22).

17. Ibid., 72.

18. Ibid., 60-66.

19. Ibid., 187–230.

Chapter 1. Ur-moments in Communication: Developing an Adult Perspective

1. Abraham Maslow, *Toward a Psychology of Being* (New York: Van Nostrand, 1968) and *Motivation and Personality* (New York: Harper and Row, 1987).

2. Erik Erikson, *Youth: Identity and the Life Cycle* (New York: W.W. Norton, 1963), 263.

3. Ibid.

4. Alfred Adler, *The Pattern of Life* (New York: Holt, Rinehart, and Winston, 1930).

5. John Bowlby, *A Secure Base* (New York: Basic Books, 1988).

6. Otto F. Kernberg, "Further Contributions to the Treatment of Narcissistic Personalities" and "Factors in the Psychoanalytic Treatment of Narcissistic Personalities"; Heinz Kohut, "Forms and Transformation of Narcissism"; and Heinz Kohut and Ernest S. Wolf, "The Disorders of the Self and Their Treatment," all in *Essential Papers in Narcissism*, ed. Andrew Morrison (New York: New York University Press, 1986).

7. Bowlby, *A Secure Base*, 11–12.

8. Margaret Mahler, *On Human Symbiosis or the Vicissitudes of Individuation* (New York: International Universities Press, 1968).

9. George Vaillant, Wisdom of the Ego (Cambridge, Mass.: Harvard University Press, 1993), 1–30.

10. Alfred Adler, *Understanding Human Nature* (Garden City, N.J.: Garden City Publishing Co., 1927).

11. Karen Horney, "Feminine Psychology"and "The Dread of Women: Problems in Marriage," in *New Ways in Psychoanalysis* from *The Collected Works of Karen Horney* (New York: W.W. Norton, 1967).

12. Ernest Hartmann, *Boundaries of the Mind* (New York: Basic Books, 1991).

13. The gold standard for understanding how babies and children develop interpersonally has been the so-called infant maternal attachment measure, which infers well-being from the reactions of babies who are temporarily separated but then reunited with their mothers. According to many experts in child development, how the baby reacts to the mother's return each time is critically important. In general, if the baby cries, goes to the mother, and is comforted, the child is securely attached. If the baby

ignores the mother and is ambivalent to her return or if the baby cries but refuses to be consoled, the baby is insecurely attached. The infant's external behavior is said to capture his or her internal model of attachment. Some psychologists view this measure as vital in determining later levels of social and emotional adjustment. Attachment theory, as it is known, is now being challenged by such researchers as Dr. Michael Lewis. See the *New York Times*, Science Section, 4 August 1998, p. 26+.

14. Virginia Woolf, *To The Lighthouse* (New York: Knopf, 1992), 35

15. F. Scott Fitzgerald, The Great Gatsby (New York: Scribner's, 1953)

16. Sigmund Freud, "Id, Ego and the Superego," In *Standard Edition of the Complete Psychological Works of Sigmund Freud,* vol. 20. (New York: W.W. Norton, 1926).

17. Carl Rogers, "A Therapist's View of the Good Life," in *A Fully Functioning Person* (Boston: Houghton-Mifflin, 1961).

Chapter 2. Getting Enough: Moving from Narcissism to Outward Focusing

1. Carl Jung, " The Stages of Life," in *The Portable Jung,* trans. R. F. C. Hull (New York: Viking Penguin Books, 1971), 3–22.

2. Anita Vangelisti, Mark Knapp, and John A. Daly, "Conversational Narcissism," *Communication Monograms* 57 (1990): 251–71.

3. Christopher Lasch, *The Culture of Narcissism* (New York: W.W. Norton, 1979).

4. Robert Bellah, Richard Madsen, William M. Sullivan, Ann Swidler, and Steven M. Tipton, *Habits of the Heart* (Berkeley: University of California Press, 1985), 142–63.

5. See Heinz Kohut and Ernest Wolf, "The Disorders of the Self and Their Treatment: An Outline," and Otto F. Kernberg, "Further Contributions to the Treatment of Narcissistic Personalities," in *Essential Papers on Narcissism,* ed. Andrew P. Morrison (New York: New York University Press, 1986.

6. Vangelisti, Knapp, and Daly. "Conversational Narcissism."

7. Ibid.

Chapter 3. Jonathan's Story: A Torn Net

1. Dan McAdams, *Stories We Live By: Personal Myths and the Making of the Self* (New York: W.W. Norton, 1993).

2. John G. Holmes, and John K. Rempel, "Trust in Close Relationships," in *Close Relationships,* ed. Cyde Hendrick (Newberry Park, Calif.: Sage Publications, 1989).

3. McAdams, *Stories We Live By.*

4. Erik Erikson, *The Life Cycle Completed* (New York: W.W. Norton, 1982).

Chapter 4. Patching Our Torn Nets: A Stable Base and Consolidation of the Affectional Self

1. See M. S. Mahler, "Volume 1. Infantile Psychosis," in *The Psychological Birth of the Infant*, ed. J. and M.S. Mahler (New York: Basic Books, 1975).

2. John Bowlby, *Attachment and Loss,* vol. 3 (London: Hogarth Press, 1980) and *A Secure Base* (New York: Basic Books, 1988), 1–19.

3. Melanie Klein, *Contributions to Psycho-Analysis* (London: Hogarth Press, 1950); W. R. Fairbain, *Psychoanalytic Studies of the Personality* (Boston: Routledge and Kegan Paul, 1986).

4. Heinz Kohut, "Disorders of the Self and Their Treatment," and Otto F. Kernberg, "Further Contributions to a Treatment of Narcissistic Personalities," in *Essential Papers on Narcissism*, ed. Andrew P. Morrison (New York: New York University Press, 1986).

5. D. W. Winicott, "Ego Distortion and the Terms of the True and False Self," reprinted in idem, *The Maturation Process and the Facilitating Environment: Studies in Emotional Development* (London: Hogarth Press, 1965), 1940–52; and Bowlby, *Attachment and Loss.*

6. Winicott, *The Maturation Processes*; and Adam Phillips, *Winnicott* (Cambridge, Mass.: Harvard University Press, 1988).

7. John Bowlby, *A Stable Base* (New York: Basic Books, 1988) and *Attachment and Loss,* vol. 3 (London: Hogarth Press, 1980).

8. Ibid.

9. Winnicott, *The Maturation Process.*

10. Winnicott, "Ego Distortion."

11. H. F. Harlow, and M. K. Harlow, "The Affectional Systems," in *Behavior of Nonhuman Primates*, vol. 2, ed. A. M Schrier, H. F. Harlow, and F. Stollnitz (New York: Academic Press, 1965); H. F. Harlow, and R. R. Zimmerman, "Affectional Responses in the Infant Monkey," *Science* 130 (1959): 421; and M. D. S. Ainsworth, M. C. Waters, and S. Wall, *Patterns of Attachment: Psychological Studies of the Strange Situation* (Hillsdale, N.J.: Erlbaum Publishing, 1978).

12. Ainsworth, Waters, and Wall, *Patterns of Attachment.*

13. Bowlby, *Stable Base.*

14. Mary Ainsworth, "Attachments beyond Intimacy," *American Psychologist* 44 (April 1989): 709–16.

15. See Erik Erikson, *Identity and the Life Cycle* (New York: International Universities Press, 1959), 97; Gail Sheehy, *Passages: Predictable Crisis of Adult Life* (New York: Dutton, 1976); D. Levinson. *The Seasons of a Man's Life* (New York: Ballatine, 1978); Bernice Neugarten, *Middle Age and Aging* (Chicago: University of Chicago Press, 1968); Winifred Gallagher, "Midlife Myths," *Atlantic Monthly,* May 1993.

16. Neugarten, *Middle Age.*

17. Winnicott, *Maturation Processes.*

18. Bowlby, *A Stable Base.*

19. Winnicott, "Ego Distortion."

20. Anita Vangelisti, Mark Knapp, and John A. Daley, "Conversational Narcissism," *Communication Monographs* 57(December 1990): 251–71.

21. Ainsworth, "Attachments beyond Intimacy."

22. Joseph Campbell, *The Hero with a Thousand Faces* (Princeton, N.J.: Princeton University Press, 1977), 1–22.

23. Karl Jung, " The Concept of the Collective Archetype," in *The Portable Jung* (New York: Penguin Books, 1976).

Chapter 5. Do the Right Thing: Moving from Victimization to Responsibility

1. W. C. Schultz, *FIRO: A Three Dimensional Theory of Interpersonal Behavior* (New York: Holt, Rinehart, and Winston, 1958).

2. R. D. Laing, *The Politics of the Family* (New York: Vintage Books, 1972) and *Interpersonal Perception* (New York: Harper and Row, 1966), 15.

3. David W. Johnson, "Communication and the Inducement of Cooperative Behavior in Conflicts: A Critical Review," *Speech Monographs* 41 (1974): 64–78.

4. George Vaillant, *The Wisdom of the Ego* (Cambrige, Mass.: Harvard University Press, 1993).

5. Freud, Sigmund, The Neuro-psychoses of Defense, in The Standard Edition of the Complete Psychological Works of Sigmund Freud, vols. 1–24, ed. J. Strachey (London: Hogarth Press, 1953–74), 43–68.

6. Vaillant, *Wisdom of the Ego.*

7. *Projection* is an unconscious process where we refuse responsibility for our feelings by assigning them to others. It is a social defense, in that it leads to an over-obsessive involvement with the enemy. Vaillant sees it as the basis of paranoia, jealousy, prejudice, and demonic possession. *Hypochondria* displaces the conflict or feelings behind the conflict onto the body. Vaillant sees this as a means of obtaining care while accusing and punishing others. While projection places the tormentor outside oneself, hypochondria places the tormenter inside. It becomes a symbolic way of expressing feeling through literally the eating out of one's own heart. *Acting out* turns anger against the self. It is linked to identification with an aggressor—achieving mastery by incorporating traits that one fears. It involves giving in to impulses in order to avoid the conscious tension that results from postponing them. The impulse becomes the action so quickly that the user escapes feeling or thinking about what she or he does. Physical abuse and violence are the result of acting out. *Disassociation* or *denial* allow

us to escape stress by denying or modifying identity. This is the use of the classic Dr. Jekyll/Mr. Hyde situation. In neurotic denial, we distort internal reality, while in psychotic denial we distort external reality. This difference mirrors the old therapeutic saying that neurotics build castles in the air while psychotics live in them. In disassociation, the inner reality become more important (more real) than the outer reality. *Fantasy* is a means of making things all right in one's head. Only the lonely are content, however, with this imaginary reality. It is a poor substitute for action and relationships. Unlike sublimation, its more mature second cousin, fantasy finds no way to embrace or connect with others. Vaillant found it correlated with bleak childhood, such as that of Jonathan, our first case study.

8. *Repression* is where we banish an idea from consciousness but preserve the effect. What is repressed returns to us in disguised forms, Vaillant believes. *Reaction formation* charts a course that is the opposite of some inner unconscious passion. The classic example is the sex fiend who becomes a priest, or vice versa. *Isolation* or *intellectualization* (which includes rationalization) is where we banish the feeling from consciousness but spare the idea. Stripped of feeling, the idea remains in consciousness but seems unimportant. This process, Vaillant believes, leads to obsession and compulsion, where the idea continues to go around in our heads. Vaillant correlates isolation with the need to adjust our inner states to a level of external denial (whereas disassociation is the need to focus on the inner details to the exclusion of the outer ones). *Displacement* is the method by which an effect is dislocated from its disturbing origin and reattached to other ideas, transferring the effect from its source to a more neutral object. The process turns mountains into molehills and is sometimes called "kick the dog" syndrome after the example of the employee who, after a bad day at work due to a troublesome boss, goes home and kicks the dog.

9. *Altruism* is getting pleasure from giving to others what you would like to receive. *Anticipation* is preparing before an event happens in order to mitigate the emotional affects of some future inner discomfort. It is like a dress rehearsal for our emotional needs. *Suppression* is holding onto an emotion until it is safe to release it. It postpones gratification and can involve minimization. *Humor* allows the idea and the effect to coexist in consciousness despite the distressing effects. It is a means of attaining pleasure. *Sublimation* makes an instinct acceptable by permitting the instinct, the idea, the object, and the emotion to remain in consciousness. When we are angry, we may choose to talk about our feelings rather than act them out by throwing a tantrum. Language, literature, and poetry are all forms of sublimation. (Displacement, by comparison, separates the emotion from the object, while intellectualization separates the emotion from the idea.)

10. See Robert Kroeber, "Study of Lives," in *Ego Psychology in Counseling,* by Paul T. King and Robert Neal (New York: Houghton-Miflin, 1968), 30–45.

11. See Anna Freud, *The Ego and the Mechanisms of Defense* (New York: International Universities Press, 1946). See also Sigmund Freud, "Inhibitions, Symptoms, and Anxiety," 75–175, and "Further Remarks on the Neuro-Psychoses of Defense," 159–85, in *Standard Edition of the Works of Sigmund Freud.* Melanie Klein also

describes what she considers to be the primitive defenses—splitting of the object, projective identification, denial of psychic reality, omnipotent control over objects—in *Developments in Psycho-Analysis* (London: Hogarth Press, 1952).

12. Vaillant, in his studies of human resiliency, identifies a supportive partner as a critical means of healing. See *Wisdom of the Ego.*

13. Freud, "Inhibitions, Symptoms, and Anxiety."

14. Karen Horney, "The Dread of Women," in *Female Psychology* (New York: W.W. Norton, 1967).

15. Alfred Adler, *Superiority and Social Interest,* 3d. rev. ed. (Evanston, Ill.: Northwestern University Press, 1979), 42.

16. This definition of neurosis is peculiar to Adler's theory and is not that generally used for psychiatric diagnosis.

17. Alfred Adler, *The Pattern of Life* (New York: Holt, Rinehart, and Winston, 1930).

Chapter 8. Escaping Our Magnetic Fields and Glass Prisons: The Oedipal Complex and Consolidating the Ethical Self

1. Sigmund Freud, "The Ego and the Id," in the *Standard Edition of the Completed Psychological Works of Sigmund Freud,* vol. 13 (New York: W.W. Norton, 1923).

2. Victoria Hamilton, "The Watching Agency," in *Narcissism and Oedipus* (Boston: Routledge and Kegan Paul, 1982).

3. Erik Erikson, *Youth and Identity* (New York: W. W. Norton, 1963).

4. Carl Jung, "The Stages of Life," in *The Portable Jung* (New York: Penguin Books, 1978).

5. J. Piaget, *The Construction of Reality in the Child* (New York: Basic Books, 1937).

6. Margaret Mahler, *On Human Symbiosis or the Vicissitudes of Individuation* (New York: International Universities Press, 1968).

7. Sigmund Freud, "The Dissolution of the Oedipus Complex," in the *Standard Edition of the Completed Psychological Works of Sigmund Freud* (New York: W. W. Norton, 1924), 13:399; and "Some Psychical Consequences of the Anatomical Distinction Between the Sexes," in the *Standard Edition of the Completed Psychological Works of Sigmund Freud* (New York: W. W. Norton, 1925), 14:28.

8. Jay Greenberg, *The Oedipus Complex and Beyond* (Cambridge, Mass.: Harvard University Press, 1991)

9. Carol Gilligan, "Women's Place in Man's Life Cycle," in *Experiencing Class, Race, and Gender in the United States* (Mountain View, Calif.: Mayfield Publishing Company, 1993).

10. Sigmund Freud, "The Myth of the Birth of the Hero," in *Standard Edition of the Completed Psychological Works of Sigmund Freud* (New York: W. W. Norton, 1923), 13:1–56.

11. Greenberg, *The Oedipus Complex and Beyond.*

12. Erik Erikson, *Childhood and Society* (New York: W. W. Norton, 1963).

Chapter 9. What We May Be: Moving from too Closed or too Open to Healthy Boundaries

1. Ernest Hartmann, *Boundaries of the Mind* (New York: Basic Books, 1991).

2. Morris Rosenberg, *Conceiving the Self* (New York: Basic Books, 1979).

3. John Bowlby, *A Stable Base* (New York: Basic Books, 1988).

4. Chris Argyris, *Interpersonal Competence and Organizational Effectiveness* (Homewood, Ill.: Richard D. Irwin Publishers, 1962).

5. Ibid.

6. Rosenberg, *Conceiving the Self.* Se also R. B. Felson, "Reflected Appraisal and the Development of Self," *Social Psychology Quarterly* 48 (1985): 71–78 and R. Haree, "The Social Construction of Selves," in *Self and Identity: Psychological Perspective,* Ed. K Yardly and T. Honess (London: Wiley, 1987).

7. C. H. Cooley, *Human Nature and the Social Order* (New York: Scribner, 1912).

8. W. H. Fitts, *The Self Concept and Self-Actualization* (Nashville, Tenn.: Counselor Recordings and Tests, 1971).

9. Dan McAdams, *The Stories We Live By: Personal Myths and the Making of the Self* (New York: Morrow and Company, 1993).

10. Winifred Galligher, "Midlife Myths," *Atlantic Monthly,* May 1993, pp.51–62.

11. I. Altman and D. Taylor, *Social Penetration: The Development of Interpersonal Relationships* (New York: Holt, Rinehart, Winston, 1973).

12. Dan Goleman, *Emotional Intelligence* (New York: Bantum Books, 1995).

13. William Rawlins, "Openness as Problematic in Ongoing Friendships: Two Conversational Dilemmas," *Communication Monograph* 15 (March 1983): 33–52.

14. Joseph Luft. and Harry Ingham, *Of Human Interaction* (Palo Alto, Calif.: National Press Books, 1969).

Chapter 10. Beatrice's Story: "Conversion"

1. Frank Sulloway, *Born to Rebel: Birth Order, Family Dynamics, and Creative Lives* (New York: Pantheon Books, 1996).

2. Ibid.

3. Erik Erikson, *Identity, Youth and Crisis* (W.W. Norton, 1968).

4. Fitts, *The Self Concept and Self Actualization* (Nashville, Tenn.: Counselor Recording and Tests, 1971).

5. Erikson, *Identity, Youth and Crisis.*

6. Erik Erikson, "Identity and Uprootedness in Our Time," in *Insight and Responsibility* (New York: W.W. Norton, 1964).

7. William K. Rawlins, "Openness As Problematic in Ongoing Friendships: Two Conversational Dilemmas." *Communication Monographs* 50 (March 1983): 28–35.

Chapter 11. Ian's Story: "Devotion"

1. Erikson, *Idenity, Youth and Crisis.*

2. Ibid.

3. Thomas Merton, *Seven Story Mountains* (New York: Harcourt Brace, 1990) and Annie Dillard, *Pilgrim at Tinker Creek* (New York: Bantam Books, 1978).

4. Sulloway, 24–55.

Chapter 12. Completing the Self: Identity Resolution and Consolidation of the Authentic Self

1. Ernest Hartmann, Boundries of the Mind (New York: Basic Books, 1991).

2. Erik Erikson, *Identity, Youth, and Crisis* (New York: W.W. Norton, 1968).

3. Erik Erikson, "Cycle of Generations," in *Insight and Responsibility* (New York: W.W. Norton, 1964).

4. Erik Erikson, *The Life Cycle Completed* (New York: W.W. Norton, 1982).

5. Erik Erikson, *Childhood and Society* (New York: W.W. Norton, 1963).

6. Ibid.

7. Karen Horney, "Problem of Marriage," in *Female Psychology* (New York: Norton, 1967).

8. Ibid.

9. Sigmund Freud, "Formulations on Two Principles of Mental Functioning," in *Standard Edition* (1911), 12:213–26 and "The Id, the Ego, and the Superego," in *Standard Edition* (1926), 20:139–207.

10. Ibid.

11. Bernard Landis, *Ego Boundaries* (New York: International Universities Press, 1970).

12. See W. Ronald Fairbairn, *Psychoanalytical Studies of the Personality* (Boston: Routledge and Kegan Paul, 1986); D. W. Winnicott, *The Facilitating Environmnet: Studies in Theory of Emotional Development* (London: Hogarth Press, 1965); and H. Guntrip' "My Experience of Analysis with Fairbairn and Winnicott," *International Review of Psycho-Analysis* 2 (1975): 145–56.

13. Carl Rogers, "A Therapist's View of the Good Life," in *The Full Functioning Person* (Boston: Houghton and Mifflin, 1961).

14. Ibid.

15. Paul King and Robert Neal, *Ego Psychology and Counseling* (Boston: Houghton Mifflin, 1968).

16. Hartmann, *Boundaries of the Mind.*

17. Ibid.

18. Ibid.

19. Erikson, *Life Cycle Completed.*

20. Erikson, *Identity Youth and Crisis.*

21. Expanding on Erikson's two poles of identity and diffusion, see James E. Marcia, "The Identity Status Approach to the Study of Ego Identity in Development, in *Self and Development,* ed. Terry Honness and Krysia Yardley (New York: Routledge and Kegan Paul, 1987). Along the same line, Orlofsky et al. have identified five levels of intimacy, which can be correlated with Marcia's stages of identity development. See J. L. Orlofsky, J. E. Marcia, I. M. Lesser, "Ego Identity States and the Intimacy vs. Isolation Crisis of Young Adulthood," *Personality and Social Psychology* 27 (1973): 211–19.

22. Erikson, *Identity, Youth, and Crisis.*

23. Frank Sulloway, *Born to Rebel: Birth Order, Family Dynamics, and Creative Lives* (New York: Pantheon Books, 1996).

24. Ibid.

25. Ibid.

26. Ibid.

27. See, in particular, Carol Gilligan, *A Different Voice* (Cambridge, Mass.: Harvard University Press, 1986).

28. Ruthellen Josselson, "Idenity and Relatedness," *in Identity and Development,* ed. Harke A. Bosma, Tobi. G. Gratosma, Harold D. Grotevant, and David J. DeLevita (Thousand Oaks, Calif.: Sage, 1994).

29. Ibid.

Chapter 13. Conclusions

1. Arlie Hotchild, *Second Shift* (New York: Avon Books, 1989).

2. Peter Kramer, cited in *Should You Leave* (New York: Penguin, 1999), 33–38.

3. Ibid.

4. Joseph Campbell, *The Hero with a Thousand Faces* (Princeton, N.J.: Princeton University Press, 1977), 11.